ERIC WALROND

ERIC
WALR

OND

THE CRITICAL HERITAGE

EDITED BY
Louis J. Parascandola and Carl A. Wade

University of the West Indies Press
Jamaica • Barbados • Trinidad and Tobago

University of the West Indies Press
7A Gibraltar Hall Road, Mona
Kingston 7, Jamaica
www.uwipress.com

© 2012 by Louis J. Parascandola and Carl A. Wade

All rights reserved. Published 2012
A catalogue record of this book is available from the
National Library of Jamaica.

ISBN: 978-976-640-295-2

Cover illustration: A section of the old St Stephen's Boys' School, Black Rock, Barbados. Photograph by Grantley Sealy.

Book and cover design by Robert Harris.
Set in Dante MT 11 / 14.5 x 27
Printed in the United States of America.

TO THE PIONEERS:

KENNETH RAMCHAND
AND
ROBERT BONE (1924–2007)

CONTENTS

Acknowledgments / **ix**

Selected Chronology of Eric Walrond / **xi**

Introduction / **1**
CARL A. WADE AND LOUIS J. PARASCANDOLA

PART 1. PIONEERING VOICES / **17**

1. The Writer Who Ran Away: Eric Walrond and *Tropic Death* / **19**
   KENNETH RAMCHAND

2. Eric Walrond: From *Down Home: Origins of the Afro-American Short Story* / **35**
   ROBERT BONE

PART 2. MODERN CRITICAL VIEWS / **55**

3. "All Look Alike in Habana": Archaeologies of Blackness across Eric Walrond's Archipelago / **57**
   MICHELLE A. STEPHENS

4. Foreign Negro Flash Agents: Eric Walrond and the Discrepancies of Diaspora / **72**
   LOUIS CHUDE-SOKEI

5. Genre, Gender and Eric Walrond's Equivocal Transnational Vision / **100**
   RHONDA FREDERICK

6   Eric Walrond and the Proletarian Arts Movement / **128**
    MICHAEL NIBLETT

PART 3. BIOGRAPHICAL SKETCHES / **147**

7   Eric Walrond and the Dynamics of White Patronage during the Harlem Renaissance / **149**
    CARL A. WADE, ROBERT BONE AND LOUIS J. PARASCANDOLA

8   A Prism so Strange: The Biography of Eric Walrond / **167**
    JAMES DAVIS

9   A West Indian Grows in Brooklyn: The Early American Experiences of Eric Walrond / **188**
    LOUIS J. PARASCANDOLA AND JAMES DAVIS

10 Exile on Main Street: Eric Walrond and Garveyism in Great Britain in the 1930s / **202**
    CARL PEDERSEN

    Selected Bibliography and Works of Interest on Eric Walrond / **215**

    Index / **219**

    Contributors / **231**

ACKNOWLEDGEMENTS

THIS ANTHOLOGY OF ESSAYS is dedicated to two scholars whose pioneering work on Eric Walrond contributed immeasurably to the editors' interest in this writer and enhanced their knowledge and appreciation of his life and work.

Kenneth Ramchand's seminal commentary, first published in 1970, initiated the process of rediscovering Walrond and establishing him as an important and accomplished writer. Forty years later, this essay still serves as an important reference point for a later generation of Walrond critics, as many chapters in this publication attest. Ramchand, professor emeritus, University of the West Indies, is best known for his ground-breaking text, *The West Indian Novel and Its Background* (1970), which was critical to the development of the study of West Indian literature as a significant academic discipline. The editors are indebted to Professor Ramchand for graciously and readily agreeing to revise his essay on Walrond for inclusion in this publication.

Robert Bone, late professor emeritus of Teachers' College, Columbia University, was another pioneer in Walrond criticism. His treatise on Walrond published in *Down Home: A History of Afro-American Short Fiction from Its Beginnings to the End of the Harlem Renaissance* represents – even now – the most comprehensive study of this writer's life and work and their interconnection, and of the accomplishments of other black exponents of the short narrative. Professor Bone's advice and the papers on Walrond which he entrusted to Louis Parascandola proved invaluable to us in our own research on this writer. His writings on various writers and topics continue to be cited extensively by scholars with an interest in twentieth-century black fiction.

Louis wishes to thank his students and colleagues at Long Island University; Dean David Cohen; Provost Gale Stevens-Haynes; his graduate helpers, Nell Del Giudice, Rajul Punjabi and Asja Parrish; his siblings John Parascandola, Judy Bilello and the late Maryann Barbieri; the memory of his parents, Ann and Louis; and especially his wife, Shondel Nero, whose constant love and support have been his anchor: faithful and always useful.

Carl wishes to thank for their encouragement and advice his daughters, Lisa Karima and Alisha Nicole Wade; his former colleagues at the University of the West Indies, Cave Hill, Barbados, especially Victor Simpson; Kendra Haynes, Ministry of Education and Human Resources Development, Barbados; his friend Jennifer Pollard; and the University of the West Indies for facilitating the research on Eric Walrond for many years.

Louis and Carl would also like to acknowledge the assistance of Dorothy, recently deceased, and Joan Stewart, daughter and granddaughter respectively of Eric Walrond; Dorothea Bone, widow of Robert Bone; Linda Speth, Shivaun Hearne and Jean Honeyghan of the University of the West Indies Press, Jamaica; the anonymous reviewers and proofreader of the University of the West Indies Press; the indexer, Elaine Melnick; Atlanta University; A'Lelia Bundles; Grantley Sealy of Barbados; the Wiltshire Heritage Museum and Library; Fisk University; Columbia University Press; and Abney Park Cemetery Trust.

SELECTED CHRONOLOGY OF ERIC WALROND

1898	(18 December) Eric Derwent Walrond is born in British Guiana (now Guyana) to William and Ruth Walrond
1906	Eric Walrond migrates with mother and siblings to Barbados
1906–c.1910	Educated at St Stephen's Boys' School in Black Rock, St Michael, Barbados
1909	William Walrond migrates to Colón, Panama Canal Zone
c.1910	Ruth Walrond and children migrate to Colón
1910–1916	Eric Walrond furthers education in Panama
1916–1918	Eric Walrond employed as reporter with the Panama *Star and Herald* newspaper
1918	Migrates to New York City via Ellis Island; secretary to Recruiting Office in the British Mission
1920	Secretary to architect, New York City; employed with *Weekly Review* run by Marcus Garvey; secretary to superintendent, Broad Street Hospital; marries Edith Melita Cadogan in New York City; union produces three daughters: Jean (Campbell), Dorothy (Stewart) and Lucille (Mathurin Mair)
1921	Wins first prize for "A Senator's Memoirs", published in *Negro World*
1922	Meets Edna Worthley Underwood, linguist and editor, who offers assistance in placing his fiction; part owner, assistant editor, *Brooklyn and Long Island Informer*; works on banana boat plying the Caribbean and Latin America

1922–1924	Assistant editor, associate editor, business and contributing editor, *Negro World;* attends City College, New York
1923–c.1924	Separated from Edith Walrond; writes Alain Locke about anxiety and depression and the lack of progress with a novel
c.1924	Moves to Harlem from Brooklyn
1924–1926	Attends Columbia University
1925	"The Palm Porch" published in the *New Negro*, edited by Alain Locke; "Drought" published in the *New Age* (London), October
1925–c.1926	Reportedly lives in A'Lelia Walker's Harlem residence and receives financial support from her
1925–1927	Business editor, *Opportunity*, journal of the National Urban League
1926	*Tropic Death* published by Boni and Liveright, New York City
1927	Receives Harmon Award in recognition of achievement in literature; second edition of *Tropic Death* published; in Panama gathering material
1928	Named Zona Gale Scholar; awarded Guggenheim Memorial Foundation Fellowship
1929	Visits Dominica, Barbados, US Virgin Islands and other countries in the Caribbean; travels to Paris and joins community of American artists in exile; Guggenheim Grant extended for six months
1931	Visits parents in Brooklyn, New York City; remains in the United States for five months
1933	Paris; interviewed by Jacques Lebar for *Lectures du Soir*; admitted to the American Hospital with appendicitis; writes to Shirley Graham Du Bois about his literary plans and expectations
1935	In Ireland as publicity manager of a "Negro revue"
1936–1937	Publishes articles in the *Pittsburgh Courier*
1936–1938	Writes for Marcus Garvey's *Black Man* (London)
1938	Arrested in London and charged with "causing grievous bodily harm"; charges later dropped

1939	Moves to Bradford on Avon in the south of England
1940	Writes letter to Henry Moe of Guggenheim, accompanying articles published since 1932, and regretting failure to honour terms of award; applies unsuccessfully for Rosenwald Fellowship
1939–1944	War correspondent for *New York Amsterdam News*
1944–1946	Publishes articles in the *People's Voice* (New York)
1948–1950	Book reviewer, *Life and Letters* (London)
1952	Admitted to Roundway Hospital, Devizes, Wiltshire, as a voluntary patient
1953	Writes letter to Henry Moe listing publications in *Roundway Review*; continues to publish in this journal until 1957
1954	Eldest daughter, Jean (Campbell), visits from Jamaica; Walrond expresses intention to donate material to Countee Cullen Collection at Atlanta University in letter to close friend Harold Jackman
1957	Discharged from Roundway Hospital
1958	"Black and Unknown Bards" – a recital of black poetry (selected by Walrond and Rosey E. Pool and arranged by Gordon Heath) presented at the Royal Court Theatre, London; book with same title published
1960	Informs Henry Moe about meetings in London with Richard Wright and W.E.B. Du Bois; expresses regret about not fulfilling commitment to Guggenheim
1965	Hospitalized following heart attack
1966	Signs contract with Arthur Pell of Boni and Liveright for reprint of *Tropic Death*; dies 8 August in London; buried in September in Abney Park Cemetery, London
1972	*Tropic Death* reissued by Collier Books, New York
1998	Publication of *"Winds Can Wake Up the Dead": An Eric Walrond Reader*
2009	Gravestone erected in Abney Park Cemetery
2011	Publication of *In Search of Asylum: The Later Writings of Eric Walrond*

INTRODUCTION

CARL A. WADE AND LOUIS J. PARASCANDOLA

OVER THE PAST FIFTEEN YEARS, interest in Eric Walrond has been steadily increasing.[1] Still, there is much that has been left unexplored about this writer, important both to Harlem Renaissance literature and to the study of the Caribbean diaspora. His short stories – particularly in *Tropic Death* (1926) – and essays helped add a transnational flavour to the Harlem Renaissance, broadening its African American base, and added a resonant anticolonial voice to Caribbean literature. This anthology, drawing on writers presenting various critical and geographic perspectives, will further increase our understanding of this enigmatic yet seminal figure, one whose lifelong concerns with the interconnecting issues of migration, identity and racial oppression remain timely today.

Walrond, whose marriage to Jamaican Edith Melita Cadogan in New York City in 1920 produced three daughters – the best known of whom was diplomat and scholar Dr Lucille Mathurin Mair – lived in or visited the anglophone, hispanophone and francophone areas of the Caribbean as well as metropolitan cities with large diasporic communities. His experiences and observations inspired much of his writing, which challenged traditional colonial ideas as well as emergent post-colonial discourses, as several of the contributors in this volume attest. Additionally, it was his short stories – and those of some of his contemporaries in the 1920s and 1930s – that first and most fully embraced the new imperatives of post-colonial writing, a feat sometimes claimed by others for the West Indian novel of the 1950s and 1960s. Walrond's pioneering experiments were at the forefront in establishing the short story, in the words of West Indian critic and contributor to this volume Kenneth Ramchand, as "the imported literary form most securely possessed and modified by the writers of the English-speaking [region]".[2] And it is *Tropic Death*, states eminent Caribbean critic Robert Hill, that is "probably the greatest short story work in the entire body of West Indian literature".[3]

Walrond's life, like that of many people from the Caribbean, was shaped by migration. He was born 18 December 1898, in Georgetown, British Guiana (now Guyana), but in 1906 his family moved to Barbados. His parents had strong Barbadian connections: Ruth Walrond was born in Barbados and her husband William was born in British Guiana, the son of Barbadian immigrants (according to the recently released US Census for 1930). Three years after that move, according to family legend, his father, William Walrond, a tailor, abandoned his wife and children and joined the great exodus of Caribbean labourers to the Panama Canal Zone. In 1910 or 1911, Ruth Walrond and her children, now destitute, were forced to migrate to the Canal Zone, seeking reconciliation with William. Walrond's life in the Caribbean affected him in various, sometimes conflicting, ways. In *Tropic Death*, set in Barbados, Panama and British Guiana, and in his other writings Walrond fictionalizes his "own experiences of the Caribbean landscape",[4] but in contrast to the tourist paradise portrayed by some writers, his depiction of the region focuses on the physical, social and economic struggles that precipitated widespread migration at the turn of the twentieth century. His youth there so thoroughly penetrated his consciousness, that even in his sixties, after not having lived in the Caribbean for decades, he frequently returned in his writing, particularly in times of financial, psychological and artistic crisis, to the world of his boyhood and adolescence. As his grandson Frank Stewart remarked, "Walrond seemed to have retained a lifelong sympathy with himself as a boy beset by the adult world."[5]

Perhaps one reason that Walrond was never able to return physically to the Caribbean was the constant outsider status he endured while living there. In Barbados he was ostracized as a "mudhead" (an insulting term describing inhabitants from British Guiana, much of which is below sea level) while in Panama he was a "chombo" (a denigrating name for a black West Indian), in Haiti "a *vieux Anglais*" (old Englishman), and in Santo Domingo, a "cocolo", a demeaning label for non-Hispanic persons of African ancestry, including those from the anglophone and francophone Caribbean. These experiences led to a permanent sense of displacement and a long-lasting, deep-seated empathy for others who were also marginalized. He felt alienated, especially while in the Panama Canal Zone, which was completely controlled by the

American presence during the building of the canal (1904–14), with its racist two-tiered structure of "silver" payment for black workers and "gold" for whites.[6]

Walrond soon began to feel stifled by the educational and vocational limitations of the Caribbean and Central America and on 30 June 1918, he participated in the great Caribbean migration to the United States, his world of "bigger endeavour". He was completely unprepared for what he encountered upon arrival: once again, as a black he was an outsider, a "nigger" in the eyes of whites and a "monkey chaser" to African Americans. The level of the discrimination he encountered, especially in the initial years of his migration when he was unable to get a job utilizing his journalistic skills, would affect him for the remainder of his life.

After his lack of success securing a job at either a white- or African American–owned newspaper, it is not surprising that Walrond turned to a fellow West Indian, Marcus Garvey, the Jamaican-born leader of the Universal Negro Improvement Association. Walrond had worked for two small Garveyite papers, the *Brooklyn and Long Island Informer* and the *Weekly Review*, before gaining employment with the weekly *Negro World*, the flagship organ of the Universal Negro Improvement Association. His participation in the paper helped provide a "potential infrastructure for the Harlem Renaissance".[7] However, despite his admiration for Garvey's black pride and his fighting spirit, Walrond was never completely comfortable with the Jamaican's separatist agenda.

After leaving *Negro World* Walrond soon became affiliated with *Opportunity*, the organ of the integrationist National Urban League, serving as the journal's business manager from 1925 to 1927, helping to stabilize the publication's finances, to bring a more international scope to the periodical and to provide a venue for several of the younger writers of the Harlem Renaissance. As Irma Watkins-Owens asserts, "Walrond helped shift *Opportunity* towards inclusion of more global perspectives, especially on developments, literary and otherwise in the colonial territories."[8] During this time, he also met Howard University professor Alain Locke and published a short story in Locke's ground-breaking anthology *The New Negro* (1925).[9] The story, "The Palm Porch", would be substantially revised in *Tropic Death*.

Tropic Death, as its title implies, intimates a Caribbean filled with both beauty and vitality but at the same time beset by conflicts and contradictions.

The book is significant in part because of its depiction of working-class Caribbean folk, providing a window into the life of a community largely unrepresented in and therefore devalued by more traditional narratives. *Tropic Death* documents the lives of ordinary Caribbean people, including their constant migration, their struggles against poverty and nature, colonial hegemony and the destructive effects of racism. As Carl A. Wade observes, "In its faithful recreation of the predicament of individual protagonists, mostly of the black peasant class, *Tropic Death* achieves a powerful indictment – however indirect – of the social, political and economic arrangements under which this group subsisted."[10]

Walrond is particularly concerned with dispelling the stereotype of a monolithic Caribbean. Consequently, he painstakingly recreates the many local dialects of the region, using language to probe the various aspects of Caribbean identity. In this way, the writer attempts to confront his own fractured identity, one shaped by often conflicting elements of European, African and American cultures, a dilemma shared by Caribbean people in general, especially those in the migrant communities. Once in America, for example, many of these immigrants experienced a sense of displacement, "a transformation that can leave one forever distanced and different from the land and people of one's origin, if also from the land of one's adoption".[11] This sense of displacement pervades *Tropic Death* and all of Walrond's writings.

The generally favourable critical reviews and financial success that greeted *Tropic Death* (it soon went into a second edition) prompted Walrond's publisher, Boni and Liveright, to provide an advance for another book, on the French involvement in the building of the Panama Canal. Riding on the success of *Tropic Death*, in 1927–28 Walrond was the recipient of a Harmon Award in literature, a Zona Gale scholarship to attend the University of Wisconsin, and a Guggenheim award (later renewed for an additional six months) to complete works of fiction on Caribbean life. This resulted in a frenetic period during which he visited several countries in Central America and the Caribbean before arriving in London in June 1929. He departed for France the next month ostensibly to complete his project on the canal, and lived there sporadically until the summer of 1933, often beset by severe financial difficulties and an overwhelming sense of artistic failure, yet frequently expressing confidence about the prospects of new writing projects including a novel on African American life and another text on Panama.

When Walrond arrived in Paris in 1929, there was a small but firmly entrenched group of black artists and writers already living there. He quickly established himself in this community, particularly renewing a relationship with Harlem Renaissance poet Countee Cullen and becoming part of the entourage of shipping heiress Nancy Cunard. While in France, Walrond socialized heavily. At the same time, he also suffered from ill health, culminating in his admission to the American Hospital in Paris with appendicitis.[12] The turmoil of those years is vividly captured in correspondence between Walrond and Shirley Graham, later the wife of W.E.B. Du Bois (Schlesinger Library, Harvard University Library).

The years 1933 to 1939 witnessed an even more unsettled lifestyle than was the norm for Walrond. In 1935, for example, he was manager of a travelling troupe – a "calypso revue" – that toured Ireland. For the most part, however, he resided in London until 1939 when he relocated to rural southwest England, primarily to escape the bombing in the capital.[13] Another reason may have been his arrest in 1938 for allegedly stabbing a man in the neck. While the charges were later dropped, the incident reveals the turbulence in his life at the time.

The small, picturesque town in which he settled from 1939 to 1952, Bradford on Avon, near Bath, promised a peaceful environment which, unfortunately, was not reflected in Walrond's personal life. Once again, as one of only a handful of black residents, he would have been an outsider. Still, he seems to have led a comfortable if uneventful existence in Bradford until 1952 when he was admitted as a voluntary patient to Roundway Hospital in Wiltshire. There is no indication of what led to his hospitalization, but clearly it was for some sort of mental illness since Roundway admitted only patients with psychological problems. Although he was, by all accounts, a charming, energetic figure, David Levering Lewis observes, Walrond "also had a brooding side, and was given to bouts of paralyzing self-doubt".[14] His disappointment and regret over his failure to honour his earlier professional obligations to the Guggenheim Foundation may well have contributed to his decision to seek help at Roundway.

But it was also during the 1930s that his radical – even Marxist – impulses came to the fore in the anticolonial articles he published in *Black Man*, edited by Marcus Garvey with whom he was now reconciled, and in other journals; in his association with other progressive forces such as *New Masses*, and in his membership on a committee to free the Scottsboro Boys. He also maintained links with George Padmore's pan-Africanist movement, and the more conservative integrationist League of Coloured Peoples headed by Sir Harold Moody. Many of the pieces published during this period attack Britain's treatment of its colonies and class structure of English society.

Ironically, it was while he was in the psychiatric facility that Walrond was most prolific; more than a dozen of his stories appeared in *Roundway Review*, the journal published by the institution. Many of these hearken back to his youth in the Caribbean, although there are also others set in England and one lengthy tale, "Success Story", that takes place largely in New York City. "Success Story", like an earlier narrative "City Love" (1927), is one of the most significant literary works on the difficult process of assimilation for West Indian immigrants. In the *Roundway* fiction, Walrond re-examines his earlier themes, including alienation, the search for identity, and the persistent problems of racism and class differences and conflicts introduced to the Americas through a legacy of slavery and colonialism. As he had been in Harlem, Walrond was one of the pioneering literary figures from the Caribbean to settle in London.

Walrond also worked on his writings about the construction of the Panama Canal, and although his long awaited book "The Big Ditch", never appeared, we do get a sense of his Panama Canal writings in "The Second Battle", a fragmentary work also published in *Roundway Review*. While it is largely a dense, scholarly text loaded with minute details of the Panama project, the manuscript is important for its continued focus on themes that had dominated Walrond's early writings, including his empathy for oppressed peoples. This subtext manifests itself, in particular, in the anti-imperialist (especially anti-American) view that pervades the work.

The writer's ability to do sustained work for *Roundway Review* and to move beyond the hospital's environs while engaging in several research projects undoubtedly gave him the confidence to leave the hospital facility in 1957 and attempt to resuscitate his literary career. Moving to London, most likely to be closer to the literary community, Walrond took a clerical position to pay expenses. In London, despite his disappointments at not finding venues for his work and dogged by poor health, he never abandoned his literary projects. As he told Guggenheim secretary Henry Moe in a letter in 1960, "in spite of age and years of silence I have not lost sight of my objectives, or the high aims with which I set out as a Guggenheim Fellow such a long time ago".[15]

Even in the 1960s, he was negotiating with Henry Pell, an editor at Liveright Publishers, for a reissue of *Tropic Death*, complete with some stylistic revisions and three additional stories. Unfortunately, however, Walrond did not live long enough to complete these projects. He died of coronary thrombosis at St Bartholomew's Hospital, Smithfield, London, on 8 August 1966 and is buried in a pauper's grave in Abney Park Cemetery in the London Borough of Hackney. A headstone marking his burial place was erected by the editors of this collection in 2009.

Walrond has until recent years been a lost figure in literary studies. He was a West Indian who spent most of his life outside the Caribbean. His greatest success came in the United States, but his representation of Caribbean folk life and language often baffled an American audience with little knowledge of the region and its customs. Thus, he has been hard to place in the literary canon. Fortunately, the recent emphasis on transnationalism has created a "home" for a writer such as Walrond, one who reflects the experience of many people, in increasing numbers, who somewhat uneasily inhabit two worlds.

Walrond has also been neglected in part because it was presumed that he had stopped writing (or at least publishing) after leaving the United States in 1929. The recent recovery of a trove of stories and essays published while Walrond was a patient in the Roundway Hospital dispels that myth. These later writings, returning to the themes he had earlier iterated so powerfully in *Tropic Death*, amply demonstrate that the talent he had shown during the Harlem Renaissance had not diminished with age.[16] The present collection of critical essays, the first of its kind, will, it is hoped, further enhance our understanding of this complex and undervalued figure, help restore him to the stature he had enjoyed during the Harlem Renaissance and situate him as an early voice of the Caribbean diaspora.

This anthology brings together a diversity of critical opinion covering forty years of Walrond scholarship, from the pioneering texts of Kenneth Ramchand and Robert Bone to the modern perspectives of scholars such as Michelle A. Stephens, Louis Chude-Sokei and others. In addition to illuminating *Tropic Death* from several perspectives, and often in dialogue with one another, the contributors discuss the important influences on Walrond's life and work and, through an exploration of his lesser-known apprentice fiction and nonfiction as well as his later *Roundway Review* writings, together provide a comprehensive critical examination of this important Caribbean American author.

In "The Writer Who Ran Away", an early seminal commentary first published in 1970 but revised specially for this anthology, prominent West Indian critic Kenneth Ramchand, through a detailed analysis of *Tropic Death*, sets out to reclaim for West Indian literature a writer he regards as one of the two major stylists of the Harlem Renaissance; the other was Jean Toomer, whom Walrond admired. Ramchand proposes Walrond – his considerable contribution to American writing notwithstanding – as the quintessential Caribbean writer, in search of home and belonging, whose narratives chronicle the peculiarities of the regional communities, their linguistic nuances, folkways, social and racial anxieties and conflicts, and the continuing malaise of Caribbean life. He contends that Walrond utilizes the common cultural and social elements of the region to create a single Caribbean society, which the writer celebrates without idealizing. Moreover, Walrond is also said to transcend the traditional Caribbean genres of social realism and protest to articulate a more comprehensive vision that foregrounds the affinities linking the physical landscape, elemental forces and West Indian folk cultures and beliefs.

Some of the early influences on Walrond's development are first identified in Robert Bone's unique and comprehensive reading of the writer's oeuvre published in *Down Home*.[17] Bone, one of the first scholars to conduct an extensive study of Walrond's life and work and their interrelationship, attributes what he considers the author's gothic imagination to his fundamentalist religious upbringing and the literary influences of Lafcadio Hearn (1850–1904) and Pierre Loti (1850–1923). Bone proposes Walrond's writing as essentially a quest to resolve the tensions and complexities of a fragmented identity shaped simultaneously by his socialization in the British colonies and in a modern metropolis. The writer's central focus, in Bone's view, is migration and transplantation and the attendant dilemmas of dislocation and cultural adjustment that confronted this quintessential "other" throughout his peripatetic life. Bone is also one of the few writers to evaluate the author's early apprentice writing, set primarily in the United States, and its significance to his fiction as a whole.

Michelle Stephens is one of the scholars at the forefront of a strain of modern criticism that locates Walrond's achievement within a larger framework of the black transnational movement of the 1930s. In "'All Look Alike in Habana': Archaeologies of Blackness across Eric Walrond's Archipelago", she examines the author's contribution to this conversation on a movement in which, as she outlines in *Black Empire*, significant black male intellectuals such as Claude McKay, Marcus Garvey and C.L.R. James imagined a black global community "united against whiteness and empire"[18] that transcended nationality. As she sees it, the meeting of African Americans and Caribbean nationals in the early years of the twentieth century became a unique moment of black intellectual encounter as these intellectuals debated the nature of black identity, its relationship to stories of the racial past, the cultural and visual entertainment technologies of the present, and the politics of the black liberation of the future. Stephens proposes that Walrond's unique contribution was a transnational perspective that historicized the specifically visual politics of blackness, race and race relations – colour consciousness, in other words, in the United States – within the broader hemispheric and colonial archaeologies.

Louis Chude-Sokei interrogates many of these and other complexities and contradictions in "Foreign Negro Flash Agents: Eric Walrond and the Discrepancies of Diaspora". Chude-Sokei argues, as he had in his influential book, *The Last "Darky": Bert Williams, Black-on-Black Minstrelsy, and the African Diaspora*,[19] that increased migration from the Caribbean has introduced varieties of black modernism that complicated notions of "race" held by black writers during the Harlem Renaissance and associated movements, since these immigrants brought understandings of race and slavery that contrasted with those of their African American counterparts. The chapter in this volume explores the contrasting ways in which Walrond and Claude McKay presented their visions of diaspora in this cultural climate. Chude-Sokei concludes that Walrond's perspective was far more prescient than that of his celebrated peer, although both were committed to a panoramic dissection of Harlem difference.

In "Genre, Gender and Eric Walrond's Equivocal Transnational Vision", Rhonda Frederick contends that, unlike many writers and theorists, Walrond evaluates the African diaspora pessimistically, if not cynically, and from perspectives that challenge and complicate the prevailing discourses, by representing the underrepresented realities of black life, especially those ethnic particularities that relate to intra- and interracial unions and masculinity. She asserts that Walrond interrogates and diverges from the somewhat simplistic ideas and ideals of race-based unity among blacks, that homogenous vision of black subjectivity. What his creative vision substitutes is a multifaceted reimagining of diasporic life, the idea of difference-in-unity. Through an analysis of some of the major female characters in *Tropic Death*, she demonstrates how the complexity of Walrond's representation is further complemented by his departure from fixed interpretations of gender that, like those perspectives on race-based-unity, permeate and undergird anglophone Caribbean men's transnational vision.

Drawing on the work of Stephens and Frederick, Michael Niblett explores *Tropic Death* in the context of the proletarian arts movement of the 1920s and 1930s which featured, among others, the work of Jack Conroy – significantly, a faithful correspondent of Walrond during the last decades of his life. Niblett highlights the destruction of Nature and the dehumanization of the folk by capitalist modernization and exploitation. Additionally, Niblett links the author's vision to that of his West Indian contemporaries such as C.L.R. James, whose writings reflected the influence of this movement, and in the views of critics such as Ramchand, ushered in the birth of modern West Indian fiction of "social realism". Ultimately, Niblett sees Walrond's text as participating in a wider aesthetic embracing writers from as far afield as Asia in its interrogation of the effects of urbanization, modernity and capitalism.

Yet another topic of continuing critical focus among literary critics and historians of the Harlem Renaissance, such as Larnell Dunkley Jr and Ralph D. Story, has been the contribution of white patronage to the work of the black artist during this period of vibrant artistic activity, and the degree to which such patronage shaped – and some contend – compromised the representation of black culture, especially as a consequence of the primitivist perspectives that influenced the agenda of many white patrons. The chapter by Wade, Bone and Parascandola, "Eric Walrond and the Dynamics of White Patronage during the Harlem Renaissance", reveals that Walrond, doubly disenfranchised as both a foreigner and black, was also dependent on the beneficence of the white establishment, although in a somewhat different way. The chapter looks at two of these unions both involving the writer – specifically those with the linguist and editor Edna Underwood and, to a lesser degree, Henry Moe, the long-serving secretary and chief executive officer of the Guggenheim Foundation – and explores the many complex dimensions of the relations between white patrons and black artists, as explicated by some critics. The chapter offers insights into the challenges created by this patronage and the artistic and other options available to Walrond and other contemporary black writers as a consequence

James Davis addresses these and other challenges in his contribution, "A Prism so Strange: The Biography of Eric Walrond", from his ambitious work-in-progress, the first biography of Walrond. While the chapter documents the attempt to reconstruct faithfully a life from disparate and not easily available sources, its larger scope is to find a central and unifying thesis for the reconstruction itself, justifying such a project of a writer considered to have produced only one major text. Davis also recounts the way in which his own perceptions and judgements of his subject have shifted as the work progresses. Additionally, he reconstructs some of the lesser-known details of those troubled years spent in Wiltshire, England, and assesses the significance of the *Roundway Review* writings, especially the lengthy serial "The Second Battle". His chapter ends with a set of questions about Walrond's life and work that the process of composing the biography has raised so far but failed to resolve.

Walrond's traumatic assimilation into New York society is the subject of "A West Indian Grows in Brooklyn: The Early American Experiences of Eric Walrond", jointly authored by Parascandola and Davis. The chapter explores the writer's apprentice fiction to chart the response of the West Indian community and that of the young writer himself to the inter- and intra-racial dynamics of life in Brooklyn's Caribbean neighbourhoods of the 1920s and 1930s, in encounters such as those dramatized in "Success Story", the six-part tale published in *Roundway Review* and recently republished in *In Search of Asylum*.

As has been mentioned, Walrond's ties with Marcus Garvey go back to the early 1920s. A little explored area of study has been the renewal of their relationship in the 1930s in England. The Walrond-Garvey relationship is the subject of Carl Pedersen's contribution, "Exile on Main Street: Eric Walrond and Garveyism in Great Britain in the 1930s". Pedersen outlines the conflict that led to a parting of the ways between the two men before their reconciliation a decade later in England. He discusses the forces that influenced Garvey's intellectual development culminating in the transnational perspective of *Black Man*, and in a rare but valuable assessment of Walrond's political writings published in this journal, addresses the writer's gradual adoption of a class-based anti-capitalist world view in preference to his mentor's black capitalism and racial politics. Pedersen concludes that this reconciliation between the two figures was, on Walrond's part, based not only on financial necessity but also to an extent on ideological kinship.

This book is intended as a deepening and a continuation of an emerging, vibrant debate on a writer whose achievements and importance to diasporic studies are only now being fully realized. Yet many facets of his personal life and his work – the fictional and nonfictional work published in *Black Man* and *Roundway Review* especially – require fuller critical scrutiny. The editors are confident that this publication of the first collection of essays on Walrond will stimulate this ongoing and very necessary dialogue.

NOTES

1. See, for example, Frank E.L. Stewart, "Eric Walrond, *Tropic Death* and the Predicament of the Colonial Expatriate Writer", *Studies in the Humanities and Sciences* (Japan) 38, no. 2 (1998): 29–88; Michael Niblett, "The Arc of the 'Other America': Landscape, Nature, and Region in Eric Walrond's *Tropic Death*", in *Perspectives on the "Other America": Comparative Approaches to Caribbean and Latin American Culture*, ed. Michael Niblett and Kerstin Oloff, 51–72 (Amsterdam: Rodopi, 2009); Rhonda Frederick, *"Colón Man a Come": Mythographies of Panamá Canal Migration* (Lantham, MD: Lexington Books, 2005); Rhonda Frederick, "Mythographies of Panamá Canal Migrations: Eric Walrond's *Tropic Death*", in *Marginal Migrations: The Circulation of Cultures within the Caribbean*, ed. Shalini Puri, 43–76 (Oxford: Macmillan, 2003); Michelle A. Stephens, "Eric Walrond's *Tropic Death* and the Discontents of American Modernity", in *Prospero's Isles: The Presence of the Caribbean in the American Imaginary*, ed. Dianne Accaria-Zavala and Rudolfo Popelnik, 167–78 (London: Macmillan, 2004); Eric Walrond, *"Winds Can Wake up the Dead": An Eric Walrond Reader*, ed. Louis J. Parascandola (Detroit: Wayne State University Press, 1998); Louis J. Parascandola, ed., *"Look for Me All Around You": Caribbean Immigrants in the Harlem Renaissance* (Detroit: Wayne State University Press, 2005); Louis J. Parascandola and Carl A. Wade, eds., *In Search of Asylum: The Later Writings of Eric Walrond* (Gainesville: University Press of Florida, 2011); Carl A. Wade, "African American Aesthetics and the Short Fiction of Eric Walrond: *Tropic Death* and the Harlem Renaissance", *CLA Journal* 42 (June 1999): 403–29; Carl A. Wade and Louis J. Parascandola, "In Search of Asylum: Eric Walrond's *Roundway Review* Writings, 1952–1957", *Journal of Caribbean Studies* 19, nos. 1 and 2 (2004–5): 21–42.
2. Kenneth Ramchand, "Andrew Salkey, 30th January 1928–28th April 1995", *Wasafari* (Autumn 1995): 82.

3. Robert Hill, comp. and ed., *Black Man: A Monthly Magazine of Negro Thought and Opinion* (Millwood, NJ: Kraus-Thomson, 1975), 19.
4. Wade, "African American Aesthetics", 415.
5. Stewart, "Eric Walrond", 57.
6. Velma Newton, *The Silver Men: West Indian Labour Migration to Panama, 1850–1914* (Kingston: Institute of Social and Economic Research, University of the West Indies, 1984), 11–29. Despite their nationality, African American labourers in the Canal Zone often faced similar discrimination as well. See Patrice C. Brown, "The Panama Canal: The African American Experience", special issue Federal Records and African American History, *Prologue* 29, no. 2 (Summer 1997): 122–26.
7. Tony Martin, "The Defectors: Eric Walrond and Claude McKay", *Literary Garveyism: Garvey, Black Arts and the Harlem Renaissance* (Dover, MA: Majority Press, 1983), 156.
8. Irma Watkins-Owens, *Blood Relatives: Caribbean Immigrants and the Harlem Community, 1900–1930* (Bloomington: Indiana University Press, 1996), 157.
9. Eric Walrond, "The Palm Porch", in *The New Negro: An Interpretation*, ed. Alain Locke, 115–28 (New York: Albert and Charles Boni, 1925).
10. Wade, "African American Aesthetics", 416.
11. Heather Hathaway, *Caribbean Waves: Relocating Claude McKay and Paule Marshall* (Bloomington: Indiana University Press, 1999), 2.
12. "Eric Walrond Sick in Paris", *Afro-American*, 11 February 1933, 13.
13. "Noted Writer Reveals Inner Glimpse of London as War Clouds Appeared", *New York Amsterdam News*, 23 September 1939, 1.
14. David Levering Lewis, *When Harlem Was in Vogue* (New York: Vintage Books, 1982), 129.
15. Quoted in Ramchand, "Andrew Salkey", 75.
16. See Parascandola and Wade, *In Search of Asylum*.
17. Robert Bone, *Down Home: A History of Afro-American Short Fiction from Its Beginning to the End of the Harlem Renaissance* (New York: Putnam, 1975). Reprinted under the title *Down Home: Origins of the Afro-American Short Story* (New York: Columbia University Press, 1988).
18. Stephens, *Black Empire*, 62.
19. Louis Chude-Sokei, *The Last "Darky": Bert Williams, Black-on-Black Minstrelsy, and the African Diaspora* (Durham: Duke University Press, 2006).

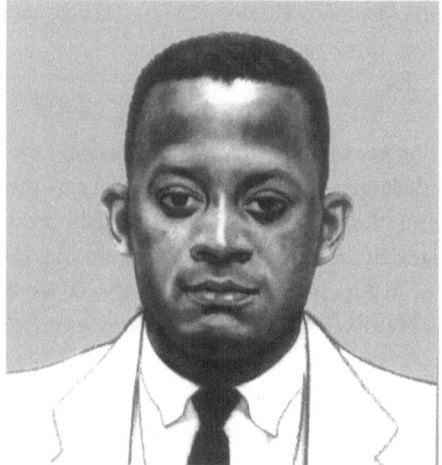

Figure 1. Eric Walrond, by Winold Reiss (pastel on board, c.1925). Fisk University Galleries, Nashville, Tennessee.

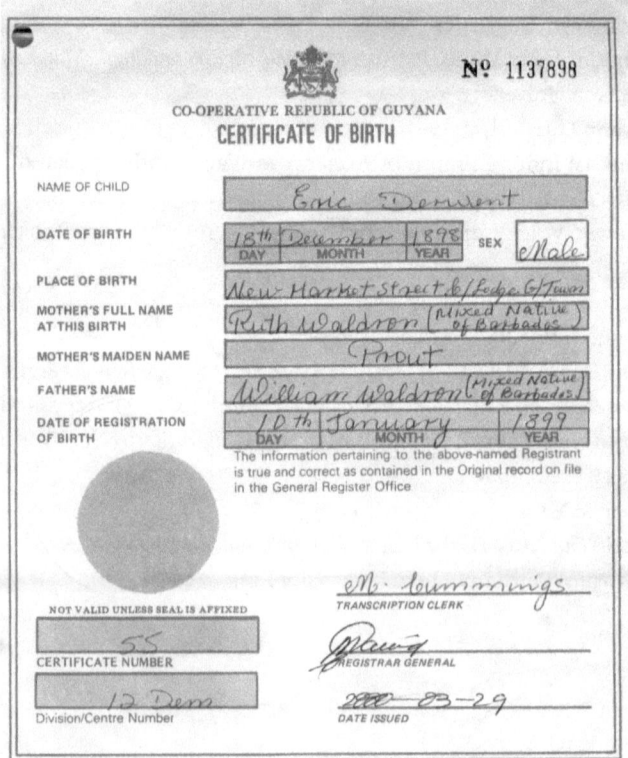

Figure 2. Copy of Eric Walrond's birth certificate. Courtesy of the General Register Office, Georgetown, Guyana.

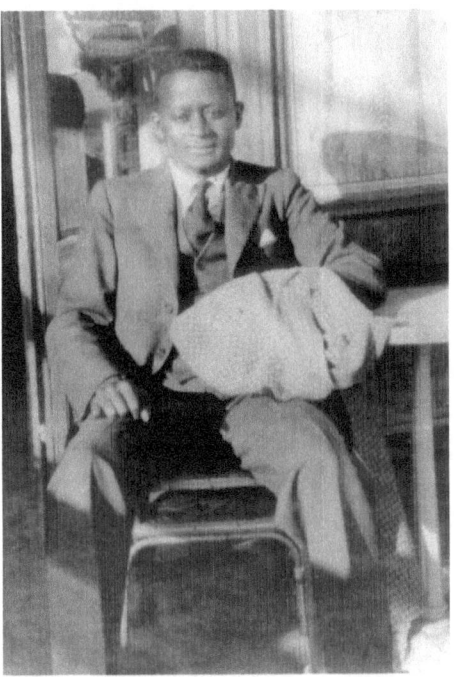

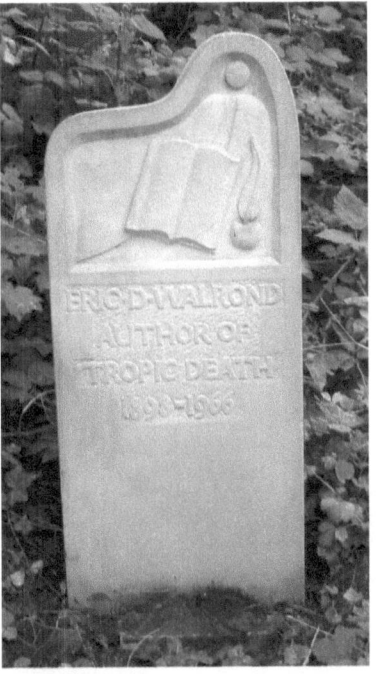

Figure 3. Photograph of Eric Walrond. Atlanta University photographs – individuals, Robert W. Woodruff Library of the Atlanta University Center.

Figure 5. Eric Walrond's gravestone in Abney Park Cemetery, London. Used by permission of Abney Park Cemetery Trust.

The City of New York.
Department of Health.
STATE OF NEW YORK.
No. of Certificate 34747
CERTIFICATE AND RECORD OF MARRIAGE
OF

(Groom) Eric D. Walrond and (Bride) Edith Melita Cadogan

Groom's Residence	2340 - 7th Avenue	Bride's Residence	399 Lex. Ave., Brooklyn
Age	21	Age	19
Color	Col'd	Color	Col'd
Single, Widowed or Divorced	Single	Single, Widowed or Divorced	Single
Occupation	Editor	Maiden Name, if a Widow	Stenographer
Birthplace	Georgetown, Brit. Guiana	Birthplace	Jamaica, B.W.I.
Father's Name	William H.	Father's Name	Albert
Mother's Maiden Name	Ruth King	Mother's Maiden Name	Alice McMahon
Number of Groom's Marriage	First	Number of Bride's Marriage	First

I hereby certify that the above-named groom and bride were joined in Marriage by me, in accordance with the Laws of the State of New York, at 2340 – 7th Avenue (Street), in the Borough of Manhattan, City of New York, this 26th of November 1920

Signature of person performing the Ceremony: Wm Stephenson Holder

Witnesses to the Marriage: William H. Walrond; Miss CelesteL.Cadogan

Official Station: Clergyman

Residence: 250 W. 136th St., N.Y.

NO MUTILATED CERTIFICATE WILL BE RECEIVED

MARGIN RESERVED FOR BINDING

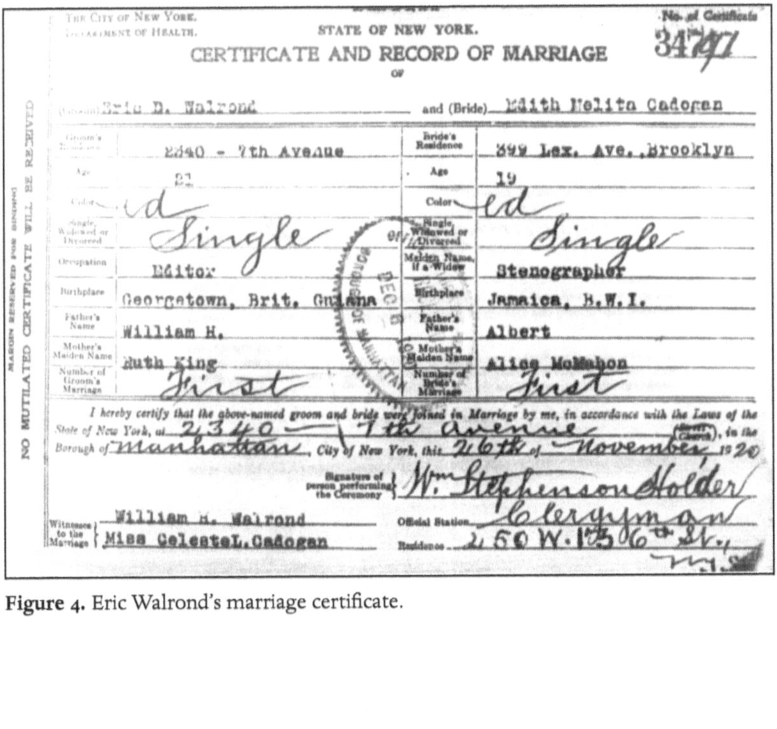

Figure 4. Eric Walrond's marriage certificate.

PART 1

PIONEERING VOICES

1

THE WRITER WHO RAN AWAY
Eric Walrond and *Tropic Death*

KENNETH RAMCHAND

ERIC DERWENT WALROND (1898–1966), who arrived in New York City in 1918, was one of our outstanding émigré writers. Like Claude McKay (1890–1948), who had gone from Jamaica six years earlier with plans to study at Booker T. Washington's Tuskegee Institute, Walrond became part of African American life; also like his fellow West Indian, he was a key figure as artist and facilitator (working through *Opportunity*) of the New Negro movement, later called the Harlem Renaissance. Both writers contributed significantly to the discourse on race and colour in America and both produced literary works that exhibited the force, freshness and vitality of African American cultural and artistic expression.

Walrond was so much a part of the African American awakening that he has tended to be regarded as a North American writer: West Indians of the present generation who have come across the name can hardly have felt the immediate special interest to explore further. He is of value to America partly because he was able to work from the inside, but mainly because he was an outsider, bringing to the American situation his own perspectives on existence and being; on race, colour and culture; on language and society; and on artistic expression. He came with ways of seeing and feeling that derived from his formative experiences in the Caribbean and Central America: childhood under British colonialism in British Guiana and Barbados ("Little England"); teenage years spent in the Spanish-speaking Canal Zone during the busiest years of

American imperialism/investment in Panama; the harshness of Nature – burning sun, molten sea and parched earth; human and economic forces adding to the trials imposed by Nature – mountain chains, forests, swamps and rivers with a life of their own subjected increasingly to order and control by the machine of progress and profit; and compassion for and insight into the lives of the enduring folk, black animate dots in an ever-widening immensity, black labour seduced from the former slave colonies and trapped in the latest embodiment of the plantation. The experiences indicated above informed his perspective and spiced his commentary on life in America. They are also what made Walrond a Caribbean writer.

Walrond's life is a tale of migration and therefore a tale of several places. He spent his first twelve years in two physically contrasting English-speaking territories. He was born in 1898 in the mainland colony of British Guiana (now Guyana), where he lived until he was eight years old. After his father left them, his mother Ruth took him to Barbados, the island of her birth. When Walrond was twelve, they moved again. He was transplanted from a rural agricultural milieu, where forms of English were spoken and vestiges of English culture had seeped down to the masses, to the industrial scene in Panama, where man was imposing his will on nature and the Americans were bullying forward the Panama Canal project. The British colonial was now living in Spanish-speaking Panama, an expanding world where "artisans from the four ends of the earth" including "hordes of Italians, Greeks, Chinese, Negroes – a hardy sun-defying set of white, black and yellow men" were helping the Americans to dig the Panama Canal. Somewhere among "the dusky peons of those coral isles in the Caribbean" who supplied "the bulk of the actual brawn for the work",[1] Ruth Walrond hoped to find and perhaps reconcile with her missing husband. The fatherless boy knew this and probably wanted it too. He lived for six years among the diverse peoples of the region itself as well as among the others who came, barefoot conquistadors or seekers of Panama gold from faraway places. All of them were under sentence of deracination or commodification.

When Walrond left Panama for the United States in 1918, he was in possession of a sound formal education, training as a stenographer, hands-on practice as a clerk in the Health Department of the Canal Mission in Cristobal, and two years experience as a journalist with the long-established *Panama Star and Herald*. But in his third social environment, the young adult could not get a job in any of the "mainstream" newspapers. He knew of the race and colour stratifications of the West Indies, the inequities of the Canal Zone based upon race and colour, and the inherited colonial tensions between Spanish colonial and English colonial. But the West Indian was shocked by the reach of racial discrimination into every sphere of life in America. Marcus Garvey was rousing the masses against dispossession. Walrond joined in.

Between 1922 and 1924 he was associate editor of Marcus Garvey's weekly newspaper *Negro World*, for which he wrote regularly, supporting and defending Garvey, pointing to significant artistic and cultural expressions, and trying his hand as a writer of fiction. All his writings, then and later, contain racial pride, a condemnation of imperialism, and a fierce opposition to white racism and capitalist exploitation. These basic motifs he had in common with Marcus Garvey. But he had his own cosmopolitan take. While working with *Negro World* he contributed to several "mainstream" journals, and to socially "respectable" black publications like the National Association for the Advancement of Colored People's *Crisis* (edited by W.E.B. Du Bois); the socialist *Messenger* (edited by A. Philip Randolph and Chandler Owen); and *Opportunity: Journal of Negro Life* (edited by Charles S. Johnson), the voice of the integrationist National Urban League. In 1925, Walrond began a three-year period as business manager of *Opportunity*, from which position he encouraged the explosion of a defiant self-expression in African American art and culture. Deviating from Garvey, Walrond wanted the New Negro to face America and take his place as an American, proud of his African origin and heritage.

Like McKay, then, Walrond was at the centre of and played an important part in African American cultural criticism and artistic life. From his prolific pen, essays, sketches, reviews and short stories seemed to flow with ease. McKay's *Home to Harlem* (1928) is for many good reasons the novel with which discussion of the Harlem Renaissance sometimes begins, but the two stylists of the movement were Jean Toomer, strange author of the single work, a neglected masterpiece, *Cane* (1923), and Eric Walrond. Although Walrond's affinities to Toomer are yet to be fully noticed and examined by literary historians of the Harlem Renaissance, his role in African American literary history is well recognized.

Walrond's high export value cannot be denied and he is still necessary to the country where he was most active (especially in his early optimism about the possibility of a society where there could be racial pride without racial discrimination). But West Indian and Caribbean people need to reclaim him from North America. His collection of stories, *Tropic Death* (1926), is one of the startling treasures in the lost literature of the West Indies. In this work he is the quintessential Caribbean writer projecting the particularities of each of the several regions of the Caribbean, and he is a prophet of a coming New World responding sensuously and politically to the ubiquitous folk imagination and to the region's submarine unity.

He is of special importance also because the buried longing for home, that life of exile, journalism and vagabondage, its promise and its strange failure is profoundly a part of the history and malaise persistent in the region of his birth. Claude McKay died in America in 1948, in poverty, obscurity and ill-health, with only the doubtful consolation of a last minute conversion to Roman Catholicism; today V.S. Naipaul and C.L.R. James [d. 1989] travel the earth, successful but ill-at-ease, and Walrond died unknown and unfulfilled in London.

How unnerving it was to me to receive back unopened a letter of 12 January 1967 that was trying to track down the vanished author. The note on the envelope read:

> Dear Sir,
> I'm sorry to have to break this news. Eric Walrond is no longer with us. He died in August 1966.
> Mrs G.E. Beard

The necessary research, for which this article is only a preliminary outline, will exhibit in passing the complicatedness of motive and impulse, the blight on the psyche which seems to descend only upon the gifted ones among us; even more to the point, such research might help us to face, a little less defensively, the true length and breadth of our present ills, since it must throw light on the nature of the society in which Walrond was born and which he did not seem to think could offer him either spiritual sustenance or asylum in his long years of crisis as a man and artist.

〜〜
〜〜

Some of the stories in *Tropic Death* may have been emotionally coloured by Walrond's experience in America from 1918, and some may have benefited from his courses at City College of New York (1922–24) and his writing courses on the short story and the novel at Columbia University (1924–26). But the first item to note is that the collection reflects Walrond's movements and experiences within the Caribbean and Central America. One story is set in British Guiana ("The White Snake"); four in Barbados, where Walrond received his early education ("Drought", "Panama Gold", "The Black Pin" and "The Vampire Bat"); three in the Canal Zone, to which he emigrated ("The Wharf Rats", "The Palm Porch" and "Subjection"); one aboard a ship heading to Jamaica from Panama or Honduras ("The Yellow One"); and one, the title story, is set in three places – Barbados, shipboard (a stage for all the world) and Panama.

Walrond had a good ear. One of the enabling achievements of *Tropic Death* is linguistic: the author is able to set down in writing convincing representations of the way his mainly peasant characters speak in each of the territories covered, and he induces us to hear both the surface differences between the regional variants and their common features. All the stories are narrated in the third person in West Indian Standard English and in a West Indian tone of voice which ensures that the narrative voice never projects itself as linguistically or socially superior to the registers in which the speech, the reported thoughts and the thought processes of the characters are conveyed. The following passage from "The Wharf Rats" shows that Walrond knew what he was trying to capture: "Like a host of the native St Lucian emigrants, Jean Baptiste forgot where the French in him ended and the English began. His speech was the petulant *patois* of the unlettered French black. Still, whenever he lapsed into His Majesty's English, it was with a thick Barbadian bias" (91).

As all the stories have a Caribbean setting, so running through them is Walrond's awareness of race and colour, and the not-unrelated impress of both the old European empires and the new imperialism that is seen bulldozing the landscape and setting up to police the Caribbean Sea as if it were an American lake. The new imperialism is stridently present in all the Panama stories as a force grinding down and gouging out the land and turning people into tools without human rights. Although all the varieties and mixtures of race, colour and nation appear in his stories, the nearest the Caribbean author comes to direct racial protest is in "Subjection" a story that seems to be sharpened by his American experience. It is a taut cinematic description of an American marine's premeditated pursuit and brutal shooting of a single black labourer as if this was the South ("I'll teach you niggers down here how to talk to a white man" [112]). This "cracker" behaviour is followed by the narrative's ironic reference to a report that is a cover-up (standard procedure) of the incident: "In the Canal Record, the Q.M. at Toro Point took occasion to extol the virtues of the Department which kept the number of casualties in the recent native labor uprising down to one" (158).

In these stories Walrond moves from simple black and white hostilities to the tangled web of nation, race and colour spun as it can only be spun in the Caribbean. The bordello run by the splendid Jamaican immigrant Miss Buckner in "The Palm Porch" is not in Harlem but in Colón. It is raw stuff smuggled in through social comedy. The haughty mulatto Madame with a wish to be white, toxic with contempt for herself and the two of her daughters who have run off with swains darker and poorer than themselves, is a diplomatic go-between orchestrating the rest of her mixed breed daughters of uncertain provenance to service the customers in her speakeasy. Here Walrond shows the levelling power of sex, which brings together a diverse clientele of different ethnicities under the cover of night and behind Miss Buckner's discreet screens. In the measured satirical portrait (such portraits are one of his strengths – see the description of the Madame [263–64]) of the entrepreneurial and pretentious organizer of the bordello, she is a lofty being removed from the power of gossip and envy, and a person of breeding, a stickler for manners and propriety above common scrutiny. But the truth Walrond shows is that Miss Buckner has no qualms about prostituting her daughters; and at the sordid climax she goes backstage and returns coolly after murdering the British vice consul, whose behaviour was threatening to interfere with the pleasures of an important Spanish captain.

Walrond draws nearly all his characters from "the motley crew recruited to dig the Panama Canal" (67) and people connected with them. In the third Panama story, "The Wharf Rats", the setting is "the low smelting cabins of Coco Té" one of the areas reserved for blacks on the Atlantic side of the canal. Here, Jean Baptiste, a St Lucian black, in Panama since the time of the French attempt to cut a canal, lives with his second wife, Celestin, a brown beauty from Martinique. A cabin away from Jean Baptiste lives a mulatto family from Tortola named Boyce. Their daughter Maura, who could be mistaken for a native señorita or an urbanized Cholo girl, dotes on the half-breed San Tie, son of a Chinese beer-seller and a Jamaica Maroon. The brooding girl, Maffi, who does the housework for Celestin, is secretly in love with Jean Baptiste's son Philip and comes from Trinidad. It is a different social segment from the world of "The Palm Porch".

While Walrond's graphic descriptions of the boys diving in shark-infested waters for coins thrown from passing ships, and of the death of Philip in the jaws of a killer shark, support the theme of poverty and economic exploitation, there are two other main interests in the story: Walrond is intent on suggesting the emotional intensities and the inner worlds of Maura and Maffi, young natural creatures in the throes of love or hormones. The second interest picked up by Walrond's fiction is the battle for the soul of the Caribbean black between Christian religion (the Plymouth Brethren in this story) and the proscribed princes and powers of the African spirit world, with whom Maffi communes. At the end Maffi hums an obeah melody and is at peace at last because she knows that Philip's death is the answer of the obeah powers to her prayers.

In his 1927 application for a Guggenheim, Walrond spoke of his plan to weave into his imaginative patterns "a considerable amount of the legends, folk tales, peasant songs, and voodoo myths abounding in the region". They are an essential part of the texture of the lives of the characters in "The Black Pin", "The White Snake" and "The Vampire Bat", which is a rousing tale of the supernatural and which significantly shows that certain aspects of the folkways are embedded early in the consciousness of whites born and growing up in the islands. It is set in Barbados, where white people and black people have lived together for generations, and where white creole children are impressed with lasting images of the worlds of their nannies, caretakers and other domestic folk. Captain Bellon Prout returning from the Boer Wars dismisses too easily Lizzie's experience of the supernatural, and he scoffs too readily at "the man in the cane", "the fire hags", "duppies" and other manifestations he had heard of as a child. Against his determined assertion of rationality, Mother Cragwell pronounces that there are two kinds of knowledge: "All yo' buckras t'ink unna know mo' than we neygas." All along Prout's dark journey to his home, Walrond shows the buckra's mind yielding to remembered childhood impressions (226, 227, 230) and he succumbs for a moment to what he deems a temptation to relapse ("barbaric obeah images filled his buckra consciousness" [228]). With his nerves on edge but desperate not to relapse any further, Prout takes into his house a black baby found sleeping in the marl. He tells himself it is another instance of a common practice among the former slave population. He pays a price for denial. His sleepless mind is tortured by images of abandoned babies, "men in the canes", "fire hags" and "weirdly interchangeable – Black Negro babes and vampire bats" (233). Next morning the young plantation owner's body is found sprawled in his hut: "With a perforation pecked in its forehead, it was utterly bloodless and white" (234). The white creole's attempt to deny the existence of early modes of feeling shared with the blacks brings down the gruesome death of Captain Bellon Prout, "a solid pillar of the Crown" (144).

Blending the legends, folk tales, peasant songs and voodoo myths in the different regions with other social and cultural features common to the region as a whole, Walrond in effect creates one Caribbean society. As we move through the different stories, we notice enforced idleness, lurking violence, the formation of ghettos no matter what the setting: the wrangling yard-type existence of "The Black Pin", the ghetto called "Bordeaux" in "The White Snake" and its larger-scale replication in "Bottle Alley" of the Panama story "Tropic Death" are examples. Everywhere, even in the countryside there are hard times, with peasants eking out subsistence from land made unyielding by burning sun and rising dust. Interestingly, the landscapes momentarily merge into one another: the opening paragraphs of "Drought", set in Barbados with "sun-crazed blacks cutting stone on the white burning hillside" and a "rock engine" driven by a buckra, might almost be the opening of a Panama Canal–cutting story. The dust that fills the air, covers the roads and enters the mouths and nostrils of the peasants at the time of drought in Barbados rises again in the Canal Zone as the land is shattered by the machines.

Walrond portrays a society in which the strains and stresses of the female are multiplied by the desperate emigration of the male. So in "Tropic Death", in the "Wha' you gwine do" passage, that incidentally illustrates Walrond's control of regional dialect, we find an overburdened Sarah Bright consulting her half-brother, Charlie Oxley, before setting out for Colón in search of Lucian Bright, the father of her children:

> "But wha' yo gwine do, ni Sarah? Wha' yuh gwine do? Yo' an' all dese chirrun yo' get dey ni?"
>
> "Oi ent stop fuh t'ink, Charlie, to tell yo' de troot. But de Lord will provide, Charlie, Oi is get my truss in Him."
>
> "But wha' kin de Lord do fo' yo' now doan heah fum dat woofless vargybin?"

"Ev'rt'ing wuks togeddah fuh dem dat truss in de Lord. Oi'll manage somehow. Oi'll scratch meself togeddah. De lil' bit of money Oi get fum de house an' de piece o' land' will jus' buy me an' Gerald ticket. Now all Oi is axin' yo' fo' do is put up de show money. Oi ent wan' no mo'. Dah is anuff. An' as de Lord is in heaven Oi'll pos' it back tuh yu' when the boat land at Colon."

"An' wuh yo' gwine do wit' de chirrun, ni Sarah? Wuh yuh gwine do wit' dum?" (252)

Walrond's stories go beyond simple hardship-and-emigration themes. The question-and-answer pattern and the repetition of Charlie Oxley's opening question suggest, through the rhythms of the folk speech, a community of feeling – grief, compassion and resolution. Sarah Bright's faith in the Lord is presented as naïve, but at the same time we can begin to discover in it the heroic capacity of the folk to hope and to endure. To put it like this is to press the point that Walrond is always moving his material away from conventional social realism and protest, and balancing or complicating the tone of the narrative by adding elements that lie outside the sphere of satire, protest or indignation.

We might as well notice that in *Tropic Death*, the depiction of a Caribbean society, for all Walrond's awareness of social and economic problems, is contained within a wider frame: the evocation of a physical world in which the seasons and the elements are dramatic agents; and the expression of a native insight into the ways of the peasant folk. Walrond's creatures inhabit a landscape tyrannized over by the sun:

> Crawling along the road to the gap, Coggins gasped at the consequence of the sun's wretched fury. There, where canes spread over with their dark rich foliage into the dust-laden road, the village dogs hunting for eggs to suck, fowls to kill, paused amidst the yellow stalks of cork-dry canes to pant, or drop exhausted, sun-smitten. The sun had robbed the land of its juice, squeezed it dry. Star apples, husks, transparent on the dry sleepy trees . . . His sight impaired by the livid sun, Coggins turned hungry eyes to the soil. Empty corn stalks . . . blackbirds at work . . . Along the water course, bushy palms shading it, frogs gasped for air, their white breasts like fowls, soft and palpitating. The water in the drains sopped up, they sprang at flies, mosquitoes . . . wrangled over a mite. It was a dizzy spectacle and the black peons were praying to God to send rain. (17–20)

The sea, too, has its anger. Out of its depths come the ravenous sharks that devour the boys in "The Wharf Rats", and the son of Sarah Bright gazes dumbly at its various faces in "Tropic Death": "To the left of him there rose the cobwebbed arch of a bridge. Under it the water lay dark and gleaming. Against the opaque sides there were scows, barges, oil tankers. Zutting motor boats, water policemen, brought commotion to the sea. Far out, where the sun kissed it, the sea shone like a sheet of blazing zinc" (239). In this fictive world, one thing spontaneously becomes the symbol of another. The frogs gasping, wrangling over a mite, and the fish in the following passage become natural symbols of man's condition: "Fish, lured onto the glimmering ends of loaded lines, raged in fruitless fury; tore, snarled gutturally, for release; bloodied patches of the hard blue sea; left crescents of gills on green silvery hooks. Some, big and fat as oxen, raved for miles on the shining blue sea, snapping and snarling acrobatically. For a stretch of days, the *Wellington* left behind a scarlet trail" (245). Of course, Walrond's stories also make the point continuously that natural disasters are sometimes aided and abetted by socio-economic forces, and natural disasters can be unleashed by man's activities.

Not surprisingly, human affairs in Walrond's stories are markedly influenced by the characters' personal relationship to the world of elemental forces. The gods still people the air, alive in the consciousness of the peasant folk and active through obeah, the supernatural, and prayer. "The dry season was at its height. Praying to the Lord to send rain, black peons gathered on the rumps of breadfruit and cherry trees in abject supplication" (17). While the decisive entry of supernatural powers in human affairs at first strikes the reader as arbitrary and in need of scientific or rational psychological explanation ("The White Snake", "The Black Pin", "The Vampire Bat", "The Wharf Rats"), Walrond's matter-of-fact treatment makes it acceptable as part of the natural order of things. In spite of the existence of more progressive or advanced tendencies in the community to cheapen or censor, the instincts rise at the proper season in this rich world of feeling: "The scent of something ripe and rich and edible – something to be tasted with the lore of the tropics deep in one's blood – something bare and big and immortal as the moon – compelling something – began to fill the air about the little boy" (179). The reader is made aware of elemental passion capable of being touched off at the slightest stimulus, even when it is as locked-in as Maffi's burning desires in "The Wharf Rats" or as apparently socially derived as the hatred that rages between the Negro and the white Cuban in "The Yellow One". It is this primal world and its ways, conveniently referred to as "folk", which Louise Bennett, Olive Lewin, Rex Nettleford and J.D. Elder have helped to capture, and which West Indian writers like Lindsay Barrett, Earl Lovelace and L. Edward Kamau Brathwaite are seeking to reintegrate.

Walrond does not write out of any simple desire to bring back the old-time days. His stories spring directly out of an existing folk community, and he is fully conscious that the old awareness and structures of belief are disappearing in the face of Westernization and industrialization. Emigration to the Canal Zone, with its promise of quick riches, brought the folk community into contact with modern industry and disturbed the old ways of life profoundly:

> Below, a rock engine was crushing stone, shooting up rivers of steam and signaling the frontier's rebirth. Opposite, there was proof, a noisy swaggering sort of proof, of the gradual death and destruction of the frontier post. Black men behind wheelbarrows slowly ascended a rising made of spliced boards and emptied the sand rock into the maw of a mixing machine. More black men, a peg down, behind the wheelbarrows, formed a line which caught the mortar pouring into the rear organ of the omnivorous monster. ("The Palm Porch", 117)

Writing about a community whose existence was still in living memory, and conscious of the changes taking place within that community, Walrond imagines it with convincingness. He celebrates the still-available positives in the community and he does so without idealizing it. (Walrond's celebrations of grounded hard-working women as well as muse-like beings who inspire men to dream dreams is a clear announcement that in his mind at least women were a valuable human resource of the region.)

"Panama Gold" illustrates Walrond's use of nature, and his intuitive grasp of the impossibility of separating out ideal folk elements from their more complicated living contexts. The story opens in the season of drought with Ella Heath, a mulatto girl too involved in life and lore to notice her loneliness overmuch:

> She would be alone at dusk, cooking, mixing flour, or tasting broth . . . "Why taste it, why? It no fo' me alone?" Yampies, eddoes, plantains . . .
> "De Bajan man him say," Ella smiled, " 'plantain an' salt fish me don't want 'um, an' de Mud-head man him say, 'me wish me had 'um, me wish me had 'um . . . ' " And moisture came to Ella's laughing eyes.

> From the plantains to the corn and the flour dumplings . . . "one o' dem would knock a man in a cock hat," she observed . . . " a man . . . a man . . ." (36)

Ella's self-sufficiency and resilience arise from her connections with the earth, and after the introduction of Mr Poyah's name and history through gossip, Walrond uses a dramatic change of season to great effect. The association of Ella with fertility rituals is obviously a celebration of her connections with the earth, but it also looks forward symbolically to the opportunity coming into her life with Mr Poyah:[2]

> Cast up on a bare half acre of land, Ella came to know the use of green, virgin things. Ore; green ore – spread over the land. Riotously nature peopled the earth about her. In front of her cabin door there was a water course. It was filled with sparrow grass. A wild, mad hectic green – the green of young sugar canes. Up and down the gap, horses, donkeys, ring-horned goats, on the way to Bridgetown to be raced, tugged at their tethers, crazy to eat up Ella's sparrow grass. It tempted the oxen carting tremulous loads of salty sugar cane grown on the swampy seaside of Barbadoes – tempted sheep, oracular, voiceless, dog-shy sheep bewilderedly on the road to market – tempted hens frizzly on the pip, and leaping, lap-eared dogs . . . Inexhaustible stems of green sprang up around Ella's domain. (42–44)

The next movement of the story returns us to the season of drought and we find Ella on the way to Mr Poyah's shop to make purchases of essential supplies. Walrond's introduction of folk legend in his stories is always functional (not decorative or exotic), and on her walk through the bushes, Ella remembers the story of the Negro who had been buried alive:

> Evergreen leaves fell swirling through the dusk upon Ella's face. She brushed them away, and into her untutored mind came a legend, "Sh, carrion crow," she cried, "me no dead yet." The evergreen leaves, caressing her face, brought it vividly to her . . . "Sh, carrion crow, me no dead yet." An old Dutch Guianese had uttered the ghastly words. Black Portuguese legend . . . For sticking his hand in a pork barrel in a Portuguese grocer's shop, a Negro had been caught and whisked off to a dark spot in the woods. His hands had been cut off and he had been buried alive, with only his head sticking out of the ground. That had happened at night. In the morning the crows had come to gouge the eyes out of his head. "Sh, carrion crow, me no dead yet . . ." Evergreen leaves on Ella's face . . . crows swirling around the head of a body buried on the Guiana mound . . . (46–47)

In her continuing loneliness, Ella is dying slowly, and though the storyline is still to be unfolded we are allowed to anticipate through the legend both that Ella will lose her opportunity with Mr Poyah, and that for all that, the will to survive shall not be defeated ("Sh, carrion crow, me no dead yet").

Ella's entry into Mr Poyah's shop is the signal for a shift of levels in the story, from ritual and symbolic to social and psychological. Social barriers begin to present themselves against what was hitherto being presented as natural gravitation between sexes. Ella's awareness of Mr Poyah's blackness and her aversion to his peg leg notwithstanding, Walrond shows us the characters sizing each other up:

> Ella's eyes deserted the old man to light upon the shopkeeper sticking his black veiny hand in the brine for the salt beef, his back to her. With a stab to the breast, she noted the protrudent tip of the cork leg . . .
>
> "Anything else, miss?" he asked, the brine dripping from his salt-crusted arm.
>
> "Gahd, he are black in troot," Ella, mulatto Ella observed to herself; then aloud, "bettah giv' me a gill o' bakin' soda, I might wan' to make a cake."
>
> "Lok out dey, Poyah," mumbled Bruin, "gwine bring down dat salmon tin 'pon yo' head too."
>
> "Oh dat can't hit me," Poyer replied, lowering the baking powder on the tip of the hook.
>
> "I's a man, man."
>
> He faced Ella, piling up the goods on the counter. "I's a man," he said, meeting Ella's frosting eyes. "I wuz a brakesman in Palama, don't fomembah dat. I wuz de bes' train hopper on de Isthmus!"
>
> "Count up de bill, quick!" Ella hastened, putting a sixpence on the counter. "It a get dark."
>
> "Frighten fo' duppies?" Poyer said, a suggestion of teasing and mockery in his voice.
>
> Island bugaboo . . . . "Who, me?" Ella's eyes blazed, "I ain't frighten fo' de livin' much mo' de dead!"

But when Mr Poyah comes courting, his presence brings out Ella's light-skinned prejudices and resistance. At the same time, however, Walrond presents the rejection of Mr Poyah as the confutation of filthy Panama gold by the wealth of the land: "All dem bag o' flour yo' 'a' got, an' dem silk shut, an' dem gold teets, an' dem Palama hats, yo' a spote round heah wid – dem don't frighten me. I is a woman what is usta t'ings. I got me hogs an' me fowls an' me potatoes. No wooden leg neygah man can frighten me wit he clothes or he barrels o' cologne" (53). So Walrond allows Ella to make her stand through those qualities associated with "the folk", even while showing her as corrupted by mulatto social awareness, the author thus refusing to invent an ideal "folk" and abjuring the easy road to satire. At the climax, Ella fights her way along rough paths and through a thick crowd, with a bucket of water on her head, brought to put out the fire raging in Mr Poyah's shop (accident, or suicide of rejected lover?) But it is too late. Mr Poyah has died and so too any chance that seemed to exist for Ella. The author's ironic compassion is aptly expressed in the wealth of implications behind the apparently simple closing sentence: "It was then that Ella realized how for-nothing was her bucket of water" (58). Walrond's multiple awareness manifests itself in a complexity of tone throughout *Tropic Death*. When his social concerns are to the fore, he is satirical and angry. But when, as is more frequent, his awareness of the severity of the world and the passing of things is in operation, the whole is tinged by a disconsolate nostalgia and overlooked by a compassionate irony. Yet, if a deep pessimism seems to underlie these stories (the title proclaims it) there is a hard optimistic layer too, based upon man's endurance in humility in the living world, and upon more domestic growths like the beginning of understanding and love such as develops in Gerald for his dying layabout father in the story "Tropic Death".

In September 1927, after the successful publication of *Tropic Death*, Walrond applied for a Guggenheim Fellowship to travel in the Caribbean and write "a series of novels and short stories on native life in the West Indies", weaving into them "a considerable amount of the legends, folk tales, peasant songs, and voodoo myths abounding in the region". The application was successful, and on a stipend of US$2,500 for the year and a six-month renewal worth US$1,250, Walrond visited the Caribbean from September 1928 until May 1929, stopping in Panama, Haiti, the Dominican Republic, St Kitts, the Virgin Islands and Barbados. He spent most of the month of June in London and arrived in Paris in July 1929. He returned to London in 1932, where he stayed until his death in 1966.

In the absence of hard biographical information we can take a chance and speculate. In the short story "Tropic Death", Gerald Bright, a boy of eight, accompanies his mother, Sarah, on a journey to Panama to find her husband and his father. Ruth Walrond and twelve-year-old Eric actually made such a journey in 1911 in search of William Walrond. William Walrond did not suffer the fate of the father in the story, and he was visited by his son in New York in 1931. But there are some parallels between Gerald and Eric, such as Gerald's memories of his days in Barbados, remembered in contrast to the wretched time he had with the boys of Bottle Alley. We can speculate that for Eric the search for a father and a home was as pressing as it was for Gerald in the story. Gerald meditates on the joys of being in the fertile family home of the Oxleys (249); he feels keenly the sense of something agitating his mother who is planning that desperate trip to Panama and he turns to her religiously as his sole protector: "He turned and there was his mother. His big bright eyes widened for her." He wanted "to breathe the holy beauty of her" (240). Ruth and Eric did not make the desired connection with William Walrond, but it is possible to argue that in the fiction the writer invents the growth of a relationship between father and son and of peace between husband and wife that stood for home. His journeyings, his exilic need to belong to something, his early fantasies about the muse, and his wonderful descriptions of unattainable women who shake the soul and heat the blood (68, 93–94) all attest to deep, unarticulated longings.

We can see the colonial's journey at last to the mother country as the final journey on a quest we can only describe as a need for home, asylum, belonging, love on the brittle earth. Arrival in England was followed quickly by disenchantment, the same disenchantment that was to be experienced by those islanders who made their London journeys to an illusion in the 1950s and 1960s. In the 1930s, in Garvey's *Black Man,* Walrond vented his disappointment and his criticisms of England. It is part of our story that those who went to England after the Second World War had no idea that he had been there before them.

All that was left for Walrond to dream about was the writing. In 1940, from a Wiltshire address, he wrote to Henry Allen Moe, secretary general of the Guggenheim Foundation: "Unfortunately, as a depression casualty I have had my ups and downs; my quest for security in a world in which nothing is stable led me astray. Yet even now, with everything more insecure than ever before, all my energies are being directed towards one end, namely to produce something which would in some small measure justify the confidence which the Foundation so generously reposed in me twelve years ago!" Walrond wrote to Moe again in 1954 ("still endeavouring to adhere to the project"), and in 1960, expressing determination "to try somehow and get on with some of my own long-neglected work.... [I]n spite of age and years of silence I have not lost sight of my objective, or the high aims with which I set out as a Guggenheim Fellow such a long time ago." Walrond wrote a number of stories and articles during the years in Europe, but when he died in London in 1966, the larger projects of this talented man, who had abandoned wife, children, mother and home in the 1930s, remained unfulfilled.

It is one of the strangest cases in our literary history. A critical biography of Walrond must explore the implications of that troubled life and measure the loss to West Indian literature, and to the short story as a genre, of one of the most imaginative and technically accomplished writers ever to come out of these islands.

AUTHOR'S NOTE

This chapter was originally published as an article in *Savacou: Journal of the Caribbean Artists Movement* 2 (September 1970. It was revised for this anthology in 2011. The original article was written quickly in 1970. Its purpose was to draw attention to an exciting "lost" West Indian writer and to present him as a casualty of a cultural situation that is still with us. In revising it for this collection, I have tried to retain that thrust. I have thickened the argument that Walrond is a Caribbean writer not a North American one though I have not attempted to insert anything that was not implicit in the original article. I have built up the literary analysis and from time to time I have added factual details to enlarge on information that was sketchy forty years ago. I have slowed up the beginning in order to argue that Walrond is of value to America because he was a Caribbean writer.

NOTES

1. *Editors' note*: Eric Walrond, "The Wharf Rats", in *Tropic Death* (New York: Boni and Liveright, 1926), 67. All quotations from Walrond are taken from this volume and subsequent citations appear parenthetically in the text.
2. *Editors' note*: Walrond uses the name Poyer in non-dialogic passages and Poyah (the phonetic spelling) in dialogue.

2

ERIC WALROND
From *Down Home: Origins of the Afro-American Short Story*

ROBERT BONE

ERIC WALROND'S FICTION HAS been described as naturalistic, but nothing could be farther from the mark.[1] His images of horror, especially of horrifying death, his fascination with the supernatural, and his obsession with the dark underside of human consciousness betray the workings of a Gothic imagination. He concerns himself, to be sure, with evolutionary doctrine – often the trademark of scientific naturalism – but not in a mechanistic or reductive way. Rather he employs the primitive or atavistic as a metaphor, a means of exploring the complexities of his black identity.

Gothic is a mode of antipastoral. It represents, in fact, the farthest limits of the countergenre. Satire counters the idyllic attitude with irony; realism with the sheer weight of actuality; the picaresque tradition with a certain roguish humor. But Gothic turns the idyll inside out; it attacks the pastoral ideal at its very source: the throne of God. To understand the inverted forms of Gothic fiction, we must scrutinize the mode in both its theological and cultural dimensions.

The pastoral ideal is associated in the Christian imagination with the Garden of Eden. In orthodox cosmology, Eden is the earthly Paradise, a reflection of the heavenly Ideal, the most that mankind has been granted as a foretaste of Perfection. The Gothic mode, on the other hand, provides us with a vision of the Garden abandoned by the Gardener, usurped by the powers of darkness. Gothic fiction is to pastoral as night to day, demon to angel, Satan to

35

Divinity, Hell to Paradise. The Castle of Otranto and the House of Usher, with their subterranean crypts and lurid tarns, are images of Hell, inversions of the earthly Paradise. . . .

The sources of Walrond's Gothic strain were both biographical and literary. He was raised by his mother in the Plymouth Brethren, a fundamentalist sect that left no doubt in the minds of its members concerning the reality of hell. As a youth of twenty and a migrant to New York, he suffered at the hands of white Americans a series of humiliations that demonstrated vividly the demonic potentialities of man. During adolescence he was an avid reader of Victorian boys' fiction, whose lurid plots were struck from the Gothic mold.[2] And in early manhood, at the outset of his literary career, he was attracted to the Gothic mode by his discovery of the books of Lafcadio Hearn and Pierre Loti.

But above all else, Walrond's penchant for the Gothic may be traced to the anguish of a fragmented self. Born in British Guiana, raised in Barbados and Panama, and growing to maturity in New York, he was beset by the problem of a multiple identity. Was he African or European; Anglo-Saxon or Hispanic; West Indian or North American? His writing is essentially an exploration of the self, moving back in time. It begins with his present circumstances in New York in the early 1920's, and moves inversely to his adolescence in Colón, his boyhood in Barbados, and his infancy in Guiana. The Gothic mode is utilized to express the primitive and atavistic features of his heritage.

Underlying Walrond's whole career is the tragic dilemma of the black Englishman. A British colonial by birth and early education, he remained throughout his life what the French would call an *évolué*. That is the inner logic of his successive moves from British Guiana to Barbados to the Canal Zone to New York and finally to London. These migrations are the outward and visible emblems of a spiritual journey: the black Briton's pilgrimage to Westminster. Walrond's life and work reveal the secret longing of the colonized black for whiteness, enlightenment, gentility, metropolitan sophistication, and similar marks of cultural "salvation."

At the same time, Walrond's traumatic exposure to American racism drove him back upon his blackness. Recoiling from a civilization that was capable of such injustice, he turned in self-defense to the myth of primitivism. Obeah, or black magic, became in his imagination a symbolic antidote to the poisons of racial hatred encountered in the Western world. It was at this point that

Walrond discovered the possibilities of Gothic as a literary mode. He employed it to express that part of his personality which remained resistant to the white man's culture: the black, African, pagan, ungovernable, unassimilable, or in a word *demonic* self that stubbornly refused to be "redeemed."

Walrond's excursion into demonism brings him to the brink of the abyss. Like Kurtz he journeys to the heart of darkness only to recoil from the horror. He is fascinated by the possibility of atavism, of lapsing into life-modes, more erotic and more indolent than those of European man. But this proves to be an unacceptable alternative because it arouses the fear of psychic dissolution. To go entirely native, to succumb to the lushness of the tropics, would be to slay his European self. It is on the rock of primitivism that Walrond's art eventually founders. In the end his anglicized sensibility prevents him from mounting a convincing demonstration of his chosen myth. . . .

LIFE AND WORK

"In every artist's life," Walrond has observed, "it is inexorable that environment – early environment – play a determining part."[3] This is manifestly true of his own career. His early manhood in New York, his adolescent years in Panama, his boyhood in Barbados, and even his infancy in British Guiana, provide the places, times, and circumstances of his tales. While it follows that a knowledge of Walrond's life will serve to illuminate his art, it is equally the case that a careful study of his art will illuminate a life about which not too many solid facts are known. Working both from the known facts and the known fictions, let us attempt an imaginative reconstruction of his inner life.

If we examine the interface of Walrond's life and art, four pressure points are evident. First, the underlying pattern of migration: from Guiana to Barbados; from Barbados to Panama; from Panama to New York; and thence to France and England. Second, the agent responsible for the earliest and undoubtedly most painful of these uprootings: an absconding, improvident, and debauched father whose life ended in defeat and failure. Third, the compensatory and somewhat hysterical ambitions of a mother whose overwrought success-drive, transmitted to her son, filled him with rebellion and ambivalence. And fourth, the racial traumas he encountered in New York which precipitated a crisis of identity.

Throughout his life, Walrond found himself in the position of the new boy on the block. He was forever on probation, forever under the necessity of proving, by gesture, style of dress, or appropriate linguistic usages, that he was worthy of admission to "the Club." Conforming to the customs of the country was imperative, for the sooner one conformed the sooner he lost his special vulnerability. The persecuted migrant, who is something like a soft-shelled crab, will pay any price for defensive armor. Hence the protestations of loyalty in Walrond's early work, which sound like Booker Washington, but have their source in the greenhorn's fear of remaining an outsider.

Human transplantation is Walrond's essential theme. Man on the move; man in process of metamorphosis; migratory man, encountering resistance and suffering the agonies of cultural adjustment, constitutes his central vision. Three of his essays are devoted to the subject of the Great Migration, an undertaking that reflects his desire to become a naturalized citizen of black America.[4] Several of his early sketches or vignettes are concerned with the dilemma of the black West Indian who has emigrated to New York.[5] And three of his best stories, "The Black Pin" (British Guiana to Barbados). "Tropic Death" (Barbados to Panama), and "City Love" (West Indies to New York) deal with various dimensions of the migratory theme.

Walrond's feelings towards his missing father are expressed in a series of portraits of ineffectual or sinister father-figures.[6] In "Tropic Death," the fullest statement of this theme, a young boy undertakes the classical quest for a father, consisting of a journey, a series or ordeals, and a descent to the under-world. Unlike Telemachus, however, Gerald Bright discovers in the object of his quest not a hero, but a rum-soaked, skirt-chasing vagabond. This fictive father is about to die of leprosy, a symbol of physical and moral dissolution. Walrond's father, as his son perceives him, is a negative model or antiself: a grim warning of the fate in store for those who succumb to the lushness of the tropics.

Walrond's father, in a word, is a backslider. To his son, he represents *blackness unredeemed* (which is to say, un-English). On the social plane, the father's indolence and irresponsibility threaten to declass his son, forcing him to live in hell (the Bottle Alley of his stories). On the psychological plane, he embodies his son's feelings of inferiority. For Walrond's fear of backsliding is at bottom a fear of failure. His father is an emblem of the worthlessness from which he flees, with the help of his mother, into white-collar respectability.

The mother-son relationship is likewise dramatized in "Tropic Death." At the age of eight – if we may take Gerald Bright as a self-projection – Walrond idolized his mother. But even as a boy, the seeds of future conflict were apparent: "By way of the Sixth Street Mission, his mother rooted religion into his soul. Every night he was marched off to meeting. There, he'd meet the dredge-digging, Zone-building, Lord-loving peasants of the West Indies on sore knees of atonement asking the Lord to bring salvation to their perfidious souls (276)."[7]

Despite the author's mocking tone, it is clear that he absorbed, from early contact with evangelical Christianity, the Protestant ethic of hard work, achievement, and success. Nor should the mission church be underestimated as an agent of acculturation, a transmission belt of Western values. Throughout his life, Walrond tended to equate being British with being saved. While he broke with his religious background during adolescence, it is accurate enough to speak of the theological framework of his art. For his imagination was profoundly shaped by his mother's harsh fundamentalism. His work constitutes, at bottom, a drama of damnation and salvation, worked out simultaneously on the personal, cultural, and theological planes.

Walrond's adolescent conflict with his mother is the basis of a story called "Subjection." In describing a youth whose life circumstances are not unlike his own, he observes, "His mother's constant dwelling on the dearth of family fortunes produced in him a sundry set of emotions – escape in rebellion and refusal to do, as against a frenzied impulse to die retrieving things. The impulse to do conquered (147)." The pressure to succeed exerted by his mother thus drove a wedge into Walrond's soul. . . . Rebelling and conforming selves were formed, with the latter momentarily ascendant ("the impulse to do conquered").

The balance of forces was reversed when Walrond moved from the Canal Zone to New York. Imagine a personality, strongly programmed for success, when it collides with the implacable barriers of caste. Imagine a young man, trained as a stenographer, and experienced in newspaper work, who cannot find appropriate employment because of the color of his skin. Imagine him, with a father's failure rankling in his heart, as the abyss of menial labor yawns beneath his feet. Recall, moreover, that this youth, who since early childhood has been moved about from pillar to post, is obsessed with gaining admission to "the Club." What would happen to his psyche on arrival in New York, where the only ticket of admission was a white skin?

He would undergo a major crisis of identity. The conforming self, thwarted by the color bar, would be incapacitated, while the rebelling self, nourished by a thousand humiliations, would take command. On the ideological plane, a process of radicalization would occur. Such was the substance of Walrond's early years in New York. He dabbled briefly in the Garvey movement, embraced for a time the socialist alternative, and in the end settled for rebellion of a literary sort, joining the New Negroes in their unprecedented celebration of Negritude. The course of his rebellion can be traced in certain of his essays, but our concern will be with his apprentice fiction.

APPRENTICE FICTION

Walrond's total output in the short-story field consists of twenty tales. Of these, ten are included in *Tropic Death*, while ten may be regarded as apprentice work. These apprentice pieces may in turn be separated into three kinds. First, a series of anecdotes or sketches or vignettes, set in the city of New York, and depicting the author's initial encounters with American racism.[8] Second, a pair of more substantial stories of Negro life in New York.[9] And third, a pair of crude fantasies set in Panama, which adumbrate the psychological landscape if not the literary power of *Tropic Death*.[10]

The sketches and vignettes may be described as pre-fiction. They represent a halfway house in Walrond's transition from journalism to imaginative literature. Trained as a reporter, he moved in stages from the factual article, buttressed with statistics, to the personal essay; thence to the vignette, and finally, the full-fledged story. His sketches and vignettes are written for the most part in the first person, and some are at first glance indistinguishable from expository prose.[11] Their anecdotal form[,] however, which absorbs increasing proportions of invention, places them in the category of pre-fiction. These pieces are thinly dramatized and crudely written, yet they encompass most of Walrond's major themes.

These early sketches dramatize the "soul pricks" and "spirit wounds" suffered by the author as a black migrant to New York. Behind the narrative voice we discern an ambitious youth whose hopes have been dashed by his exposure to the color bar. At a deeper level, Walrond is concerned with the nature of evil: with the process of initiation into a social order that is evil, and the loss of innocence that this entails. What strikes him most about the racist madness is its irrationality, its capriciousness, its fundamental absurdity. He perceives it correctly as demonic. Philosophically, this leads him to challenge the rationalist view of human nature that derives from the Enlightenment. Esthetically, it prompts him to explore the Gothic mode.

What troubles Walrond most above the racist mentality is its relentless categorization. People are judged, so to speak, by the backs of their necks, rather than their faces.[12] They are threatened psychologically with facelessness – with a humiliating loss of individuality. Depersonalization is the essence of the crime. It is to cope with this phenomenon that Walrond becomes a writer. For if race categorizes, style particularizes. The desire to individuate is the key to Walrond's flamboyant style: "In front of me is a jet black trollop. Her hair is bobbed. I snort at the bumps – barber's itch – I am forced to see on the back of her scraped neck."[13] Art forces us, in other words, to view reality in all of its uniqueness and complexity.

But art alone is not enough. Implicit in Walrond's early fiction are the values of racial consciousness and racial solidarity.[14] These are seen as a defensive armor necessary to protect the self from a fatal innocence and vulnerability. "Vignettes of the Dusk" provides a brilliant image of this vulnerability. The narrator enters an expensive restaurant in the Wall Street area where he orders oyster salad and "a vanilla temptation," only to be brought his food in a paper bag and hustled out. To resist the vanilla temptation – the unconscious desire to be white – is essential to the black man's health and sanity. This theme is given full expression in Walrond's first real story.

"Miss Kenny's Marriage" (*The Smart Set*, September 1923) is the story of a businesswoman of a certain age who invites disaster by marrying a man of twenty-five. She is the owner of a hair parlor on Brooklyn's Atlantic Avenue, where she has amassed a small fortune selling a preparation called Madame Kenny's Tar Hair Grower. Her intended, Mr. Ramsey, is a young lawyer belonging to one of the oldest colored families in Brooklyn, who regard as riffraff anyone who cannot trace his ancestry to the Battle of Long Island. Miss Kenny's social aspirations, however, prove to be her undoing, for Counsellor Ramsey, some three months after the wedding, absconds with his spouse's bank account.

In form, the story is a travesty; its theme, the pretender brought low. Miss Kenny embodies various forms of pretentiousness: linguistic, cultural, and social. She feels herself superior to other blacks, her pride, and bigotry being the antithesis of racial solidarity. Walrond takes an obvious delight in pulling his protagonist down from her empyrean heights, and to this end he employs a wide range of deflationary stratagems. These include a series of reductive metaphors comparing Miss Kenny to a horse, a wolf, a ferret, or a squirrel: a series of descriptive details which undercut her lofty notions by setting forth the grubby facts of her existence; and a series of bathetic devices such as constitute the common arsenal of travesty.[15]

The thrust of this story is similar to that of Claude McKay's Harlem tales. It portrays the assimilationist impulse as a psychological disaster. Miss Kenny maintains a false front for the benefit of whites; hers is a self-disparaging and inauthentic mode of life. By implication, Walrond calls upon his black readers to resist assimilation and cultivate their Negritude. This is the appropriate response to the racial onslaught depicted in his pre-fiction. Miss Kenny is, in short, a negative exemplar or antiself. By means of travesty, which is at bottom a form of ridicule, Walrond hopes to exorcise "the vanilla temptation." Not without a certain awkwardness, this early tale is nonetheless a portent of stronger work to come.

"City Love" (*American Caravan* 1927) is one of Walrond's most effective stories.[16] It is a solidly constructed work consisting of three sections, arranged in the musical progression ABA. The first and third sections (or main plot) are concerned with an extramarital affair between Primus, a married man, and Nicey, his paramour. The middle section (or subplot) depicts Primus in his domestic relations with his wife and son. They are recent migrants from the island of St. Lucia to New York, where Primus is employed as a longshoreman. Harassed and bullied on the docks, he tries to save some vestige of his manhood through his sexual adventures, and through bullying his wife and son.

As the story opens, Primus is trying to seduce Nicey in St. Nicholas Park, but she insists on being taken to a room. At his first attempt to purchase privacy, Primus is turned away because they have no bags. Having returned to his own apartment for a battered suitcase, he tries again, but this is time is rebuffed because the lady is without a hat. "Why don't you people come right?" the black landlord demands. Angry and embarrassed, Nicey takes flight, but is persuaded to return after Primus buys her a bonnet. In the final scene they are escorted down a moldy corridor and warned by the proprietor,

"Don't forget . . . that if you want hot water in the morning, it'll be fifty cents extra."

The exacting nature of society (represented by the Harlem landlord) is Walrond's theme. Its demands on the greenhorn are relentless, even down to the pettiest detail. These demands reflect the iron law of metamorphosis by which an immigrant becomes a naturalized citizen. Nor is society erroneous in imposing such harsh terms. For the newcomer represents a threat to social order. His blunders tend to undermine the commonly accepted fictions on which society depends for its stability. Everyone understands that Primus and Nicey are not married, but the amenities, or outward forms, must be preserved. Nicey's hatlessness is an affront because it lacks verisimilitude: "Don't they know that folks don't travel that-a-way?"

It is only on second reading that the close articulation of subplot and main plot becomes apparent. The structure of the story invites us to compare two kinds of bullying. Thus the father's abusive treatment of his infant son in Section Two is an ironic echo of the treatment he himself receives at the hands of the host society. Immigrants, like children, are often bullied by those more knowledgeable, and hence more powerful than themselves. Walrond embodies this perception in a metaphor, portraying the migrant as an orphan child, naked and defenseless. In this impressive tale, he universalizes the migratory theme, removes it from the realm of racial melodrama, and invests it with an unanticipated poignancy.

In the early phase of his apprenticeship, Walrond's imagination was primarily engaged with the racial situation in the city of New York. Commencing in 1924 and 1925, however, he turned increasingly for his material to the Caribbean countries of his youth. This major shift of focus was accompanied, on the esthetic plane, by a corresponding shift from realism to romanticism, and more precisely to the Gothic mode. For Walrond was in process of embracing the myth of primitivism, whose fundamental movement was away from the metropolitan centers of occidental civilization, and toward a tropical environment such as he inhabited for the first twenty years of his life.

Walrond's first attempt in this direction was a pair of tales entitled "A Cholo Romance" and "The Voodoo's Revenge." From their titles it would seem that he intended to explore the Indian and African features of his Caribbean heritage. But in moving from his early manhood in New York to his adolescent years in Colón, something went awry. Repressed emotions were released, associated with his parents and his adolescent sexuality, with which his art was not prepared to cope. The result is raw fantasy. These tales are flat failures, yet they adumbrate the Gothic atmosphere of mystery and horror that permeates the pages of *Tropic Death*.

"A Cholo Romance" (*Opportunity*, June 1924) is a drama of backsliding and redemption, stemming from that period in Walrond's life when he was poised on the edge of the abyss. The possibility of atavism, or reversion to savagery, is embodied in Maria, a Cholo girl threatened with white slavery by Baxter, her putative father. She is saved from degradation in the nick of time by a clean-cut hero named Enrique Martin. This lurid melodrama contains the seeds of one of Walrond's finest stories, "Tropic Death." They share a common setting (a shabby boardinghouse in Bottle Alley), overlapping characters and the crucial presence of an evil and corrupting father-figure. In "Tropic Death," however, Walrond masters these materials artistically.

In an essay called "Imperator Africanus," Walrond describes the rise of Garveyism after World War I:

> Fresh from the war, from the bloodstained fields of France and Mesopotamia, the black troops, bitter, broken, disillusioned, stormed at the gates of the whites – pleaded for a share of that liberty and democracy which they were led to believe were the things for which they had fought. And it was of course a futile knocking. Hardened by the experience of the conflict, the negroes . . . rose in all their might to create for themselves those spoils of war and peace which they knew they could not hope for from the ruling whites.[17]

"The Voodoo's Revenge" (*Opportunity*, July 1925) may be read as a parable of Garveyism, whose psychological foundation was loyalty betrayed. A Panamanian editor, Nestor Villaine, is treacherously jailed by a politician he has helped to place in office. In revenge, he hires a young St. Lucian to kill the Governor by poisoning. The youth is then disposed of in order to conceal the crime. The repressed emotions at the heart of this crude fantasy are revolt and rebelliousness. Villaine is Walrond's Bigger Thomas – a "baad nigger," as his name implies. The clash between the author's conforming and rebelling selves is nowhere more apparent than in this embittered loyalist, practitioner of voodoo, and emissary of revenge. . . .

TROPIC DEATH

Tropic Death consists of ten stories, set for the most part in Barbados or in Panama. The settings are symbolic of a vast upheaval in the lives of the Caribbean peoples. The village of Black Rock represents the dying vestiges of the plantation economy established by the British, while the city of Colón embodies the forces of industrialization set in motion by the building of the Panama Canal. Awakened from their ancient, rural way of life by the promise of greater economic opportunity, the black peasants of *Tropic Death* are flocking to the crowded cities of the Canal Zone. Walrond has contrived, in short, a Caribbean version of the Great Migration.

In addition to their common historical setting, the tales are linked by the motif of sudden death. Existence is precarious in Walrond's fictive world, and he employs the lethal dangers of the tropics to undermine our faith in Western rationalism. He is concerned with those dimensions of reality – accident, disease, and natural disaster – which Western man is under the illusion of having conquered through machine technology. From the depths of his Gothic sensibility, Walrond challenges the notion that man has won his freedom from physical nature by means of the machine. His snakes and sharks and vampire bats, his droughts and fires and tropical diseases, serve as grim reminders of mankind's tenuous position in the universe.

Technological optimism having been discredited, Walrond proceeds to explore the realm of the demonic. Always a hazardous enterprise, such a course traditionally involves a descent to the underworld. The movement of *Tropic Death* is perpetually downward into turbulence and chaos. Typically we descend from the deck to the bowels of a ship, from the sparkling surface to the murky depths of the sea, from civilized to primitive courses of conduct, or from the human to the reptilian plane of being. Only in the final story, "Tropic Death," does the self complete the cycle of descent and return, and having visited the lower depths, emerge triumphant.

The quality of the collection is uneven. Certain of the stories contain lumpy autobiographical ingredients inadequately metamorphosed into art. Others, while more successfully distanced, are lacking in coherence and design. As Robert Herrick writes of Walrond in the *New Republic*, "He is careless of composition, as the younger writers of the day often are, disdaining unity and coherence in their effort to seize a deep reality."[18] Yet the stronger tales in *Tropic Death* must be counted among the most effective of the Harlem Renaissance. Five of these stories, discussed in some detail, will serve to illustrate the range and power of Walrond's art.

"Drought" is the story of a natural disaster and its impact on the lives of a Barbadian peasant family. Leading at best a marginal existence, the family of Coggins Rum is reduced by the drought to a state of near-starvation. Despite repeated warnings from her parents, the six-year-old Beryl persists in eating marl to relieve her hunger pangs. Like some imp of the perverse she refuses to be disciplined and subsequently dies, her stomach bloated by the coral dust she has ingested. Her blighted life, which mirrors on the human plane the devastated landscape, is emblematic of the cramped, impoverished, and desperate circumstances of the Caribbean peasantry.

Walrond's theme is the intractability of nature and human nature. The drought no more responds to the peasants' prayers than the child to the parents' pleas or imprecations. Coggins Rum, his "brow wrinkled in cogitation," is a symbol of human reason. But the universe that he inhabits is envisioned as a jagged rock and human life a stubbed toe. "Yo' dam vagabond yo'!" Rum exclaims as he lacerates his naked toe. Yet the child is no more to be governed than the wayward toe. Sexual waywardness in fact produced her: yellow Beryl, "the only one of the Rum children who wasn't black as sin." The tale is concerned, in short, with those elements of human experience which defy reason.

"Hard-ears," the child is called, and the fruit of her stubbornness is a hard belly. The story is dominated by images of stones and rocks and petrifaction. Coggins Rum works in a quarry where throat and lungs are filled with stone dust. His children kill birds with "touch-bams," hollow pipes rammed with stones and gunpowder. Beryl rams herself with marl until she bursts, and an autopsy reveals the calcium deposits in her stomach. If the story has a villain it is Rum's wife, whose heart is hardened against her daughter's suffering. The spiritual danger of these peasant folk, the imagery suggests, is coming to resemble inwardly the hard, unyielding qualities of their environment.

Migration and resistance to migration is the subject of "The Black Pin." It is a subject deeply embedded in Walrond's life experience. . . . His recognition that xenophobia is a universal human trait enables him to elevate his personal humiliations to the plane of myth. He understands only too well what it means to be resented as a trespasser on the territory of another, to be treated as an untouchable, to be the innocent victim of un-provoked assault. In the confrontation between April Emptage and Zink Diggs, he creates an archetypal image of the immigrant's ordeal.

April and her four children have fled from British Guiana to Barbados in quest of a better life. They buy an old shack and settle in a tiny plot of land where they begin subsistence farming. Their nearest neighbor, Zink Diggs, is not long in opening hostilities. She strikes a child, takes a goat hostage, and in the course of a boundary dispute, levels April's crops to the ground. Her poisonous hatred is symbolized by a black pin, soaked in "some demon chemical," and employed as a voodoo fetish. When the pin threatens to ignite April's shack, she redirects the poisonous smoke toward the house of her tormentor and Zink Diggs – in a brilliant image of retaliatory hatred – is destroyed by her own malice.

Structurally speaking, the story possesses an admirable symmetry. Each woman has a favorite song: in April's case, a hymn of universal love, "An' crown Him Lahd av ahl"; in Zink's, a folk-song, "Donkey wahn de watah, hole 'im Joe," which in context means "hold back the immigrant." One woman represents constructive; the other, destructive energy. April's name is suggestive of her spring plantings, while Zink's is associated with the "buzzing and zimming of a saw." Poison is balanced by counterpoison, as Zink's murderous intentions boomerang. Her determination to burn out the migrants is countered by April's peasant tenacity, her strongest weapon in the struggle to survive.

The title story, "Tropic Death," is a parable of lost innocence. The story opens with the image of a boy, standing on a dock in Barbados, and dressed in the fashion of the Victorian middle class. Unlike the ragged street urchins with whom he is contrasted, the boy has obviously led a sheltered life. He is about to embark with his mother on a quest for her missing husband. At the end of his voyage to Colón, Gerald finds himself installed in Bottle Alley, the slum and red-light district of a booming harbor town. There is no protection from its noise and dirt, poverty and disease, violence and sensuality. The boy's migration from Barbados to Colón is thus a rite of passage from boyhood into manhood, an abrupt transition from the state of innocence to that of fallen man.

The fate in store for Gerald and his mother is adumbrated by a shipboard incident. The Bishop of the West Indies, a red-jowled Scotsman, deserts the comfort of the upper deck to bring the Word of God to the black deckers. Piously avoiding grime and filth, he is the accidental victim of an ill-timed gob of spit. Like the Bishop's perilous descent into chaos, Gerald and his mother are about to descend to a lower level of the social scale. Declassed by the weakness and ineffectuality of his father, the boy must learn to live amid the grime and filth of Bottle Alley. At the same time, compensating factors are at work in the form of a new resiliency, a greater maturity, and a wider experience of life. The story thus is a recapitulation of the Fortunate Fall.

In its central image of the Garden, the story illuminates the dynamics of inversion that link the pastoral and Gothic modes. As the boy observes the sordid life of Bottle Alley, the sun, striking a galvanized roof, reflects the brilliant colors of a tropical garden: "It created a Garden of the roof. It recaptured the essence of that first jungle scene (267)." This image of *reflected glory*, as in Milton's description of the fallen angels, vividly conveys the boy's sense of loss. For the main burden of "Tropic Death" is the loss of Eden (or childhood in rural Barbados), and its replacement by the Gothic horrors of Bottle Alley in the city of Colón.

Following her husband's deportation to a leper colony, Sarah Bright takes refuge in the English Plymouth Brethren, a dissenting sect which promises redemption from the world of Bottle Alley. She attempts to impose a rigid fundamentalism on her son, but he is moving to the rhythm of a different drum. Transformed by his father's sufferings, the boy develops greater insight and sensitivity. Increasingly he withdraws into a brooding isolation. A protective detachment becomes his defense against the world. Out of unendurable catastrophe, the artistic temperament is born. Compassion will be the instrument of Gerald Bright's redemption, but compassion expressed not through religious but esthetic forms.

In "A Midsummer Trip to the Tropics," Lafcadio Hearn envisages a bitter struggle for survival in the Caribbean:

> But with the disappearance of the white populations the ethnical problem would still be unsettled. Between the black and mixed peoples prevail hatreds more enduring and more intense than any race prejudices between whites and freedmen in the past; a new struggle for supremacy could not fail to begin, with the perpetual augmentation of numbers, the ever-increasing competition for existence. And the true black element, more numerically powerful, more fertile, more cunning, better adapted to pyrogenic climate and tropical environment

would surely win. All these mixed races, all these beautiful fruit-colored populations, seem doomed to extinction. . . .[19]

This passage forms the conceptual basis of Eric Walrond's widely anthologized story, "The Yellow One." His heroine, "La Madurita," is a symbol of those beautiful fruit-colored populations which the Europeans left behind them in the Spanish Main: "She was lovely to behold. Her skin was the ripe red gold of the Honduras half-breed (68)." She meets her doom on a voyage from Honduras to Jamaica, when caught up in the deadly hatreds of a coal-black Negro from the Florida coast and a Cuban who is a mestizo like herself. Their savage brawl, in the course of which she is trampled to death, takes place in the sizzling ship's galley, whose heat is emblematic of that "pyrogenic climate" which so impressed itself on Hearn.

"The Yellow One" reverberates with echoes of Caribbean history. La Madurita's husband, for example, is a Jamaican mulatto named Alfred St. Xavier Mendez. His middle name reminds us of the sixteenth-century Jesuit who missionized the Spanish Main. Walrond's point is that the vaccination didn't really take. Christianity remains a thin veneer among the Caribbean peoples, while just "below decks," sex and violence tempt the psyche to resume its pagan ways. When La Madurita goes below, she is descending into the Caribbean past, into the cauldron of hatreds which are the chief legacy of white colonialism. The brawl that she unwittingly provokes is rendered in images that stress the atavistic tendencies in Caribbean life.

Alfred, who lies lethargically on deck while his wife is being killed below, adds a new dimension to the theme of atavism. A delinquent father and husband, he represents the indolence and irresponsibility that Walrond associates with his own father. Not for nothing is Alfred from Jamaica, which has been described by Walrond as "a land with as many color distinctions as there are eggs in a shad's roe." In his essay on Marcus Garvey, Walrond writes that "In Jamaica, as elsewhere in the United Kingdom, England differentiates between the full bloods and the half bloods. In Garvey's Jamaica, the mulattoes were next in power to the whites. The blacks, who outnumber them three to one, have actually no voice politically or economically."[20]

This background will help to explain the central image of the tale: "The sea was calm, gulls scuttled low, seizing and ecstatically devouring some reckless, sky-drunk sprat (69)." For a sprat (or herring) to be "sky-drunk" is to aspire to an alien element, the air. The penalty for such presumption is to be devoured by a gull. So with the mestizo class, created by miscegenation, who are intoxicated by the social layer just above them. Oriented toward whiteness, holding themselves aloof from ordinary blacks, and forever putting on airs, they expose themselves through their anti-black bias to the risk of psychic death.

"The White Snake," which is Walrond's most impressive tale, displays his talents at their most Gothic. We are plunged at once into the world of nightmare, as a black Guyanese servant-girl cries out in her sleep that "a white snake [is] crawlin' up me foots (186)." The tale that follows amounts to an objectification of her dream. Seenie, who has been seduced and impregnated by a mulatto adventurer named Jack Captain, takes refuge on the sparsely populated isle of Waakenham near the delta of the Essequibo River. There she finds employment in the household of a Negro constable. And there, in a primitive hut deep in the Guiana woods, she fulfills her motherhood by rearing Water Spout, her illegitimate child.

One night, returning to her hut after work, Seenie drops off into an exhausted sleep beside her infant son. Awakened by his hunger cries, she nurses him – half asleep, and surrendering to the sublime mammalian passivity of breast feeding. Later on she reawakens, feels a reassuring presence at her breast, but puzzled, hears her son crying on the floor: "Was he a dual being? Here he was at her breast, gnawing away at it. And there he was down on the floor, howling (206–7)." The cold head at her breast suddenly recedes, and she jumps up, screaming out in horror. Next morning, one of the constable's men drags in "the fresh dead body of a bloaty milk-fed snake the sheen of a moon in May (208)."

It is crucial that the episode takes place at night, in a twilight zone between sleep and waking: "Cycles of the day sped through Seenie's head. There was a fugitive line between them and the half-realized happenings in a dream (203)." That thin and fragile line is basically what interests Eric Walrond. Psychologically, it is the boundary between the conscious and unconscious mind; culturally, between civilization and savagery; morally, between angelic and demonic tendencies in man. The story is concerned, in short, with the precarious nature of the human enterprise. Seenie's hut, located in an isolated clearing on the edge of the jungle, is emblematic of the constant danger of declining to a lower plane of being.

Civilization remains in jeopardy because nature, including human nature, is recalcitrant to human will and purpose. On the Essequibo Coast, river timbers buried in the mud overturn the boats of miners returning from the gold fields. Sheep dogs mutiny at night, devouring their own charges. And the omnipresent snakes, abandoning the coral road to man only during daylight hours, reassert their immemorial dominion after dark. Human nature is no less intractable: Seenie has been missionized, but gives birth to an illegitimate child; she is tyrannized by her employers, but subtly resists their authority. The White Snake may thus be seen as the embodiment of those ungovernable cosmic forces which lie beyond the reach of progress or policemen.

Walrond's White Snake, like Melville's White Whale, is an emblem of the dual nature of the cosmos. Thus the White Snake and Water Spout are manifestations of the same reality: "Was he a dual being?" This image of the child-serpent, with its Melvillean blend of innocence and terror, is fundamental to Walrond's cosmology. Jack Captain, who sired Water Spout in a moment of "dismal oversight," is described as hermaphroditic. His sexual ambivalence, projected on the cosmic plane, becomes a symbol of Divine Ambiguity. For the cosmos confronts us principally with mystery, so that groping in the dark toward the child-serpent, we can only scream with Seenie, "Oh, me Gawd, me Gawd (207)."

Tropic Death was a remarkable achievement for a man of twenty-eight. It remains to inquire why, after so promising a start, Walrond was reduced to silence. We know very little of his private life, and nothing that might account for the disconcerting fact that shortly after *Tropic Death* appeared, and at the height of his literary fame, he left New York for Europe, never to return. Of his writing, we know only that he labored unsuccessfully on a history of the Panama Canal which he planned to call *The Big Ditch*. Perhaps one day letters, diaries, or manuscripts will come to light which will dispel the mystery. In the meantime, we must rely on the internal evidence provided by his stories.

A survey of Walrond's fiction reveals a fundamental contradiction in his art. On the one hand, he adopts the myth of primitivism and works within its terms. Influenced by the writings of Loti and Hearn, and encouraged by the climate of the times, he explores the theme of atavism in its various ramifications. On the other hand, in his secret heart he endorses the missionary point of view. He believes in racial progress up the evolutionary ladder into some ineffable White Heaven. In consequence, he cannot really bring himself to celebrate the primitive. *Tropic Death* is in fact the veiled confession of a colonized black that he cannot return to his primitive sources.

In terms of Walrond's artistic development, *Tropic Death* turned out to be a dead end. Like Toomer's *Cane*, the book was essentially a backward glance, whose aim was the consolidation of identity. As a "return to beginnings," both personal and cultural, it generated a considerable power. But it failed to lead anywhere, leaving its author bereft of an artistic future. Yet despite its limitations, *Tropic Death* will be remembered as a notable achievement of the Harlem Renaissance. And it will be particularly treasured, by American Negroes of West Indian descent, as a pioneer attempt to grapple with the complex fate of hailing from the Spanish Main.

ACKNOWLEDGEMENTS

From *Down Home: Origins of the Afro-American Short Story*, by Robert Bone. Omissions are marked by ellipses, and note numbering has been changed from the original to conform to the text used in this edition. © 1988 Columbia University Press. Reprinted with permission of the publisher.

NOTES

1. See Sterling Brown, *The Negro in American Fiction* (Washington, D.C.: The Associates in Negro Folk Education, 1937), 154–55; and Hugh Gloster, *Negro Voices in American Fiction* (Chapel Hill: University of North Carolina Press, 1948), 180–83.
2. Walrond's early reading of such serials as "Dick Turpin," "Old Sleuth" and "Dead Wood Dick" is alluded to in his story, "The Voodoo's Revenge," *Opportunity*, July 1925, 212.
3. Eric Walrond, "El Africano," *Crisis*, September 1923, 169.
4. See "The Negro Comes North," *New Republic*, July 18, 1923; "The Negro Exodus from the South," *Current History*, September 1923; and "From Cotton, Cane, and Rice Fields," *Independent*, September 24, 1926.
5. See "On Being Black," *New Republic*, November 1, 1922; "Cynthia Goes to the Prom," *Opportunity*, November 1923; and "Vignettes of the Dusk," *Opportunity*, January 1924.

6. See, for example, Baxter of "A Cholo Romance," Alfred of "The Yellow One," and Primus of "City Love."
7. Page numbers in parenthesis throughout this chapter refer to the Boni & Liveright edition of *Tropic Death*.
8. See "On Being Black," "On Being a Domestic," "The Stone Rebounds," "Cynthia Goes to the Prom," and "Vignettes of the Dusk."
9. See "Miss Kenny's Marriage" and "City Love."
10. See "A Cholo Romance" and "The Voodoo's Revenge."
11. See especially "On Being Black" and "On Being a Domestic."
12. For Walrond's employment of the neck as metaphor of race, see "The Stone Rebounds" and "Vignettes of the Dusk."
13. Eric Walrond, "Vignettes of the Dusk," *Opportunity*, January 1924, 20.
14. See especially "Cynthia Goes to the Prom" and "Vignettes of the Dusk."
15. Miss Kenny, for example, is described as the tar queen: what the author confers with one hand he retracts with the other.
16. Published some months after *Tropic Death*, this tale should not perhaps be viewed as apprentice work. It is treated here because, like the pre-fiction and "Miss Kenny's Marriage," it deals with the New York scene.
17. Eric Walrond, "Imperator Africanus," *Independent*, January 3, 1925, 8.
18. Robert Herrick, review of *Tropic Death*, *New Republic*, November 10, 1926, 332.
19. Lafcadio Hearn, *Two Years in the French West Indies*, 97.
20. This and the above quotation may be found in Eric Walrond, "Imperator Africanus," *Independent*, January 3, 1925, 9.

PART 2

MODERN CRITICAL VIEWS

3

"ALL LOOK ALIKE IN HABANA"
Archaeologies of Blackness across
Eric Walrond's Archipelago

MICHELLE A. STEPHENS

IN 1923, THE WRITER ERIC WALROND commented on the death of fellow West Indian Bert Williams in the pages of Marcus Garvey's *Negro World*. Williams, who migrated to the United States from the Bahamas in the 1890s to become one of the most popular and infamous blackface minstrel performers of the early twentieth century, had passed away quietly in 1922. Walrond used the occasion of the publication of a posthumous biography to comment on the most striking feature of the comedian's career, "Bert Williams' dominant melancholia". In 2005, when Caryl Phillips,[1] another Caribbean author, offered a fictionalized account of Williams that emphasized his battles with alcoholism and depression, he answered the call Walrond had made over eighty years earlier when he stated in his tribute: "Some day one of our budding storywriters ought to sit down and write a novel with a Negro protagonist with melancholia as the central idea. Bert Williams had it."[2]

Eric Walrond himself could have written that story, however, for despite his current lack of visibility, in the early 1920s Walrond was a well-known contemporary of fellow Caribbean writer Claude McKay and many of the other creative artists of the Harlem Renaissance. Despite this fleeting fame, Walrond does not stand out as a prominent figure of 1920s black history, an absence he shares with Bert Williams. Louis Chude-Sokei argues that West Indian men such as Walrond and Williams represented and embodied cultural and ethnic forms of blackness that were literally unrecognizable, and therefore unmarketable, to American audiences of the 1920s. In response, Caribbean immigrants in Harlem during the 1920s were forced to assume African American racial identities as the only recognizable way of being black. Chude-Sokei identifies this as another, unremarked-upon, form of racial passing, as a "particularly black West Indian process and strategy of passing as an African American through the mastery of black vernacular speech and symbolic/cultural codes". Throughout the New World more broadly, he continues, blacks "appropriated [the minstrel mask]" and other sanctioned performances of black masculinity, "in order to construct a face", that is, in order to be recognized in the United States. In the early years of the twentieth century, West Indians' assimilation into American society was represented precisely by their willingness to become not Americans so much as African Americans, to substitute African American racial identities for their Afro-Caribbean ones.[3]

This image, of Caribbean American immigrants acquiring an African American "face", aptly highlights the significantly visual and scopic dimensions of American performances of blackness that were evident in the blackface minstrelsy of the turn of the century, but also, in the negative experience of "colour consciousness" many black intellectuals described in the 1920s. In "The Paradox of Color", an essay Walter White wrote for Alain Locke's *New Negro* anthology, he describes "colour consciousness" as a distinctly different and more negating form of racial experience than race consciousness. Colour consciousness reflected attitudes of mind that fixated on the colour of one's skin, attitudes that characterized *both* racism from without and insidious forms of internal prejudice located within the African American community.[4] Passing, too, was considered a symptomatic form of colour consciousness for it was based on the negative experience of one's racial identity through the colour, or in this case, lack of colour, of one's appearance.

Bert Williams chose to negotiate his own cultural invisibility as a West Indian by literalizing in blackface the visual politics that shaped perceptions of blackness and understandings of race in United States society. As a writer, Walrond chose instead to situate his fictional narratives in a black New World space of difference, an archipelagic Americas in which blackness could be perceived and performed in multiple modes, genres and registers. His fiction and essays are the artefacts of alternative, travelling notions of blackness that circulated between black America and the Caribbean during the 1920s. In his fiction, Walrond was unique in his attempts to extract African Americans, with their narratives of racial history intact, from the United States context, relocating them in a New World of colour, an American archipelago, that made visible the hemispheric and colonial genealogies within which various national racial stories were created in the first place.

Walrond's fiction and journalism reflects the circum-Atlantic landscapes and seascapes he wrote within, part of a black, oceanic, interculture that existed in the diasporic space between the African American New Negro and the Caribbean New World Negro of the 1920s and 1930s. This was a space where black New World cultures created themselves in each other's presence. Outside the nation, in this oceanic space of black intercultural interaction, multiple cultures of blackness in the New World have created dialogues concerning the nature of the relationships between race, slavery, colonialism and modernity, and their implications for the future construction of black selves.

Notwithstanding the cogency of Chude-Sokei's arguments concerning cultural relations between African Americans and West Indians in Harlem from the beginning of the twentieth century through the 1920s, the critique of the cultural power of African American ideas of race can overemphasize US hegemony in the Americas without taking into account West Indian subjects' own reasons and desires for redefining themselves according to certain aspects of blackness signified in and by African American history. Men such as Walrond, Williams and McKay, formed politically by the discourses of sovereignty they inherited as colonial subjects from the European empires, found in African American blackness an alternative political language of freedom with which to identify, a freedom, ironically enough, symbolized and embodied by the struggles of the American slave. Belinda Edmondson has demonstrated how West Indian males used, in the very beginnings of the twentieth century, Victorian notions of gentlemanliness to construct a gendered language of blackness that focused on the colonial subject's capacity for self-government.[5] As such, West Indians were borrowing from tropes of sovereignty and conceptual political frames that were part of the legacy of European imperial discourse. However, multiple political strands travelled across both Europe and the Atlantic over the course of transatlantic history and it is in some of these alternative strands that we find a convergence between understandings of race in the Caribbean and the United States. This convergence also functioned as an intercultural meeting point between West Indian immigrants and southern migrants in Harlem in the early decades of the twentieth century.

In the 1970s, Michel Foucault traced the genealogy of an alternative political discourse in Europe that ran alongside the reframing of monarchical sovereignty in revolutionary republicanism. Instead, this alternative drew its evocative charge from the discourse of race war. For Foucault, modernity represented precisely the moment when political struggle, the defence of the rights of both the individual and the nation-state, were evoked not in the name of *the* people but in the name of *a* people, a special, chosen people in world history, and the struggle against sovereignty also meant protecting this chosen race from conquest, tyranny, oppression and slavery.[6] Drawing on a narrative of "the history of the race struggle" for its political legitimacy, this mode of political speech has a distinctive, hortatory tone, as Foucault further described: "the story of the race struggle will of course speak from the side that is in darkness, from within the shadows. It will be the discourse of those who have no glory . . . a disruptive speech, an appeal. . . . We came out of the shadows, we had no glory and we had no rights, and that is why we are beginning to speak and to tell of our history."[7] This form of political speech has a definite resonance in African diasporic discourse, often taking the form of the racial "revolutionary romance" which, as David Scott has described, has "a fairly recognizable structure [beginning with] a dark age of oppression and domination . . . followed by the emergence of the great struggle against that oppression and domination, and the gradual building of that struggle as it goes through ups and downs, temporary breakthroughs and setbacks, but moving steadily and assuredly towards the final overcoming, the final emancipation".[8] In the 1920s, certain features of this racial discourse, and tropes of this intercultural, racial revolutionary romance, were shared by West Indians and African Americans alike. The latter's articulation of their own history as an American minority racial group resonated with the experiences of West Indian immigrants as colonial subjects, shaping the affinities with African Americans experienced by immigrants such as Walrond and McKay.

In "The Paradox of Color", Walter White echoed this language of race struggle when he stated: "The constant hammering of three hundred years of oppression has resulted in a race consciousness among the Negroes of the United States which is amazing to those who know how powerful it is."[9] This historical consciousness of race, whose dimensions included "that deep spirituality, that gift of song and art, that indefinable thing which perhaps can best be termed the over-soul of the Negro", also provided the driving rhetorical force of Du Bois's earlier turn-of-the-century classic, *The Souls of Black Folk*, another textual attempt to articulate this "indefinable thing"– this race essence generated out of a particular New World history.[10]

For Walrond and his West Indian contemporaries, intellectuals and artists of the 1920s and 1930s such as Claude McKay, or C.L.R. James, this counter-discourse of racial freedom developed with great political force within African American communities for one very specific historical and cultural reason – the interracial context of racial conflict and warfare in the United States. As the Martinican Frantz Fanon, writing thirty years later than the Harlem Renaissance but reflecting back upon the significance of African American history and identity within diasporic politics, also stated: "the American Negro is cast in a different play [than that of the colonial]. In the United States, the Negro battles and is battled. There are laws that, little by little, are invalidated under the Constitution. There are other laws that forbid certain forms of discrimination. . . . There is war, there are defeats, truces, victories. 'The twelve million black voices' howled against the curtain of the sky."[11] The meeting of African Americans and Caribbean nationals in the early years of the twentieth century represented a unique moment of *political* encounter and diasporic *ideological* formation, when black intellectuals and artists from different locations in the New World engaged back and forth in a conversation about the nature of black identity, its relationship to stories of the racial past, and the politics of black liberation in the future.

Walrond's specific contribution to this discussion was that he offered a black transnational perspective that historicized the specifically visual and scopic politics of blackness, race and race relations within the United States. In his writings Walrond contextualized the power of the white gaze – imprinted on the black subject as his or her "colour consciousness" – within the broader hemispheric and colonial genealogies that shaped race consciousness. Louis Parascandola's important edited collection of Walrond's writings begins in the 1920s with Walrond's defence of the awarding of the literary prize, the French Prix Goncourt, to the first black colonial author, Fanon's fellow Martinican René Maran, for his novel *Batouala*. One is immediately struck in this piece by Walrond's invocation of the race-war narrative as relevant across national and linguistic boundaries, as an essential feature of the diasporic condition of the New World Negro and consequently his art of the

Americas. In his defence of Maran and black art more broadly, Walrond captures the monumentalizing tone of discourses of racial freedom from oppression: "The Negro, for centuries to come, will never be able to divorce himself from the feeling that he has not had a square deal from the rest of mankind. His music is a piercing, yelping cry against his cruel enslavement. What little he has accomplished in the field of literature is confined to the life he knows best – the life of the underdog in revolt."[12] As Walter White did in his essay, Walrond again echoes here the hortatory, jeremiad-like tone Foucault described as characteristic of "the story of the race struggle [that] will of course speak from the side that is in darkness, from within the shadows . . . a disruptive speech, an appeal".[13]

Over the course of the 1920s, Walrond's essays reveal his sense that there were two different kinds of black art and, consequently, two different visions of the race. One form of art was genealogical and diachronic, driven by the jeremiad of the revolutionary romance; the other was epidermal and synchronic, driven by colour consciousness and a politics of the skin. In his own creative writing of the 1920s prior to the story collection *Tropic Death*, Walrond constructed genealogical tales, short fictions that offered a political narrative for the meaning of blackness in global history. In the 1921 story "A Senator's Memoirs", for example, the context of world war very much shapes a black senator's understanding of the fate of the race in a grander story of humanity, and the race's future salvation against the degeneration of others. The senator proclaims:

> As I turn back to the period of adolescence in the history of the darker races; as I behold the strong men of the earth flying at each other's throats over the spoils of a wretched war; as I gaze upon the spectacle of nations born and bred in the cradle of chivalry sinking their claws into the treasure-chests of bedridden Africa . . . God, how the memory of this oppresses me! – as I imagine the pageant of the crimes and blasphemies perpetuated against us for ages and ages – I shudder at the thought of the fate and future of a 'backward' race.[14]

The story's inevitable plot turn towards race war – "as the shadows of darkness fell . . . three men – a Japanese, an East Indian, and a Maroon descendant – knelt and plotted the doom of the white world" – is justified through the language of liberty: "the age of freedom. There is a spirit of love and equality and righteousness about it that thrills me. . . . for three miles I saw nothing but myriad brown-faced people. From the banks of the Zambesi, from across the Nile, from South Africa, Liberia, Hayti, America – they stood, a free and redeemed people!"¹⁵ It is this multi-racial, "brown-faced" people, whose bodies of colour become the bearers of a historical narrative that stretches from "the banks of the Zambesi" to America, who are now united as a new, special and redeemed race.

Walrond's interest in Bert Williams's melancholia during this period had at its heart a deep concern about the conversion of racial history into epidermal performance, the scopic aspect of blackness guiding the political vision of African Americans and maybe even their sense of self. Henry Louis Gates Jr has made the point that in creating the trope of the New Negro, black artists and intellectuals of the 1920s were also attempting to reconstruct the "image of the black".¹⁶ As they attempted to provide new meanings for the colour of the race, they also engaged in a much more visual semiotics, where race also became a politics of the skin. Describing Williams's melancholia as a "nostalgia of the soul", Walrond also worried that the West Indian's comedic performance reduced the soul of the race to the colour of the skin – "Is it really worth it – lynching one's soul in blackface twaddle?"¹⁷ Thus in the 1922 story, "On Being Black", the visibility of blackness and the scopic gaze of the white Other become the central themes shaping the plot and the protagonist's "color-ordeal", setting up a clear tension between narrative and visual forms of apprehending race and racial meanings.

The story begins with the following scene: "I go to an optician and ask for a pair of goggles. My eyes are getting bad and my wife insists upon my getting them. For a long time I have hesitated to do so. I hated to be literary – that is, to look literary.... [But] I need them.... the lights in the subway are blindingly dark [and] the glitter of spring sends needles through my skull."¹⁸ When the protagonist arrives at the optician's he is "confounded" by the variety of "new fangled" glasses and "styles", as if the world of the visual, its apparatus and equipment, has become ever more confusing. As he looks at one pair of spectacles he thinks, "Here is a new one on me", but the joke ceases to amuse him when the optician, with his "snow-white" head bent over a tray of glasses, mistakes the protagonist for a "colored chauffeur". Afraid to offend, the protagonist takes great "pains... to be discreet" as he attempts to correct the man, but the interaction becomes unbearable and he is forced to walk out. What specifically becomes unbearable is the face of the optician that is directly in his line of sight, his expression revealing how much he is entertained by this "coloured" dilemma, as the protagonist observes: "I can see his face wrinkle in an atrociously cynical smile. But I cannot stand it – that smile. I walk out."[19]

The story "On Being Black" then continues in this vein, with equally excruciating scenes of interracial interaction in which the visual continues to play a key role. At employment agencies the narrator is self-consciously aware that he is "black, foreign-looking and a curio". As he determinedly eradicates his "sensitivity" to being seen, he is suddenly no longer seen – "they do not see me. I am just one of the crowd." When he tries to escape "to the tropics", as described in a "sheaf of booklets telling me all about the blueness of the Caribbean, the beauty of Montega Bay", he still has to pass through the racial gateway expressed in the travel agent's question, "White or colored?", and when he enters the booking agency "a dozen pairs of eyes are fastened upon me. Murmuring. Only a nigger." While it ends with the protagonist "limp, static, and emotionless", overall the story reveals a plot strategy that Walrond will continue to employ, one of releasing his fictional protagonists from the phenomenological clutches of colour consciousness in the United States by relocating them to the Caribbean. This move does not allow Walrond's protagonists to escape their race, however, but rather, to reframe it, in another, more deeply historical and *lateral,* diasporic light.[20]

Walrond often moves his African American characters literally away from the United States geographically – to New World spaces where the black American subject is no longer the only sign of blackness, neither to himself nor, as importantly, extra-textually, to Walrond's American readership. In this small way, Walrond attempted to denaturalize American forms of colour consciousness where black skin becomes the only and absolute signifier for what it means to be black and what it means, more broadly, to be raced. In Walrond's fiction the world of colour, composed of a variety of "darker" races, is fragmented into so many shades and cultures that American and African American understandings of blackness do not disappear but are reframed within different geo-historical contexts.

Walrond's American archipelagos of blackness, for example, also included the Spanish-speaking world. In the story "I Am an American", he relocates a black American from Georgia to Cuba.[21] Chude-Sokei argues that West Indians in the United States in the early decades of the twentieth century engaged in a form of racial masquerade, one that ultimately revealed the "silencing of a history of black cultural distinctiveness" and illuminates "the often painful processes by which African American self-assertion has the secondary effect of marginalizing and subsuming multiple black othernesses".[22] In "I Am an American", Walrond complicates not only blackness, but also, African Americanness, describing an encounter between a Cuban and an African American man who has been forced to readjust to his own cultural marginalization as a black expatriate on the Spanish-speaking isle. The African American responds to the narrator's question, "the Spaniards treat you all right, don't they?" – by saying, "When I came here first I had a hell of a time. New, green – you know. Called me 'Negro Jamaicano.' Sure got it in for the Jamaicans here."[23] The point of the story is not to present the Caribbean as a racial paradise, free from discrimination in contrast to a racist United States. As the African American's comments reveal, Cuba is not without discrimination, but what it lacks is precisely that sense of colour consciousness – the apprehension of race through the scopic signifier of the colour of one's skin. Instead, as the African American points out, "All look alike in Habana."[24]

"I Am an American" is also the first story in Parascandola's collection in which Walrond uses a word that appears throughout his writings, often enough to be ascribed the quality of a signature in his depiction of New World peoples and histories. The story ends with the narrator responding to the black Georgian's story, "And, quite sepulchrally, I said, yes, yes, yes." Earlier in the narrative, before his encounter with the African American, the narrator drifts along el Avenida Italia, noticing and describing the tropical Cuban scene that surrounds him:

> On I drifted. In the middle of every block I saw native laborers sleeping on the piazzas. In dark shadowy halls, black folk, ulcered, leprous, unwashed, victims of the hideous wiles of brujeria, sat and crooned and rocked their knees while they fondled statuettes of the Virgin. . . . [I] gazed across the bay at the dark outlines of Morro castle. Violet-like was the blueness of the Caribbean. It licked the black rocks at my feet.[25]

When the African American appears, the languorous pace and tone of the story shifts, and descriptive language is replaced with direct speech and dialogue between the characters. Their encounter is staged, however, against this backdrop Walrond describes earlier, that of a much older, black and colonial world that lays like a racial palimpsest underneath each character's impressions of where they belong in this modern, American landscape.

In his account of Walrond as a figure of the Harlem Renaissance, David Levering Lewis commented on the gloominess of the landscapes evoked in his stories. Parascandola quotes Lewis's description of Walrond's stories as unfolding on a "dying archipelago in the margin of modern civilization". The suggestion of the grave in this Caribbean landscape, however, references not so much the dying as the undead. In this setting, the "native labourers" are not the figures of a marginal, Third World peasantry crushed under the force of modern industrial society represented by the United States. Rather, the "ulcered, leprous, unwashed" bodies of the black folk represent the continued eruption of submerged racial histories onto the colonial landscape, and the exposure of the bones of history that lie beneath epistemologies of the skin. The image of the sepulchre suggests the need for archaeological approaches to racial discourse in the New World, a digging deeper into the catacombs of coloniality that undergird synchronic, cross-cultural encounters between various racialized subjects throughout the Americas.

The word "sepulchral" appears again in the 1923 story, "The Stone Rebounds", where "dark Harlem" is now the setting as two men, one white, the other a "Negro playwright", walk together "along Seventh Avenue" to a club in Harlem. Their jaunt is precipitated by their discomfort with the prejudicial stares that accompany them on their trips together into white spaces: "at the restaurant, the theatre, on the bus, in Greenwich Village; yes, it had followed us, like a starving wolf". In flight from this collective stare, they soon find themselves descending into a basement from a "dark, maple-shaded street" in Harlem, the atmosphere inside as gloomy as the street without. Inside, the narrator becomes "conscious of an enveloping silence", and once again, the silence is "sepulchral". Surrounded by that silence, the story ends as the narrator looks around and rejoices, somewhat manically, in the reversal of the gaze, "On me a houseful of eyes is cast. I do not feel out of place. I rejoice in the reaction. I know why they are staring at me. I am white."[26]

In the 1924 story, "Vignettes of the Dusk", a naïve immigrant of colour finds himself in "the heart of America's financial seraglio". As he marvels at the modern "beauty that is America", the language he uses evokes the splendour and grandeur of Old World civilizations: "It reminds me of a mediaeval palace. Mirrors, flowers, paintings, candelabra; waiters in gowns as white as alabaster; and at the table a row, two deep, of eager, bright faced youths and maidens." However, it is the newness of America that takes the narrator's breath away: "To me it offers exhaustless possibilities. It opens up entirely new and unexpurgated editions to life." Of course, when the waiter brings him his lunch in "a nice brown paper bag with dusky flowers on it" and asks him silently to leave, the narrator "sepulchrally" pays the cheque and "waltze[s]" out, recounting for the remainder of the story the paradoxes of life in coloured America. On the one hand he is amazed at Harlem's "conglomerateness. . . . Quadroons, octoroons, gypsies, yellows, high and low browns, light and dark blacks, of all shades and colors of shades". On the other hand, he is surrounded by neighbours measuring the blackness or whiteness of others by staring at the backs of their necks.[27]

Within the context of American and other national cultures, the semiotic consequences of gleaning meaning from racial surfaces can be deadly. As Paul Gilroy describes, "identity ceases to be an ongoing process of self-making and social interaction. It becomes instead a thing to be possessed and displayed."[28] The meaning of blackness is frozen and reified as an aesthetic and semiotic attribute of the body, a process Gilroy has also described as "epidermalization", the inability to think race beyond the skin. In the 1920s, Walrond was attempting to tell stories of race that could go beyond blackface both literally and figuratively, beyond physiognomy and epidermis. His use of metaphors of death captured the melancholic resonances of black New World identities and cultures converted in modernity into mere racial appearances.

As the New Negro movement picked up speed, Walrond focused more of his journalistic attention on the specific conditions of the New Negro in the United States. In "The New Negro Faces America", he placed the African American "at the crossroads of American life . . . pinning everything on the hope, illusion or not, that America will some day find its soul [and] forget the negro's black skin".[29] Throughout his 1920s essays he followed the New Negro North from the South, watched Harlem develop as both "The Black City" and "a city of dualities"; observed Marcus Garvey voicing the racial historical narrative bound within the New Negro's soul.[30] During the First World War, he marked the moment when blacks "from the Old and New Worlds", first meeting on the battlefields and as labourers in Europe, solidified their conviction that a submerged "history of the race struggle" was shaping their shared victimization: "The negroes met and exchanged and compounded their views on the whites, their civilization, and their masters.... And when the blacks rose from the resulting pyre of disillusionment a new light shone in their eyes – a new spirit, a burning ideal, to be men, to fight and conquer and actually wrest their heritage, their destiny from those who controlled it."[31] In his account of Garveyism, Walrond recognized the potential for this political narrative of the race to become a "medium of violence".[32] However, in contrast, Walrond also emphasized the intercultural potential of the Black Star Line to nourish and develop "the oceanic genius of the blacks".

In a variety of stories leading up to *Tropic Death,* Walrond made it his special task to convey a genealogical connection between the mainlands and islands of the Americas. This connection was based on sepulchral histories, and called for the death of naturalized visual and scopic tropes of colour as the primary way of understanding race in the New World. In Walrond's archipelagic Americas, transnational and transatlantic racial histories were the framework within which national histories of race were forged. Walrond's arcane language represented his attempt to look beyond the borders of modern nations and colonial territories to the lost "continent" of the New World, that prized object of European discovery and early modernity, that lay sunken beneath.

The 1924 story "The Godless City" opens with the image of a ship, representing the United States, but embedded in a thick, Caribbean sea. Aboard this ship, the white captain and his black American crew observe the fiery destruction of a Panamanian city. The city has been destroyed twice before on a seemingly regular cycle, as one black Jamaican crew member describes further: "God's doings, that's what it is. Every ten or twelve years the city's got to be cleaned – wiped out – destroyed. A plague – a fire – something.... Just acres of smoking ashes – ashes of flesh – ashes of bone – ashes of wood." Despite this cycle, the Caribbean city continues to resurrect itself, and while it is described as the home of the dead, this island sepulchre is actively vibrant and possessed by the undead: "ghosts and legends and scarecrows were the order of the night. It was voodoo-stricken. It smacked of witches and hobgoblins. The very calm sombreness of it was uncanny." Despite every effort of the ship's captain, not even the modern, enterprising spirit of the United States of America can stop this black cycle of birth, violence and rebirth that characterizes Aspinwall as a city of the archipelagic Americas, where time moves in cycles characterized by the passing on of some histories and the arrival of others.[33]

Hemispheric analyses of interactions between various black cultural forms can tell us, in and of themselves, something about the nature of the intellectual conversations that have passed between black diasporic New World subjects through the archipelagic space of the Americas throughout the twentieth century. Here I do not mean to describe comparative perspectives or approaches that treat African American communities and Caribbean populations as isolated, separate worlds unto themselves, that can then be compared with or contrasted to each other. Nor do I mean to imply the opposite, that African Americans and Caribbean nationals can be seen as one united population of colour in the Americas, unaffected by deep divisions and differences of race, culture, political economy and the like. Rather, I am suggesting that very specific stories of the race emerge when we shift our geopolitical and geocultural perspective to one that sees the "black" Americas as a regional, circum-geographic space, one that accommodates both the similarities and the differences that criss-cross between US America and the Caribbean Americas, in a space that on any given day one could find oneself surrounded, "On all sides [by] the Dutch of Curacao, the Latins of the Pass, the Africans of Jamaica, and the Irish of Barbadoes."[34]

Amid this cross-cultural diversity, I say "black" specifically to suggest that the geo-historical link between these spaces and imagined communities would be their racial formation, as spaces deeply impacted, even if in different ways, by the history of colonialism and the variety of political discourses of power and freedom that have shaped the New World. Eric Walrond's writings both described and served as the very epitome of a process in which black New World cultural forms have continually migrated outward from their points of origin to join a very distinctive conversation about race in the Americas that has been circulating among black populations since the early years of the eighteenth century. Tropic death, then, as a central trope of a diachronic narrative of the race as a conquered and enslaved people, should really be seen as a trope celebrating the undead, the turn away from the resonant power of what can be seen, visual tropes of blackness, and the resurrection of what remains (to be seen), the sepulchral origins of race in histories of conquest and discourses of power.

NOTES

1. Caryl Phillips, *Dancing in the Dark* (New York: Alfred A. Knopf, 2005).
2. Eric Walrond, "Bert Williams Foundation Organized to Perpetuate Ideals of Celebrated Actor", in *"Winds Can Wake Up the Dead": An Eric Walrond Reader*, ed. Louis J. Parascandola (Detroit: Wayne State University Press, 1998), 64–65.
3. Louis Chude-Sokei, *The Last "Darky": Bert Williams, Black-on-Black Minstrelsy, and the African Diaspora* (Durham: Duke University Press, 2005), 104, 14.
4. Walter White, "The Paradox of Color", in *The New Negro: Voices of the Harlem Renaissance*, ed. Alain Locke (New York: Atheneum, 1992), 366.
5. Belinda Edmondson, *Making Men: Gender, Literary Authority, and Women's Writing in Caribbean Narrative* (Durham: Duke University Press, 1999).
6. Michel Foucault, *"Society Must Be Defended": Lectures at the College de France, 1975–1976*, trans. David Macey (New York: Picador, 2003), 59, 61.
7. Ibid., 70.
8. See David Scott interviewed by Stuart Hall, *BOMB Magazine*, no. 90 (Winter 2004–5), http://bombsite.com/issues/90/articles/2711. Classic African diaspora texts, such as C.L.R. James's *The Black Jacobins: Toussaint L'Ouverture and the San Domingo Revolution* (London: Allison and Busby, 1989) and Frantz Fanon's *The Wretched of the Earth* (New York: Grove Weidenfeld, 1963), rely on this narrative structure to tell a history of the race that legitimates black revolutionary action.
9. White, "Paradox of Color", 366.
10. Ibid., 364. Also see W.E.B. Du Bois, *The Souls of Black Folk* (New York: Penguin Books, 1996).
11. Frantz Fanon, *Black Skin, White Masks*, trans. Constance Farrington (New York: Grove Weidenfeld, 1967), 222.
12. Walrond, *"Winds"*, 54.
13. Foucault, "Society Must Be Defended", 70.
14. Walrond, *"Winds"*, 71.
15. Ibid., 72.
16. Henry Louis Gates Jr, "The Trope of a New Negro and the Reconstruction of the Image of the Black", *Representations* 24 (Fall 1988): 129–55.
17. Walrond, *"Winds"*, 65.
18. Ibid., 76.
19. Ibid., 77.
20. Ibid., 77–79.
21. Ibid., 81.
22. Chude-Sokei, *Last "Darky"*, 15.
23. Walrond, *"Winds"*, 83.
24. Ibid.

25. Ibid., 82.
26. Ibid., 87, 88, 89.
27. Ibid., 90, 90–91, 92–93.
28. Paul Gilroy, *Against Race: Imagining Political Culture Beyond the Color Line* (Cambridge, MA: Harvard University Press, 2000), 104.
29. Walrond, *"Winds"*, 111–12.
30. Ibid., 116, 117.
31. Ibid., 122.
32. Ibid., 125.
33. Ibid., 163, 165.
34. Ibid., 257. See Mary Renda's *Taking Haiti: Military Occupation and the Culture of US Imperialism, 1915–1940* (Chapel Hill: University of North Carolina Press, 2000), for a discussion of the term US America as a way of designating the United States' bounded place within and claim to the term, the Americas.

4

FOREIGN NEGRO FLASH AGENTS
Eric Walrond and the Discrepancies of Diaspora

LOUIS CHUDE-SOKEI

> Sometimes, on returning, at the end of the eventful night, they would find their skins salted – by the enemy – and, unable to ease back into them, the wretches would inquire, "Skin, skin yo' no know me?" And for the balance of their thwarted lives they'd go about, half-slave, half-free, muttering: "Skin yo' no know me, Skin yo' no know me?"
>
> – Eric Walrond, *Tropic Death*

BEFORE THE DIVERSE LITERARY products and cultural legacies of the African diaspora become too safely retrofitted by a contemporary new world notion of "the diasporic" – one arguably at odds with the current historical sensibilities of blacks in a post-/neo-/omni-colonial world, not to mention an Africa that it continually marginalizes – it might be helpful to return to before that heuristic structure had become a fait accompli. It might be helpful to return to before the variegated violence of New World black genesis had begun to ossify its cultures into a politics that depended on African anteriority but arrogated to itself cultural and discursive primacy. This arrogation manifested itself particularly in America, with a sequence of black movements and ideologies that depended on "Africa" to establish notions of racial solidarity across geo-cultural dispersal while simultaneously depending on the cultural power of the United States. Due to this latter much ignored and eagerly denied irony, "the diasporic" has come to function too often as a wishing away (or silencing) of the multiple aporias of black-on-black cross-culturality.

Though it is true that "the diasporic" is generally used with the assumptions of black cultural and historical difference buried within and therefore enervating it, it is not true that we have accepted the injunction to think of "blackness" as an open if not contested signifier.[1] Those internal differences are not in practice given the destabilizing centrality that they deserve and are instead usually subsumed into a larger politics of racial solidarity generated less by diaspora than from specific zones and modes of cultural privilege within it. What we are then left with is a context in which "the diasporic" has become mere epistemological shorthand, an uncritical method of transnationally articulating race rather than as a consistent conceptual *problem* for blacks in a modernity that due to dispersion has rendered race and Africa as multiple, their meanings divergent, their value culturally contested. With diaspora as a conceptual and political problem then – one both liberating and threatening to local black racial orthodoxies and as crucial to racial formations as is racism – it is necessary to re-examine writers who, in a sense, saw this new regime coming and perhaps worried about its implications.

The primary figure of concern here is the Caribbean journalist, essayist, acclaimed short-story writer and erstwhile novelist Eric Walrond whom David Levering Lewis aptly described as "one of the world's most uprooted species, the Anglo–African Caribbean *déraciné* – a British Guianan from a broken home, carted by a genteel mother to Barbados where Saint Stephen's Boys' School contoured his psyche to an English mold, and then to Panama where he completed secondary education in Spanish schools and under private tutors".[2] As such a species – one even more common today than it was then – Walrond's work was produced at that very moment when "the diasporic" could not be taken for granted, when it was still debatable, being fragmented and contested at each point of its geopolitical and socio-historic articulation. Though he was neither the first nor the only to present discrepant versions of black dispersal as a challenge to racial orthodoxies, particularly those in black America, like his peer Claude McKay he witnessed and suffered from orthodoxies that used "race" or "the diasporic" to affirm and maintain local, First World cultural hierarchies and political priorities.[3] Also like McKay his views of dispersal from the perspective of a black immigrant were deployed explicitly against such gestures of racial vanguardism particularly considering the deeply assumed cultural exceptionalism of the Harlem movement.

For example, Walrond too was caught in the sometimes-petty hostilities between the rival pan-Africanisms of W.E.B. Du Bois and Marcus Garvey as well as the grassroots, street-level cultural and social tensions between African Americans and black immigrants in New York. But the difficulties that he and other Caribbean – not to mention African – writers faced were themselves central to the formation of pan-Africanism, that significant articulation of a black diasporic vision that though rarely named is at the core of the "Black Atlantic" or contemporary figurations of black or African diaspora. They occurred simultaneously with cultural attempts to wrest "Africa" from colonial and racist imaginings and to reject social orders and policies based on those imaginings. Also, these intra-racial tensions were concurrent with the movement to actively deploy "Africa" as a primary and resistant frame of reference for geographic dispersal, cultural expression and political protest. It is good to remember here V.Y. Mudimbe's argument in *The Invention of Africa*, that this period in question was effectively a new episteme, marked by significant epistemological mutations around the term/icon/concept of "Africa" and the implications that such a mutation had for racial and colonial politics throughout the world.[4] For blacks in places ranging from Harlem to Paris, Jamaica to Cuba, these mutations were prototypically modern in that they were produced within a larger context: of that once-medicalized desire for a lost homeland called nostalgia, that assumed hunger for an ever-evasive past that, though common for a time of rampant immigration and border crossings, would for blacks always be figured specifically in a language of race. This would be the case despite their ambivalence towards African origins and the complexities of their intercultural relationships.

However, the simultaneity between the black New World construction of an African dispersal and the tense cultural rivalries and historical differences at work among multiple black ethnicities and migrant communities continues to be the most potent threat to both the assumption of a shared nostalgia, a common yearning, and to "the diasporic" as a valuable gesture of stability or continuity. So to name this moment of return within which Walrond's reputation flared and failed, it is broadly that of black literary and cultural modernism when "the diasporic" was merely a problematic anthropological assertion of retentions, a radical yet suspect claim on transhistorical continuity and a quasi-religious dream of utopia ironically guaranteed by an ambivalent anteriority. It is the moment of Ethiopianism, pan-Africanism, Negritude, Negrismo and so many other movements, tendencies, ideologies. More specific to this chapter, it is the moment of the Harlem Renaissance, where it was clear to Walrond and McKay that the crises of black modernity were racism and colonialism but also the raw terror of the African diaspora's own incalculable and potentially *unrepresentable* diversity.

As it is well known, the various cultural products of Harlem's modernism were littered with – one could say obsessed with – references to Africa, diaspora and immigration, particularly from the American South. However, it was primarily black immigrant writers from outside the United States who understood the implications of international black migration and the liberating threat that its cross-cultural conflicts posed for race, America or the "pan" gesture as a heuristic structure or political and historical paradigm, particularly in a context such as Harlem, which was increasingly defined by the interaction of radical black differences due to shifts in immigration patterns as the borders of the British Empire began to spill over into those of America. The implications of these black border-crossings have long been belied by the tendency to continually over-fetishize a monumentally "black" relationship to whiteness or the West; but it is precisely those still rarely engaged black-on-black cross-cultural relationships that Walrond and McKay so excelled at exploring and depicting. For them race and migration were in fact highly *competitive* discourses in the black diaspora, despite being grounded in deceptively shared assumptions. For them also, this *was* black modernity. Despite the general bio-cultural assumption of racial commonality that held at the time, they actively used what we now call "the black diaspora" to enact a praxis of black-on-black cross-culturality that emphasized the discrepant, and gloried in the incommensurable and its oftentimes violent interactions. But where McKay's discrepant diaspora depended on a more marketable and politically viable African American centrality, Walrond's vision of race and migration went so far afield from that centre that it effectively disappeared.

≈

Though only footnoted by scholars of the Harlem Renaissance and occasionally of Caribbean literature, the publication of Walrond's *Tropic Death* was a significant event in an era where the very publication of *any* book by a black writer was greeted with both curiosity and deep interest, particularly one from one of the lesser-known British colonies in the Caribbean and who, despite his avowed love of America, thought himself "spiritually a native of Panama".[5] But in the evolution of black cross-cultural literary poetics and cultural politics in the United States, its presentation of distinct black experiences and languages was enough to impress and baffle readers becoming increasingly trained to equate black experiences and responses with exclusively African American ones. *Tropic Death* challenged a great many readers with its self-conscious ellipticism and what many thought to be its linguistic excesses. But its arrogant daring to express a mythic vision of black migration in multiple non-American black dialects, vernaculars, folkways and world views is what may have sealed its fate as the great "lost" work of that period. That choice to leave imaginatively the contours of an American-based movement or cultural tendency like the Harlem Renaissance, to imagine it as secondary to a larger process of black cultural transformations, is key to the book's disappearance.

Read as a myth, or a mythic rendering of black dispersal, *Tropic Death* flaunted its foreignness in a literary climate where "black migration narrative" was being almost exclusively associated with the post-slavery movement from the American South to its rapidly industrializing urban North, not so much with the migration of Afro-Caribbean peoples into America, many arriving due to their labour on the Panama Canal. The book in fact begins with what could be called a fracturing statement of intent. In describing the setting – one very obviously Caribbean, since we are told that the peasants are "West Indian", the whites English, the food distinctly Caribbean, the dialect non-American and the songs "Bajan", – the narrator suddenly and enigmatically points out that this "wasn't Sepia, Georgia, but a backwoods village in Barbadoes [sic]".[6] This line expresses less as a narrative need than a cross-cultural demand that the reader dislocate those equations being made between black and African American, migration and "the South" in the literature and cultural politics of the time. Yet despite its exoticism and self-avowed foreignness, this collection of "tropical" stories, for which the Panama Canal provided the broader political setting, was not published without a welcoming American context. The collection arrived in the midst of a Caribbean/black immigrant literary and cultural flourishing in New York, a cultural burst that could be described as a modernist cross-current or a movement within a movement. It energized Harlem's renaissance and was crucial to its process of intra-racial identity formation as well as to black America's understanding of its relative place in a much broader black world of cultural and political activity.

Setting the tone and shaping the ground for this cross-current, Claude McKay's much-lauded "If We Must Die", had appeared in 1919 and was followed in 1922 by his *Harlem Shadows*. Though the Jamaican polymath Joel Rogers's *From Superman to Man* had appeared in 1917, it was McKay's collection, with its poems of migration, alienation and nostalgia that caused a stir. It included a number of poems that spoke directly to Caribbean migrants while also offering a great deal to African American readers ill at ease in the metropolis and the increasing opacity of its racial politics. Poems such as "To One Coming North" was clearly so split in its signifying to migrants from the American South and newcomers to North America from "the changeless southern isles".[7] This North may have been shared, but the relative *Souths* were as distinct as the journeys from them. It was in *Harlem Shadows* that McKay's well-known calypso-cum-poem "The Tropics in New York" appeared, managing to transform the specific longings of a Caribbean migrant into the "transcendental homelessness" of modernism as well as into a criticism of American economic and racial power structures rooted in an implicit African primitivity:

> Bananas ripe and green, and ginger-root,
> Cocoa in pods and alligator pears,
> And tangerines and mangoes and grape fruit,
> Fit for the highest prize at parish fairs. . . .
> My eyes grew dim, and I could no more gaze;
> A wave of longing through my body swept,
> And, hungry for the old, familiar ways,
> I turned aside and bowed my head and wept.[8]

Perhaps more prosaically, McKay's romanticizing of specific Caribbean fruits, vegetables and products and a lush island landscape was not as exotic as it may seem. It was due to an increasing awareness of how present, if not familiar, Caribbean culture and its public presentations of nostalgia were on the streets of Harlem. But it is unlikely that most African American "arrivants" had the kind of "mystical" nostalgia for the violence-prone Jim Crow South that many Caribbean immigrants had and actively cultivated for their home islands upon arrival: in that former context, that last quatrain is particularly difficult to digest. For another example, though McKay largely maintains a placeless, unspecified metaphor, "To One Coming North" does not easily translate cross-culturally:

> Like me you'll long for home, where birds' glad song
> Means flowering lanes and leas and spaces dry,
> And tender thoughts and feelings fine and strong,
> Beneath a vivid, silver-flecked, blue sky.[9]

The black subject and the peculiarities of its longing are in question here; and the black modernist desire to construct a universal racial voice is delimited by differential if not incommensurable histories. For one thing, where Caribbean migrants were notorious for refusing American citizenship, and so could always deploy their longings and nostalgia as a psychological escape clause from the racial drama of the nation, African Americans were constrained by the political need to assert a political and historical place within the borders of a country that consistently refused to acknowledge their belonging to it.

Perhaps in a generation the South would be remembered thus by black Americans, once the realities of arrival ceded to the needs and luxuries of nostalgia. Yet it is true that the pastoralizing of the American South and its plantation economies was too suspiciously present in a racist climate that worked hard – particularly via blackface – to maintain the fiction that the American Negro's rightful home *was* in the South. And there was clearly a counter-pastoralizing in African American modernist poetics, at work most notably in Du Bois's *The Souls of Black Folk* but most conspicuously in Jean Toomer's *Cane*, a work to which *Tropic Death* was and is most often compared. This latter form of pastoralizing would claim the South as Negro homeland but as a link to both Africa and a political consciousness rooted in the experience of slavery. But in McKay's work the language of a Caribbean pastoral and its unique diasporic nostalgia was the most blatant expression of a black immigrant attempt to speak a universal language that was inevitably split between a culturally dominant black America and other black cultural priorities and racial categories. Walrond, however, was never much of a pastoralist even though his work was fundamentally split in precisely this way, between a universal Negro and multiple, specifically Caribbean ones, between the need for solidarity against racism and colonialism and the desire to attend to – and glory in – the often painful intricacies of cultural and historical differences.

Walrond also never pandered to that prelapsarian utopia which was McKay's stock-in-trade: one in which the Caribbean and Africa became a romantic and sometimes cartoonish singularity. Instead, he was resolutely "anti-tropical" in his representations of the Caribbean. (His book is called *Tropic Death* for very good reasons.)[10]

Compared to the work of McKay, *Tropic Death* does violence to the very suggestion that the Caribbean could breed any kind of simplistic poetic reverie or romantic nostalgia. Beginning with a sharp image of "parched, grim, sun-crazed blacks cutting stone on the white burning hillside", it continues with this vision of the landscape of black migrant origins:[11]

> Crawling along the road to the gap, Coggins gasped at the consequences of the sun's wretched fury. There, where canes spread over with their dark rich foliage into the dust-laden road, the village dogs, hunting for eggs to suck, fowls to kill, paused amidst the yellow stalks of cork-dry canes to pant, or drop, exhausted, sun-smitten.
>
> The sun had robbed the land of its juice, squeezed it dry. Star apples, sugar apples, husks, transparent on the dry sleepy trees. Savagely prowling through the orchards blackbirds stopped at nothing . . . Turtle doves rifled the pods of green peas and purple beans and even the indigestible Brazilian *bonavis*. Potato vines, yellow as the leaves of autumn, severed from their roots by the pressure of the sun, stood on the ground, the wind's eager prey. Undug, stemless – peanuts, carrots – seeking balm, relief, the caress of a passing wind, shot dead unflustered eyes up through sun-etched cracks in the hard, brittle soil. The sugar corn went to the birds. Ripening prematurely, breadfruits fell swiftly on the hard naked earth, half ripe, good only for fritters . . . Fell in spatters . . . and the hungry dogs, elbowing the children, lapped up the yellow-mellow fruit.[12]

The wonderful eccentricity of his perhaps too self-consciously modernist language conveys a natural world that is as stunning as it is punishing, as bursting with life as it is withering with exhaustion. It is a vision of a world and a people "ripening prematurely", though "robbed of its juice" and "severed from their roots"; a world where dogs compete with children and birds make away with what little bounty there is. *Tropic Death* is littered with such images, of a Caribbean world profoundly unlike McKay's in that it was not external to American imperialism or closer to "Africa"; nor was it within the zone of a British empire that so many Caribbean migrants still held sacred, sometimes even as a way of rejecting the ambivalent commonalities of an environment shared with African Americans. And in *Tropic Death* Walrond presents a series of images and stories of such lurid racial, sexual, psychic and intra-racial violence that one hopes and prays to one day discover a conversation or correspondence between him and Jean Toomer.[13] But the very impact of McKay's poems like "Flame Heart", "Home Thoughts", "After the Winter", "I Shall Return", "Outcast" and many others in *Harlem Shadows* was significant to Walrond. It made clear that within the larger cultural context of the Harlem movement and the fetishized tensions of black and white there was another discourse at work that fed, borrowed from and in some cases went against the grain of that being erected in the formal and active spaces of black renascence.

Crucial to the historical parameters of this movement-within-a-movement in which "foreign Negroes" – to use Walrond's preferred mode of reference – and native African Americans catalysed each other, *Harlem Shadows* was published the very year that the great Caribbean blackface performer Bert Williams died.[14] Though Williams was and continues to be read and remembered through the lens of an explicitly American racial politics (though now with more obligatory bows to his Caribbean origins), he was and is the ultimate icon of the multiple masks that black immigrants must wear in engaging white and black America and the distinct forms of assimilation required by both. Walrond described Williams as "an ambassador across the border of color" and one of "the great artists of the theatre of all time". He attributes much of the cultural zeitgeist to Williams, arguing that his legacy was, in 1923 only "beginning to bear fruit".[15] Adding to this cultural fruition, the Garvey movement was at its peak alongside the growing "Garvey Must Go" campaign, which to a great many Caribbean immigrants had a distinctly anti-Caribbean/black nativist slant.[16] This black, anti-black foreigner bias was fed by Du Bois (who notably called Garvey an "illiterate foreigner") and others of the African American elite despite the fact that much of the "Garvey Must Go" campaign was spearheaded by West Indian radicals in Harlem who had established themselves as far back as 1919 with the founding of the African Blood Brotherhood.

So by the time of *Tropic Death* much of Harlem life had been effectively *tropicalized* by the social and cultural presence of "foreign Negroes". In his fine study of the Caribbeanization of the Seventh-Day Adventists, R. Clifford Jones writes:

Their distrust of each other notwithstanding, West Indian and black American cultures did affect each other in early twentieth century America. In the religious sphere, voodoo and obeah from the West Indies did intermingle with conjure, which had made its way to Harlem from the South. In time, West Indian fruits and vegetables decorated many Harlem food stores and tables. So great was the demand for these tropical products that a profitable business was spawned to make them available. Black Americans even took to West Indian music, finding in the rhythmic, pulsating tempo strains of Africa with which their souls connected and resonated. One song, "Sly Mongoose", could be heard being belted out on phonographs as early as 1915, and calypso music grew in popularity through the 1920s. So, too, did West Indian comedians and entertainers.[17]

Yet despite the fact that McKay was *the* Caribbean literary lion and black radical *du jour* in this tense and productive moment of black-on-black cross-culturality, *Tropic Death* actually appeared two years before his history-making best-seller *Home to Harlem* (1928). It was arguably a significant influence on McKay's second novel *Banjo* (1929) in its radical departure from the borders of an African American dominated cultural setting and its stylistic migration as far from social realism as was possible for the less talented fiction-writer McKay, who could only ever manage his impressionism in short, ecstatic bursts.[18] It is worth then joining the dots between all of these events and publications to carve out a concurrent, yet overlapping and discrepant space of black immigrant modernism. This is of particular importance since the West Indian vogue in Harlem was not just in music, food and colourful clothing and exotic dialects. It translated into political and literary activity in which both West Indians and African Americans used diaspora as a way of framing not just resistance to a global colonial sprawl but also of managing a social world that was increasingly culturally fragmented and at times socially divided, largely due to the immediate presence of immigrants from that sprawl. It must be emphasized that as real as was the resistance to racism and colonialism, it is this tense and competitive intimacy between black immigrants and native African Americans that conditions the emergence of pan-Africanism and will propel various transformations of American immigration policy.[19]

But it is tempting to imagine Walrond and McKay as silently colluding in the performed skin of an African American modernism, both being noted denizens of Harlem's demimonde and both in and out of the institutional folds of Garveyism. And that they both disappeared from Harlem before its Renaissance could produce a backlash also links them, in that their disappearances suggest both a petering out of their commitments to black American renascence and a frustration with its cultural limits. Indeed, much of *Home to Harlem* – particularly as voiced by the Haitian character Ray – features exhaustion with the limits and conventions of race in America and its black leadership, which precipitates the movement away from Harlem at the end of the novel. Much of *Banjo* is an explicit and at times gossipy attack on the same, and here McKay names names as the central African American character becomes decentred in the novel by a deluge of non-American black concerns and interests. This rambling "sequel" to *Home to Harlem*, however, mounts its innumerable black-on-black cross-cultural criticisms from a perspective that is less a vision or exploration of black immigrant life than of "vagabondage". As portrayed by McKay, this romanticized black wanderlust is much closer in fact and in narrative structure to the "errantry" described by Edouard Glissant in *The Poetics of Relation*. For "the troubadour" (Banjo or McKay) "errantry is a vocation only told via detour", and *detour* – as in decentred narrative sprawl – is the name of the game in *Banjo*, famously subtitled, in McKay's bid for experimental modernist kudos, "A Story without a Plot".[20] And for Glissant – as for McKay and certainly for Walrond – "this thinking of errantry, this errant thought, silently emerges from the destructuring of compact national entities that yesterday were still triumphant and at the same time, form difficult, uncertain births of new forms of identity".[21]

In their work, a frustration with "compact national entities" is obvious, as is a shared fascination with the new forms of racial and social types produced by the global intersections of colonialism and racism. But otherwise, there was very little between the two writers personally beyond a good degree of the kind of bad blood that qualifies them as authentic participants in a modernist literary movement. In a letter to Nancy Cunard during his penurious time in North Africa writing his "peasant saga" *Banana Bottom* (1933), McKay made clear his feelings towards the other conspicuous Caribbean modernist in Harlem.[22] This should help betray any suggestion here of there being an essential Caribbean solidarity vis-à-vis an African American cultural and social context, especially since big island/small island rivalries were alive and well in Harlem up until the failure of the West Indies Federation in 1962. What

McKay writes of Walrond (and of Arturo/Arthur Schomburg) needs to be quoted at length for how it contextualizes the intra-racial micro-politics of Harlem's modernism:

> No, I dislike Eric Walrond. And he does me too. Think he is very pretentious light-weight. Knew him when I was on the Liberator with Max Eastman & he on the Negro World with Garvey. 1922. Garvey had given me hell and more in his paper (he had a grudge about me for showing up the preposterous side of his movement in the Liberator) . . . Eric came to see me and give some inside dope on Garvey's character for me to make a comeback attack – the crassest moral stuff & besides he was working for the man . . . Next time I heard from him was 1925 in France he wrote asking me to read stories for a competition in the Negro magazine "Opportunity" for which he was assistant editor & offered to place some stuff for me. I was glad to do it for I was quite broke . . .
> But my ultimate success with "Home to Harlem" after years of struggling brought all the black venom out against me. I was told that Walrond said "I knew how to exploit people." And my friends of the "enemy race" whom I have shamefully exploited have never to my knowledge complained. I was called every damned thing. (Schomburg especially amazed me. Because he was always a young old dog. Full of naughty tales. Couldn't imagine him sitting well with Du Bois. But I supposed he slated me to curry favor with the Aframericans, being West Indian . . .) . . . Walrond (in a widely reprinted article) said I had been invited to Russia by the Soviet government and the impression was that I had become a bolshevic agent. A lie . . .
> What maddened the American [indecipherable word] was my making money out of my novel, because the whole intelligentsia crowds have a wards-of-charity mentality – a helpless looking to the powerful philanthropist for awards and scholarships. I told Walrond he ought to have use[d] his scholarship to try and achieve liberty of mind and freedom of expression. I have gone carefully through his stories and stripped of their journalistic verbiage they reveal nothing but the average white man's point of view towards Negroes.[23]

What is most fascinating here is each writer's (according to McKay) quickness to proclaim the other either an exploiter of the race or manifesting a "white man's point of view", fascinating not just for its early dependence on the seemingly timeless rhetoric of "blacker than thou", but due to the fact that *both* of them had earned a spot on Marcus Garvey's infamous list of "Literary Prostitutes".[24] These were black writers who were being exploited by white publishers to defame the Negro in the name of newness and, perhaps most importantly, against the aesthetic restrictions of Garvey himself. Strangely enough W.E.B. Du Bois is on that list, though this had less to do with the actual "scandal" (or newness) of his work than his well-known competition with Garvey for a cultural and political power that depended on a symbolic and discursive control of the African diaspora. One imagines that Walrond's praise for Carl Van Vechten's notorious *Nigger Heaven* (1926) – in many ways the template for McKay's novel – made them suspicious as well.[25] But despite his difficulty with the ellipticism of *Tropic Death* and no doubt its vision of black life far beyond the American racial binaries that dominated his thinking, Du Bois eventually acknowledged it as "on the whole . . . a human document of deep significance and great promise".[26] This grudging endorsement is significant because it comes from someone whom Walrond had always bitterly attacked for having no sympathy for the black masses and whose pan-Africanism was hardly creditable since Du Bois "put national above racial consciousness".[27] Du Bois's endorsement also appears in the midst of a black racial climate hell-bent on political and cultural consolidation, what Walrond ambivalently described as an "ethnological oneness", a solidarity that is ultimately a "desperate striving, after a pigmentational purity".[28] The climate was one in which white America was dependent on the clear-cut determinism of chromatic difference. In between these two forces, *Tropic Death* garishly and luridly celebrated characters of a racially "mystical heritage".[29] These men and women either display or intimate the impossibility of innocence in "a society where everything – color, culture, race, and even destiny – has become indeterminate".[30]

One wonders if Walrond's much more general social acceptance among the African American literary elite – particularly with the strong support of *Opportunity* editor Charles Johnson – had something to do with McKay's antipathy. McKay was noted for his relationships primarily with the Greenwich Village left, Max Eastman, his sister Crystal, and others in and around the *Liberator*. He is known also for relentlessly celebrating a working-class authenticity continually at odds with an intellect that threatens that vital, primitive authenticity. His relationships with African American intellectuals were never as smooth as were those of the genteel Walrond. Since McKay had at this time chosen to masquerade his work in the primary signifiers of African American culture and not yet write specifically of the Caribbean in his fiction, one wonders if Walrond's work was possibly threatening for its unrepentant linguistic and socio-cultural "foreignness". It is this unrepentant fetishizing of black linguistic and historical *otherness* that makes Walrond ultimately the strongest figure in a black immigrant modernism, one that depends on America as merely one node in a broader set of cultural flows and is not obliged to a discourse of citizenship or national belonging. It is perhaps due to McKay's much more commercially viable black-on-black masquerade that *Home to Harlem* was wider known though less admired than *Tropic Death*. It provided readers with recognizable African American settings and racial types despite its many attempts to complicate them with Caribbean themes and characters. No doubt this is why the book tends to be comfortably remembered as an African American text and its primary black-on-black criticisms ignored in favour of its critique of American racism. For McKay, *Banjo* would be the true departure, but by then Walrond had embarked on "The Big Ditch", his regrettably never-completed work about the Panama Canal. He was also on the verge of leaving America never to return, except for a visit in 1931.

Another important detail in the letter is that the 1925 competition McKay refers to is in fact the *Opportunity* competition which helped announce a formal literary Renaissance, the one where Langston Hughes took first-prize for his poem "The Weary Blues", where Zora Hurston took a second for her short story "Spunk", and where other winners included Sterling Brown, E. Franklin Frazier, Countee Cullen and, of course, Eric Walrond, whose brilliant precursor to *Tropic Death*, "The Voodoo's Revenge", placed behind "Spunk". There was another important player in Harlem's literary cross-culturality involved in the *Opportunity* awards: the legendary king of the Harlem underworld and influential pan-Caribbean nationalist Casper Holstein, an immigrant from St Croix whom Walrond described as "some sort of messiah" among Virgin Islanders.[31] At the end of the awards dinner he was announced as the official patron of the next contest, and it was to him that *Tropic Death* was initially dedicated. As is well known what emerged from the *Opportunity* awards and the special issue of *Survey Graphic* (*Harlem: Mecca of the New Negro*) that had appeared the month before was the collection *The New Negro*. Edited by Alain Locke, this anthology included McKay's work but featured also "The Palm Porch" from *Tropic Death*. This story would be disparaged in the above letter to Nancy Cunard as essentially a black man's version of a white man's story – coming from McKay such criticisms shouldn't fail to surprise.

J.A. Rogers was included in *The New Negro* but more prominent was an essay by his fellow Jamaican W.A. Domingo, one of the founders of the African Blood Brotherhood. Domingo's "Gift of the Black Tropics" was the closest to a foreign Negro manifesto then possible, though it only mentions "voluntary pilgrims" from the African continent in passing.[32] With its stress on the "black foreigner" with "an alien heritage" and its focus on the tensions between black immigrants and native blacks, Domingo's essay only articulates what had long been the focus of Walrond's work for organs such as *New Republic, Negro World, Crisis, Current History, Opportunity, Messenger* and a plethora of others.[33] As Irma Watkins-Owens points out, as a business manager with a good degree of influence over content, "Walrond helped shift *Opportunity* towards inclusion of more global black perspectives", publishing the work of writers who would participate in Negritude as well as Negrismo.[34] In his work up to *Tropic Death*, Walrond presents if not a foreign Negro manifesto then a set of profiles and psychic, cultural portraits of America as experienced by black immigrants. But because the native African American discourses of race were so dominant as to render others invisible, and because this historical period is when those discourses began to transmute their specificities into absolutes, it was necessary for him to balance his nationalism with an equal commitment to the intricacies of "foreign Negro" assimilation and its dispersed affiliations.

This balancing of immigrant politics with cross-cultural poetics would most directly inform *Tropic Death* despite its exotic Caribbean setting. Harlem was, after all, his "sociological *el dorado*", a "seething spot of the darker races of the world".[35] Rather than accept that its denizens were simply "Negro", Walrond celebrated this "human mardi gras" filled with "heterogenous people".[36] But who was this "foreign Negro" so vividly present and participant in black American modernism? What was this archetype, how did it function and what (or rather, how) did it see? Domingo describes the early street level context of this movement-within-a-movement:

> Ten years ago it was possible to distinguish the West Indian in Harlem, especially during the summer months. Accustomed to wearing cool, light-colored garments in the tropics, he would stroll along Lenox Avenue on a hot day resplendent in white shoes and flannel pants, the butt of many a jest from his American

brothers who, today, have adopted the styles that they formerly derided. This trait of non-conformity manifested by the foreign-born has irritated American Negroes, who resent the implied self-sufficiency, and as a result there is a considerable amount of prejudice against West Indians. It is claimed that they are proud and arrogant; that they think themselves superior to the natives. And although educated Negroes of New York are loudest in publicly decrying the hostility between the two groups, it is nevertheless true that feelings against West Indians is strongest among members of that class. This is explainable on the ground of professional jealousy and competition for leadership.[37]

Though our perennially unreconstructed nationalisms forbid us from excavating intra-racial prejudices (ever conveniently attributing them exclusively to white racism), it is true that just as early-twentieth-century America was not an easy place for blacks, early-twentieth-century Harlem was not an easy place for black immigrants: "The West Indians' penchant for colorful clothes and unmistakable twang made him the target of crude jokes and comic misrepresentations in private and public. Street vendors particularly relished ridiculing West Indians, whom they sometimes physically assaulted."[38] But as Domingo and Clifford Jones point out, despite the differences and the occasional violence, there was, if not a synthesis of cultures, an eventual awareness of shared presence and some degree of catalysis between the groups. In the years after *Tropic Death*, Walrond reflected on his errantry and his arrival in America in similar terms:

> I settled in the Harlem Negro quarter. I found the community fairly evenly dominated by Southern Negroes and West Indian emigrants. A wide cleavage existed between the two groups. The West Indian with his Scottish, Irish or Devonshire accent, was to the native Black who has still retained a measure of his African folk-culture, uproariously funny. He was joked at on street corners, burlesqued on the stage and discriminated against in business and social life.[39]

Though rarely acknowledged, this is also the primary setting and the much-misunderstood political context for *Home to Harlem*. McKay's intra-racially fragmented New York features "foreign Negroes", black migrants and quasi-stateless vagabonds: Jamaicans, Haitians and migrants from the American South and more skin tones than any chromatic scale could contain. *Banjo* then goes much further in constructing a stateless place where *all* blacks are foreign: to each other and to the West itself. In this highly sexualized and unbelievably masculinized anarchistic space (wine and sex being the true cross-cultural, pan-African priorities), McKay argued for a kind of freedom from "compact national entities" and from sedentary notions of racial identity and politics.

However, the primary setting of *Banjo* was merely chosen by McKay to one-up and intensify the black cross-cultural complexity of early-twentieth-century New York, to push it beyond its national limits and cultural biases. In Marseilles he created a mythic space where there were no culturally dominant, local black natives and where the presence of white power was so decentralized as to be manageable. Marseilles was a space where competition around resources did not upset the balance of power between and among black linguistic and cultural differences. The Vieux Port in Marseilles is that mythic space of "barbarous international romance":

> In no other port had he ever seen congregated such a picturesque variety of Negroes. Negroes speaking the civilized tongues, Negroes speaking all the African dialects, black Negroes, brown Negroes, yellow Negroes. It was as if every country of the world where Negroes lived had sent representatives drifting in to Marseilles. A great vagabond host of jungle-like Negroes trying to scrape a temporary existence from the macadamized surface of this great Provençal port.[40]

There are a great many passages such as this in *Home to Harlem* and *Banjo* that present an intra-racial, cross-cultural or international panorama of black social and historical types; some of the most memorable and vivid sections of these novels are comprised of such moments, sometimes ad nauseum. As will soon be discussed, Walrond's work depends also on these wide-angle shots. What matters here is that Marseilles was ultimately McKay's escape from Harlem. However, it was an escape facilitated by *Tropic Death*, published prior to *Home to Harlem* and *Banjo* and which truly one-upped the cross-cultural complexity of New York by representing the Caribbean and the Panama Canal as zones of unrivalled black linguistic and cultural diversity, unparalleled black modernity: "Considering the physical limits of the region, there is hardly to be found elsewhere in the Atlantic a richer fusing of cultures than has been at work in the sunny coral isles of the West Indies."[41] As Watkins-Owens points out, it was there where Caribbean migrants first encountered other types of blacks – particularly African Americans.[42] That being the case, it is important to note that it was in the Canal Zone that Afro-Caribbean migrants encountered also Jim Crow-esque modes of racial classification as well as the American practice of deliberately encouraging "intraracial hostility in order to prevent the formation of labor unions".[43] As one observer noted: "The Jamaican [is told] that because some Caucasian blood flows through his veins he is better than the Trinidadian. The Barbadian has been taught that because he is more nearly of pure Negro blood he is better than the mixed people of Jamaica. . . . Thus they go, ever fighting, ever hating each other. The Barbadian hates the Jamaican, the Trinidadian hates the Barbadian and the Jamaican hates them all."[44]

Unlike Walrond in *Tropic Death*, McKay would significantly tone down the kind of intra-racial hostility at work in his utopia, though it is as present there as it is in *Home to Harlem*. But his overall "foreign Negro" vision can easily be overlooked due to his pedantic primitivism, his commitment to provocative representations of sex and race – often in a puerile attempt at courting offence from the African American intelligentsia – and a highly romantic socialism. It becomes less "foreign" than highly idiosyncratic. But what matters is that his "vagabondage" was informed by Walrond's work up to and including *Tropic Death*, particularly that which consistently fragmented "the Negro" into constituent and panoramic parts: native and immigrant, foreigners and African Americans, all of whom had distinct histories, modes of racial self-comprehension and innumerable biases towards each other. Walrond would in fact hone in on what he saw as the *felix culpa* of a larger colonial modernity, one that facilitated black-on-black cross-cultural contact in advance of the Panama Canal Zone:

> In Egypt and Palestine and other parts of the war area the black troops of the Western Hemisphere met other blacks – native Africans. It was the first mass contact of the negro from the Old and the New Worlds. Here something which the white war lords had not bargained on resulted. The negroes met and exchanged and compounded their views on the whites, their civilization, and their masters. Here the policies of France and Britain and Belgium and the United States with regard to their black wards were put in the scales. And when the blacks rose from the resulting pyre of disillusionment a new light shone in their eyes – a new spirit, a burning ideal, to be men, to fight and conquer and actually wrest their heritage, their destiny from those who controlled it.[45]

This vision of black modernity too becomes central to McKay's *Banjo*, most of which is an extended conversation about different types of whites, distinct forms of Negro identity and multiple comparisons of colonialism, black cultures and differential forms of inter- and intra-racial prejudice. Unlike much of the material produced in and around the Harlem Renaissance, it is notable that this is a black modernity that sees *actual* Africans as participants. But what is most valuable about Walrond is that he consistently historicizes the various biases in these interactions, refusing to reduce them to anything so monolithic as "racism" or the vagaries of skin colour as would McKay; and he certainly does not reduce them to an ultimately black male process of cross-cultural bonding.

〜〜〜

Despite the various intra-racial biases at work in the context of a harshly racist social and political environment, the very presence of the "foreign Negro" in Harlem was a catalytic one. Like Ray's influence on Jake in *Home to Harlem* and the impact on the character Banjo of a ragged, gloriously uncontainable sprawl of black cultures and languages, the "foreign Negro" was central to the politics of a black-on-black cross-culturality that is too often neglected in histories of American racial formation. After all, "blackness" in this climate was as much produced in relation to whiteness as it was vis-à-vis other types of blackness, and the consolidation of one had its impact on the articulation of others. The "foreign Negro" was therefore a distinct kind of racial subject, one that even white racism had identified: "The white man in America, strangely, does not consider the West Indian a 'nigger'. He is to him a 'foreigner'."[46] This distinct type of Negro can be described by Edouard Glissant's term, "flash agent":

> What is a flash agent? To conceive the question we must first consider the age-old ways in which cultures have interacted each time they have been in contact. Not just the interaction of their tendencies towards attraction or repulsion but the workings of their inner structures that become modified each time – the network of similarity or osmosis, or rejection or renaturing, that formed, manifested itself, canceled itself out . . .
>
> . . . flash agents are the relay agents who are in tune with implicit violence of contacts between cultures and the lightning speed of techniques of relation. They send consciousness hurtling into the sudden certainty that it is in posses-

sion of the obvious keys of interaction or, usually, into the assurance that it does not need such keys.[47]

Taking seriously the very notion that pan-Africanism and diasporic thinking was and is in large part an active attempt at a politics of relation – in which the multiplicities of black cultures, sensibilities, histories and concerns interact in the hopes of becoming interrelated, if not singular – and acknowledging now the need to extend largely First World assumptions of unanimity, the "foreign Negro" is that relay agent central to Walrond's work. Taking seriously also Glissant's faith in a transcendental process of cross-culturality that surpasses historical coding or political motivation, foreign Negro flash agents operate in the work of Walrond and McKay, effecting a cultural transformation that exceeds any attempt to channel or even claim it. They are in excess of Garvey and Du Bois and of diaspora as it is generally conceived as a structure bound essentially by race and generated increasingly by formations that are rooted in bi-chromatic, First World racial critique.

Unlike many of his peers in Harlem, Walrond was comfortable with racial and historical uncertainty and much more at ease with the violence of cultural transformation. But in tune with the necessary uncertainty of mutual transformation, his work argues for what George Lamming described as a distinct Caribbean immigrant "way of seeing" within the United States. The "foreign Negro" makes relation – race, in fact being a product and sign of relation – possible. An early story features this particular brand of black subjectivity, this non-bi-chromatic way of seeing race and history. Published in 1922 in the *New Republic*, it begins as a description of the tragic mundanities of racial prejudice and its impact on self-definition. That it is entitled "On Being Black" is important because after an introductory section where the reader is made to assume that the main character's personae is a familiar one, the sort of "blackness" shifts and fragments as it does in the first pages of *Tropic Death*. This occurs when the reader is told that the narrator though black, is also "foreign-looking and a curio".[48] The reader is then presented with a scene that complicates the "network of similarity" by revealing that this character's racial self-identification is far more prismatic than that expected of an African American socialized within a largely black/white framework:

> As I enter a dozen pairs of eyes are fastened upon me. Murmuring. Only a nigger. Again the wheels of life grind on. Lots are cast – I am not speaking

metaphorically. The joke is on the Latin. Down in Panama he is a government clerk. Over in Caracas, a tinterello, and in Mexico, a scientifico. I know the type. Coming to New York, he shuns the society of Spanish-Americans. On the subway at night he reads the New York Journal instead of La Prensa. And on wintry evenings, you can always find him around Seventy-second Street and Broadway.[49]

The "foreign Negro" reads race across a transnational landscape, perceives multiple histories behind masks, compares, contrasts and teases out the traces of relation, even when it is being denied. Because of the subject's participating in various histories of race and migration – Spanish, Caribbean and American in this case – "black" here means something quite distinct from African American and is located in a much broader network of affiliation and disaffiliation. A great many of his stories and essays in the years before *Tropic Death* featured this attempt to "renature" how racial identity functioned in Harlem by presenting a distinct form of specularity unique to black immigrants. For example, "I Am an American", features an African American from Georgia adrift in Cuba where he has learned the differences between the experiences of blacks in Cuba, Jamaica and America.[50] Or, there is the staggeringly good "Vignettes of the Dusk", which features "foreign Negroes" attempting to assimilate into African America via "philological assimilationism" despite being vilified by the native African Americans.[51] This latter piece echoes his discussion of the "dialectical oppression" faced by non-native blacks in Harlem discussed in "The Black City".[52] Then there is "The New Negro Faces America", where he imagines the "foreign Negro" as "the stokesman in the furnace of Negro ideals", and "The Negro Literati" which suggests that "as a foreigner" he – and others – are far less "obsessed by the inferiority complex" and therefore much less "enslaved spiritually" than American blacks.[53] Or there is 1927's brief but dense "The Color of the Caribbean", a remarkable exploration of the varied racial types and social meanings of race across a Caribbean landscape, one that due to its complexity renders the black immigrant "bewildered" by what he or she finds in America: "On coming to the United States, the West Indian often finds himself out of patience with the attitude he meets here respecting the position of whites and Negroes."[54]

What ultimately comes across in most of Walrond's stories, reviews and essays is the idea that due to migration (and in the case of Caribbean immigrants, often *multiple* pan-Caribbean, pan–Latin American migrations, not to mention the orienting experience of various empires) black immigrants have access to a kind of specularity that exceeds the limited "double consciousness" of Du Bois and the facile universalism of most uses of "the diasporic". As argued elsewhere, Du Bois's paradigm has been fetishized primarily as the guarantor of an African American exceptionalism that operates in the name of diaspora.[55] Though this prismatic specularity is present in Walrond's journalism and essays, it is at the centre of the fiction. In the stories he presents a panoramic racial specularity that is intimate with the distinct networks of "rejection and renaturing" that comprise race and diaspora. It is also quite overwhelming, especially for those constrained by an American framework. For example, in his *Opportunity* prize-winning "The Voodoo's Revenge", the white American and African American readers were no doubt dazzled by its variety of colonial and racial types and histories not to mention his use of Spanish, French and Creole terms to designate them. In panoramic terms he describes French creoles "who had left the service of the Americans to go into business for themselves"; "Antillian canal diggers" and "Silver City Negroes who spoke *patois* – blacks and brunettes from St Lucia and Trinidad and Martinique".[56] There are "pretty Negresses from the isles of the Caribbean who wore flame-colored skirts and East Indian earrings and heavy silver bangles reaching up to their elbows. Some, those of 'higher caste,' wore in their bosoms cameos and pearls and Birds of Paradise feathers to ornament their already gorgeous head dress".[57] Also, "Chombos", gold-toothed obeahmen, practitioners of voodoo in whom "one saw a transplantation of the ancient culture of Europe" and in whom "was a lingering strain of those heroic men who set out at the beginning of the Nineteenth Century to conquer in the name of France the tropic isles of the Caribbean".[58] And there are characters like the mulatto "Born in the Cayman Islands" and who had "been to Liverpool, Calais, Bremen" and fancied himself "a cosmopolitan".[59]

In "The Godless City", another story set in the Canal Zone, we have American Negro sailors and a captain who was the "last of that tribe of black Vikings, the Maroons of Jamaica".[60] They encounter "Negroes from St Lucia and Martinique, who cut roses and dug graves" and who "went to the heart of Africa for their music" which, in a wonderful cross-cultural irony, could only be played "as the French Negro colonials know how".[61] There is talk also of "Negroes of the Guianas" and "Bush Negroes from Paramaribo" and "'Big Tree' men of Jamaica", not to mention "Chinese lottery ticket vendors and Japanese candy makers".[62] And this is only a brief sketch, since Walrond is so exuberant in his lush descriptions of not just racial differences but cultural and historical ones. This latter point is what differentiates him from McKay, whose *Home to Harlem* and *Banjo* similarly celebrate black differences in such panoramic terms, but reduce them to the varieties of skin colour. In Walrond the fetish is for micro-histories and cross-cultural distinctions *made possible* by skin colour and the way they interact. However, it must be remembered that *Banjo* is directly informed by these stories and by *Tropic Death* with its "pauperized native blacks" clinging "to the utmost vestiges of the Crown".[63] McKay was no doubt influenced by its panorama of Honduran peasants and black Maroons; New Orleans creoles prejudiced against its Porto Ricans and Cubans; Italians, Poles, Greeks, Chinese, Trinidadians and European tourists; and its very many characters worshipping not only voodoo and obeah, but also Condomblé and forms of Brujeria.

But hold on: there are also characters like the St Lucian "black as the coal hills he mended", who "forgot where the French in him ended and the English began" but who "whenever he lapsed into His Majesty's English, it was with a thick Barbadian bias".[64] There are "Tortola mulattoes" and "half breed" Chinese Maroons.[65] Then, "Zigaboos", "Cholo Indians", Hindus, and "docile, half-white San Andres coons".[66] This is not to mention a great many characters that are of utterly indeterminate ethnicity and seem strangely free to then choose or create themselves despite the seeming inevitability of prejudice, violence and death. Especially Caribbean women. In keeping with his interest in women as narrative centres, they are as powerful as they are tragic whereas the men all fade, disappear and die. Walrond's panoramas are in fact gendered in a far more sophisticated way that McKay for whom women were largely threats to a homo-social vagabondage.[67] But even in his most exoticizing moments women are key to his wide-angled cross-culturality as central figures of diaspora and its infinite crossings:

> Up on the verandas there dark, bright-skirted flame-lipped girls, the evening before, danced in squares, holding the tips of their flimsy dresses to the *coombia* of creole island places. Creole girls led, thwarted, wooed and burned by *obeah*-working, weed-smoking St Lucian men. Jamaica girls, fired by an inextinguishable warmth, danced, whirling, wheeling, rolling, rubbing, spinning their posteriors and their hips, in circles, their breasts like rosettes of flame, quivering to the rhythm of the *mento* – conceding none but the scandalously sexless. Span-

ish girls, white ones, yellow ones, brown ones, furiously gay, furiously concerned over the actualities of beauty.[68]

But this is all merely a selection from two or three of the stories. One's consciousness as a reader is sent hurtling into indeterminacy by the range of categories, modes of racial self-knowledge, distinct historical experiences, and possible forms of identity covered by this panoramic and dizzying cross-culturality. It becomes difficult if not impossible to contain or frame this kaleidoscopic vision by an abstract universalism like diaspora, one that despite its capacity to assume and maintain internal differences is itself fractured by the intersections of so many *other* diasporas evident in the tongue and in the skin. The question Walrond's work seems to ask is this: What is the value of diaspora if *everyone* is "diasporic", or produced by multiple diasporas? And since all diasporas intersect, the true historical and conceptual problem may be the very assumption of origins, common or otherwise, and the idea of an abstract category for such movement and transformations.

Yet even though the radically hybrid and polyglot societies represented in *Tropic Death* were clearly Caribbean, they were intended to signify within and against the racial politics of Harlem, United States. *Tropic Death* is less the exotic, colourful and grotesque vision of a tropical elsewhere that many claim it to be and which it in fact initially seems to be. It should be read less as a collection of black exotica, despite Walrond's clear preference for such modes of representation, but instead as an attempt to denature the increasingly bi-chromatic system of racial values at work in American modernism in quite mythic language and terms. Its mythic qualities are quite obvious: elusive, fragmented and almost preciously "modernist" language which evades the social realism so prized among most writers of his generation; its blurring of the Caribbean and Latin America into one dreamscape of violence, cruelty and unimaginably suggestive beauty; and the fact that despite the distinct narratives within each story, they each flow into each other so easily that it is not unusual to hear it described as a novel in much the way that Jean Toomer's *Cane* often is. However, the themes and concerns of *Tropic Death* are only more exaggerated and narratively well developed than the clunkier experiments in social realism and Garveyite racial romanticizing that came before it.

Despite its Caribbean provenance, *Tropic Death* was meant to function within an America that was beginning to consolidate its primary if not governing understanding of race around two specific poles: black (that is to say, African American) and white (the construction of which is too a by-product or after-effect of waves of European immigration, as distinct ethnic groups become catalysed and transformed into a mythic and dominant "whiteness"). It is the case that far too much discussion about American racial formations tends to coalesce in these structures, neglecting the complex and equally significant intra-racial, cross-cultural tensions at work in African America. But against these centripetal forces, Walrond offered a myth of racial dispersal that countered "the great migration" with the Caribbean movement into the United States and supplemented the involuntary movements of an increasingly abstracted "middle passage" with the concrete, voluntary migrations of black immigrants. Indeed, Walrond's work primarily stages and layers "the diasporic" via encounters between what the late Nigerian anthropologist John Ogbu labelled "voluntary" and "involuntary" minorities, two groups who may share a racial category but who have marked differences in their fundamental conceptions of race and culture, and in their patterns of affiliation and strategies of assimilation.[69]

Read without the driving expectations of American racial preferences, *Tropic Death* also asks profound questions about the relationship between those for whom diaspora is a historical abstraction and those for whom it is and continues to be a social and cultural reality due to various migrations. And such migrations, it must be stressed, were central not only to modernism, which is why Walrond's work is so resonant today and demands a critical return. These migrations are the defining issue in a contemporary world of black natives, immigrants and refugees whose paradigms of self-knowing, cultural belonging and political affiliation do not fit easily into, say, American or African American categories of race. These are peoples also whose migrations are not so easily contained by black First World histories of "the diasporic" and their attendant political assumptions. To completely historicize the deployment of a black concept of diaspora in American literature and cultural politics, it is necessary to return to this work. Such a return is not to diminish a history in which the geographical sprawl of blacks after the slave trade was being plaited into mutually sustaining cultural and politically productive sets of synchronies and similarities – that "invention of Africa" that was and is largely a product of black diaspora. Instead, this return is necessary to keep contemporary notions of "the diasporic" open to contestation, suspicion and questioning by taking seriously the discrepant views of diaspora that constitute it and the multiple types of migration that give it cultural force and historical value.

NOTES

1. This is especially the case since the impact of Paul Gilroy's *The Black Atlantic: Modernity and Double Consciousness* (Cambridge, MA: Harvard University Press, 1993), which so ardently rendered necessary the constitutive presence of black difference in discourses of race, history and culture.
2. David Levering Lewis, *When Harlem Was in Vogue* (New York: Oxford University Press, 1979), 128.
3. Central to this critique of the black West is the early-twentieth-century classic, *Ethiopia Unbound: Studies in Race Emancipation*, 2nd ed. (London: Routledge, 1969), by Sierra Leonean barrister and "godfather" of African nationalism, J.E. Casely-Hayford.
4. V.Y. Mudimbe, *The Invention of Africa: Gnosis, Philosophy and the Order of Knowledge* (Bloomington: Indiana University Press, 1988).
5. Eric Walrond, *"Winds Can Wake Up the Dead": An Eric Walrond Reader*, ed. Louis J. Parascandola (Detroit: Wayne State University Press, 1998), 332.
6. Eric Walrond, *Tropic Death* (New York: Boni and Liveright, 1926), 20.
7. Claude McKay, *Selected Poems of Claude McKay* (New York: Bookman Associates, 1953), 19.
8. Ibid., 31.
9. Ibid., 19.
10. Richard J. Powell, "The Picturesque Miss Nottage and the Caribbean Sublime", *Small Axe*, no. 25 (February 2008): 164.
11. Walrond, *Tropic Death*, 19.
12. Ibid., 23–24.
13. Jon Woodson does point out that both Walrond and Toomer were acquainted, however, through the former's participation in the latter-led group of Harlemites devoted to the study of the work of post-Blavatskian mystic G.I. Gurdjieff. Jon Woodson, *To Make a New Race: Gurdjieff, Toomer, and the Harlem Renaissance* (Jackson: University Press of Mississippi, 1999).
14. Walrond wrote a favourable review of *Harlem Shadows* in *Negro World*, 6 May 1922, 4.
15. Walrond, *"Winds"*, 65.
16. Ibid., 127. See also Louis Chude-Sokei, *The Last "Darky": Bert Williams, Black-on-Black Minstrelsy and the African Diaspora* (Durham: Duke University Press, 2006);

Irma Watkins-Owens, *Blood Relations: Caribbean Immigrants and the Harlem Community, 1900–1930* (Bloomington: Indiana University Press, 1996); Winston James, *Holding Aloft the Banner of Ethiopia: Caribbean Radicalism in Early Twentieth-Century America* (New York: Verso, 1998).

17. R. Clifford Jones, *James K. Humphrey and the Sabbath-Day Adventists* (Jackson: University Press of Mississippi, 2006), 77.
18. Walrond wrote a favourable review of *Banjo* in the *Clarion* (London) (July 1929), reprinted in *In Search of Asylum: The Later Writings of Eric Walrond*, ed. Louis J. Parascandola and Carl A. Wade (Gainesville: University Press of Florida, 2011).
19. For more on West Indians during the Harlem Renaissance see Watkins-Owens, *Blood Relations*; James, *Holding Aloft the Banner*; and Louis J. Parascandola, ed., *"Look for Me All Around You": Anglophone Immigrants in the Harlem Renaissance* (Detroit: Wayne State University Press, 2005).
20. Edouard Glissant, *Poetics of Relation* (Ann Arbor: University of Michigan Press, 1997), 15.
21. Ibid., 317–18.
22. Cary D. Wintz, ed., *The Harlem Renaissance 1920–1940: The Politics and Aesthetics of "New Negro" Literature* (New York: Garland, 1996), 495.
23. Ibid., 317–18.
24. Theodore G. Vincent, ed., *Voices of a Black Nation: Political Journalism in the Harlem Renaissance* (Trenton, NJ: Africa World Press, 1991), 358–59. Reprinted in Walrond, *"Winds"*, 135–37.
25. Walrond wrote a favourable review of *Nigger Heaven*, "The Epic of a Mood", *Saturday Review of Literature*, 2 October 1926, 153. Reprinted in Walrond, *"Winds"*, 135–37.
26. W.E.B. Du Bois, "Five Books", *Crisis* 33, no. 3 (January 1927): 152.
27. Walrond, *"Winds"*, 126–27.
28. Ibid., 117.
29. Walrond, *Tropic Death*, 91.
30. Levering Lewis, *Harlem*, 190.
31. Watkins-Owens, *Blood Relations*, 157.
32. Alain Locke, ed., *The New Negro: Voices of the Harlem Renaissance* (New York: Simon and Schuster, 1992), 342.
33. Ibid., 341.
34. Watkins-Owens, *Blood Relations*, 157.
35. Walrond, *"Winds"*, 116.
36. Ibid., 129.
37. Locke, *New Negro*, 346.
38. Jones, *James K. Humphrey*, 75.
39. Walrond, *"Winds"*, 281.

40. Claude McKay, *Banjo: A Story Without a Plot* (New York: Harper and Brothers, 1929), 68–69.
41. Walrond, "Winds", 142.
42. Watkins-Owens, *Blood Relations*, 14. See also Rhonda D. Frederick's impressive *"Colón Man a Come": Mythographies of Panamá Canal Migration* (Lantham, MD: Lexington, 2005), 15.
43. Heather Hathaway, *Caribbean Waves: Relocating Claude McKay and Paule Marshall* (Bloomington: Indiana University Press, 1991), 15.
44. Ibid., 15.
45. Walrond, "Winds", 121–22.
46. Ibid., 281. For more detail see also Chude-Sokei, *Last "Darky"*.
47. Glissant, *Poetics*, 165–66.
48. Walrond, "Winds", 77.
49. Ibid., 79.
50. Ibid., 83.
51. Ibid., 92.
52. Ibid., 118.
53. Ibid., 130.
54. Ibid., 146.
55. Chude-Sokei, *Last "Darky"*.
56. Walrond, "Winds", 94.
57. Ibid., 94–95.
58. Ibid., 95.
59. Ibid., 100.
60. Ibid., 162.
61. Ibid., 164.
62. Ibid., 165–66.
63. Walrond, *Tropic Death*, 29.
64. Ibid., 68.
65. Ibid., 70.
66. Ibid., 101.
67. This also takes into account the various attempts at or assertions of a queer reading of McKay and his peregrinations, the most notable (though problematic for its sometimes valuation of a complex reading of suggestive possibilities in favour of evidence) is the nevertheless engaging and intriguing *Claude McKay, Code Name Sasha: Queer Black Marxism and the Harlem Renaissance*, by Gary Edward Holcomb (Gainesville: University Press of Florida, 2007).
68. Walrond, *Tropic Death*, 108.
69. John Ogbu, *Minority Education and Caste: The American System in Cross-Cultural Perspective* (New York: Academic Press, 1978).

5

GENRE, GENDER AND ERIC WALROND'S EQUIVOCAL TRANSNATIONAL VISION

RHONDA FREDERICK

Black empire narratives constitute an important feature of a modern black transnational imaginary. They represent a desire on the part of marginalized modern black subjects to tell global stories of the race in the context of empire and conquest.
   —Michelle Ann Stephens, *Black Empire*

Some [Negroes] feel that with a strong native Government flourishing on the shores of Africa, evils like lynching in Georgia and exclusion laws in Australia would be dispensed with. Others, and these are in the majority, cannot see beyond the shores of the Hudson. They haven't any international vision.
   —Eric D. Walrond, "The New Negro Faces America"

Western invocations of a "family of man" have undeniably been platitudinous, ahistorical, and self-serving . . . In a now increasingly discredited form, the oneness of humanity produces a mythological universality that closes off understandings of the significance of human differences and masks western involvement in the active creation of human injustices. In this sense, the concept alludes to a timeless, unchanging essence that provides "the solid rock of a universal human nature" . . . But the idea can serve other ends. Taking the oneness of humankind only as a compass point, we can use it to guide the multifaceted, particular, and hence historical creation of a more liveable human future, although the dimensions, landscape, and qualities of that future are as yet imperceptible.
   —Charles Carnegie, *Postnationalism Prefigured*

UNLIKE WRITERS WHO GENERALLY celebrate Caribbean landscapes[1] and theorize a (more or less) unified African diaspora, Eric Walrond's evaluation of places occupied by black peoples is strikingly pessimistic. The interpersonal relationships he fictionalizes are similarly cynical. Yet Walrond's pessimism reflects not only a desire to de-mythologize the value of the land in relation to "the folk", but also conveys his interest in representing underrepresented features of black people's realities, ones that characterize their confrontations with nature/geography, migrations and myriad oppressions. Contemporary reviews of Walrond's *Tropic Death*, however, de-emphasized these thematic strains in favour of descriptions of the writer's "impressionistic style" and "eye for exotic detail".[2] Critical attention to his writing style and subjective readings of his stories appear to have overwhelmed rather than complemented the author's creative and extra-literary preoccupations and the "black content" of his stories.

By reading content through form, and by interpreting Walrond's fictional and non-fictional depictions of anti-black racism, intra-racial and interregional prejudices, and man-made and natural forces that affect African-descended peoples in the Americas, readers can come to critical conclusions about his oeuvre that account for his extra-literary investments. When one attends to Walrond's form, themes and concerns, she or he finds that explorations of black transnationalism come to the fore, a driving ideological concern the author shares with Caribbean writers associated with the Harlem Renaissance.[3] Where black transnationalism, as a socio-political philosophy, evolved out of contemporary discourses on anticolonialism, nationalism and internationalism, Walrond's fiction reflects an orientation that foregrounds black ethnic particularities and, therefore, complicates ideas about unity among blacks in the African diaspora. Analyses of Walrond's autobiographical and fictional pieces reveal images of migrating blacks, but ones often depicted from the perspective of contentious intra-racial specificities. In other words, his representations of heterosexual as well as intra- and extra-racial relationships insist that readers consider formations of a black, inter-/transnational community as "multifaceted [and] particular".[4] What this vision might reveal is occluded by visions of transnational blackness simply "united against whiteness and empire",[5] namely, how integral white/European racism was to a homogeneous vision of black subjectivity.[6] Taken collectively and viewed across genres, Walrond's body of work rethinks black community from a different base. A transnational black community, re-presented in this author's fictional and non-fictional narratives and articulated out of friction, highlights the possibility that this community can be "thought" outside of a reaction to white/European racism.

In highlighting complexities in Walrond's body of work, it can be seen that particular characters represent the "contradiction [that] often adds power and poignancy to his work".[7] Walrond's female characters are often contradictory or they demonstrate the consequence of unexamined forces with which other characters should contend, leaving readers to consider the import of their far-ranging characterizations. I focus on Walrond's female characters in this chapter to explore interpretive consequences that result when we insert the author's experiences and creative vision into the critical contexts of black inter-/transnationalism and identity formation. Where some have depicted black inter-/transnationalism as a patriarchal, global and (largely) sanguine ideological perspective, through Walrond's women we find a vision of the possibilities of a vexed though enabling black subjectivity.

In *The Practice of Diaspora*, Brent Edwards makes a case for rethinking the US geographic and ideological orientation of some scholarship on the "Harlem" Renaissance.[8] Citing W.E.B. Du Bois's speech at the Pan-African Conference (1900) and Alain Locke's internationalist intentions for the "New Negro" (1925), Edwards joins a cadre of critics who argue that the "[Harlem] Renaissance was international in scale both in terms of where its contributors came from and in terms of its being merely the North American component of something larger and grander".[9] Marking the United States as *the* site from which the tidal wave of early-twentieth-century black cultural and ideological production emanated results in "US-bound themes of cultural nationalism, civil rights protest, and uplift" overwhelming the internationalist/transnationalist aspect of this narrative-based movement. Exchanging Paris for the United States in this same period, he argues, significantly extends physical and ideological boundaries of this renaissance: "[T]o ask about the function of Paris is to ask a broader set of interrelated questions about the role of outer-national sites even in texts that are putatively the canonical literature of 'Harlem'. It is as though certain moves, certain arguments and epiphanies can only be staged beyond the confines of the United States, and even sometimes in languages other than English."[10] Where blacks from different parts of the globe, and speaking/writing in a range of languages, converged on Paris between the world wars, a complex black internationalism resulted.

Edwards's argument resonates intimately with my reading of Walrond's oeuvre, specifically as the former identifies

> a vision of internationalism, perhaps, though not exactly "worldwide black unity": in these transnational circuits, black modern expression takes form not as a single thread, but through the often uneasy encounters of peoples of African descent with each other. The cultures of black internationalism are formed only within [a paradoxical view of pan-African unity], with the result that – as much as they allow new and unforeseen alliances and interventions on a global stage – they also are characterized by unavoidable misapprehensions and misreadings, persistent blindnesses and solipsisms, self-defeating and abortive collaborations, a failure to translate even a basic grammar of blackness.[11]

Borrowing from Stuart Hall's concept of "articulation", Edwards represents the products of a Paris-informed theory of African diaspora as, simultaneously, "unified" and contentious, "African" and "not African" (in what it borrows from discourses of Jewish diaspora),[12] and that straddles geographical and linguistic spaces. "Articulation", he writes, "functions as a concept-metaphor that allows us to consider relations of 'difference within unity,' non-naturalizable patterns of linkage between disparate societal elements".[13] Edwards continues: "In a transnational circuit, then, articulation offers the means to account for the diversity of black takes on *diaspora*, which Hall . . . explicitly begins to theorize . . . as a frame of cultural identity determined not through 'return' but through difference."[14]

Michelle Wright's *Becoming Black* explores black diasporic identity formation versus Edwards's ideological and narrative constructions of this diaspora, but they nonetheless reach similar conclusions. Wright observes that while peoples on the African continent understood themselves as variously diverse before European contact (in terms of culture, language, ethnicity and geography and the like), after this contact and in the diaspora, African and African-descended peoples were made, homogeneously, "black". Yet Wright does not represent the inherent contradiction between the multi- and unifaceted nature of black identity as that which best defines subjectivity in the "African diaspora"; instead, perhaps in addition, she writes of the "'in between' space that Blackness seems to inhabit: within contradiction . . ., the material and the abstract . . . , and the struggle between Black identity's individual and collective aspects".[15] People in search of a "black self-consciousness" negotiate this complex as they process meanings of individual and collective blackness.

By describing a process of identity formation likely engaged in by *people* in search of self definition, Wright offers insight into the difficulty scholars faced in theorizing diaspora: "while scholars have scratched their heads over how to negotiate these extremes to produce Black self-consciousness . . . Black writers and thinkers living in the West have been producing their own answers".[16] Creative narratives, therefore, hold complexities that have been tricky to maintain in critical works. By devising a fictive critical frame, Wright maps African diasporic intellectual traditions as they progress through stages, the last of which grounds the thesis of *Becoming Black*. She describes a "first-generation of theories" as appearing in the first half of the twentieth century and as "counterdiscourses that directly opposed nineteenth-century French, German, British, and American discourses, all of which posited the Black as Other to the white subject". The second generation appears in the late 1960s and similarly challenges the notion of blacks as "other", but also takes issue with the masculinist and nationalist black subject espoused by first-generation intellectuals of the African diaspora.[17] Wright remarks on philosophies that limit the first generation's black subjectivity to "male" and "nation", and poses an extensive critique that would "[compare] subject formation across a range of sociopolitical categories (race, nation, gender, and sexuality)".[18] To put it succinctly, *Becoming Black* seeks

> to understand "Blackness" as a unity of diversity. By producing a comparative analysis of how subject formations by African American, Afro-German, Black British, Black French, and Anglophone and Francophone writers countered those discourses that produced Blacks as Other to the (white) Western subject – an analysis that also looks at how gender and sexuality inform the construction of these diasporic subjects – this project seeks to understand how Black theories of subjectivity both differ and remain the same across the African diaspora.[19]

Conceptualizing blackness in this way also understands identity as a social category produced through – and not excluding – gender and sexuality, so that "we arrive at theories of the Black subject that successfully negotiate the ideal and material formations that must predicate Black subject formation".[20]

In responding to Western discourses in which the white male citizen/sovereign was defined against a black (male) other, Wright observes similarly patriarchal impulses in black challenges to this "othering". In other words, challenges to the black, African "antithesis" of the white, European "thesis" operate out of a hetero-normative masculinity that leaves little room for discussion of white or black femaleness. After identifying commonalities in some processes of white/European and black/African diasporic subject formations, Wright concludes that first-generation theorists, "explicitly, as in [W.E.B.] Du Bois, or implicitly, as in [Aimé] Césaire, [Léopold Sédar] Senghor, and [Frantz] Fanon, the first counterdiscourses of subjectivity (re)produce a patriarchal world view in which men give birth to men, or the one produces the one". Out of this trope of "male mother"/"male birth" second-generation writers and thinkers highlight "this fallacy of a nation of men giving birth to other men and [acknowledge] the active role of the Black female in both subject construction and the nation so as to bring the Black female into being".[21]

Wright and Edwards accept complexities in theories of diasporic black self-consciousness and ideologies, and place significant emphasis on the ability of literature/creative narratives to reflect "difference in unity". As Wright details:

> The texts I discuss range from dense philosophical treatises to experimental poetry, and I read through a range of dialectic and dialogic subject formations to show how this tradition of African diasporic counterdiscourses on the subject is not only directly engaged with those European discourses of the white subject and Black Other but in fact subverts and revises some of their most central tenets. Through this methodology, I show how African diasporic theories of subjectivity, *although often ignored or misrecognized as works of fiction bereft of theoretical content*, are an undeniable art of nineteenth- and twentieth-century theories of subjectivity.[22]

Eric Walrond, most prolific about one hundred years before Edwards and Wright, anticipates the concept of "difference in unity". His writing, perhaps informed by his personal experiences, captures African-descended peoples in different locations (Barbados, Panama, United States, in transit) and under different pressures (of gender, class, race and modernity). Walrond's female characters are particularly illustrative of his (predominantly) creative representation of African diaspora-as-complex, an interpretive truth that distinguishes his body of work from that of his US-based contemporaries.

In a work "interested in how male intellectuals from the Anglophone Caribbean attempted to imagine a transnational form of black nationality that could both transcend nationalism and reimagine the state itself", Michelle Ann Stephens centrally places gender in her analysis of black transnationalism.[23] Early narratives written by African Americans and US-based anglophone Caribbean writers employed gendered tropes in order to reflect the differences between a more open-ended vision of the diaspora as a virtual global nation, linked culturally, historically and emotionally, and a more territorial sense of the race as a transnational political community consolidated through the power of a sovereign state.[24]

In *Black Empire*, Stephens defines "black transnationalism" as a discourse that "references both the construction of a global imaginary that drew from the masculinist rhetoric of sovereignty essential to both imperial and national visions of the state and an alternative set of tropes and symbols representing clues to alternative ways of imagining black freedom, alternatives that deviated from the paradigms of empire".[25] The physical devastation in Europe after the First World War gave way to the ideological reconstitution of European countries as separate "nations", and ideas about possibilities of class-based identities activated by the Russian Revolution were circulating at about the same time. Black North American and Caribbean intellectuals privy to these ideological revolutions deployed them to theorize a prescriptive politics for black liberation across the globe. Yet, according to Stephens, "the white, modernist, and nationalist formations dominant during the 1910s and 1920s were not... the only sources for the twentieth-century New Negro's primary identifications". Intellectuals such as Marcus Garvey, Claude McKay and C.L.R. James availed themselves of "the traces of alternative forms of identification that developed among hybrid, multinational, and multiracial populations travelling in the spaces between the New and the Old Worlds, throughout the centuries of colonial settlement and imperial development".[26]

Thus positioned between political, geographical and ideological locations, Caribbean proponents of black transnationalism revealed how the prejudices and disenfranchisements existing in colonial and pre-national worlds extended into new national ones. Yet despite the fact that key features of empire seeped into new narratives of nation and democracy, theories of black transnational subjectivity relied upon features of "empire" and masculinist discourses even in challenging the new political organization's democratic efficacy. To put it another way, some features of empire – particularly, for my purposes, fixed notions of gender – permeated the transnational visions of black, anglophone Caribbean men.

Though Walrond's writings have not typically been read as being ideologically *prescriptive* (as the work of his contemporaries has been), reading them through a critical frame informed by Edwards, Wright and Stephens's perspectives on diaspora highlights contrapuntal perspectives in Walrond's oeuvre. The creative writer's work, therefore, demonstrates a critical point of departure that unseats fixed ideas about masculinity and empire as organizing principles for black subjectivities across borders.

〜〜
〜〜

Themes that manifest in Walrond's creative work are also visible in his nonfiction writing. Tracing these reverberations across genres reveals the author's attempt at imaginatively rendering anglophone Caribbean realities forged in colonial, imperial and migratory crucibles. Permeating the author's work are ambivalences that call into question simplistic conceptions of unity among African-descended peoples, particularly as these ground theories of "a black state, a black empire".[27]

Where the subjects of Stephens's analyses in *Black Empire* base their theories of black solidarity on conceptions of a unified black community-across-borders (the "black race" defined by a purportedly shared experience of white supremacy, black Caribbean intellectuals – enabled by not-yet-formed "nations" – blend different critical models to imagine new critical forms for black freedom/subjectivity, and thus de-emphasize intra-racial differences but emphasize some forms of patriarchy), Walrond begins from a creative/theoretical perspective that questions whether an uncomplicated race-based unity can sufficiently ground a global black community. Thus, any review of Walrond's body of work must embrace the idea of a black transnational solidarity from the perspective of difference, if not discord. Readers must ask: How might black transnationalism be construed when blacks' traditional and historical challenges are taken into consideration? And if in narratives of black empire "educated leaders, either as individuals or as the heads of black and internationalist organizations, negotiate a dialogic relationship with Euro-American imperial organizations and nation-states",[28] then what do we make of Walrond's characters – pre-modern people facing modernity, relating to themselves and to others, and living – who form the theoretical centre of the transnational imaginings in his work? I approach answers to these questions by interpreting Walrond's depiction of heterosexual relationships, ones fraught with misunderstandings, prejudices and flaws in character. The multiple colonial and imperial locations in Walrond's personal and fictive worlds, as well as the intra- and extra-regional migrations in both, result in narrative complexities that provide insights into identity and ideology for African-descended peoples in the diaspora. These, in addition to the author's expressed feelings of dis-location in various spaces, his attacks of depression and self-doubt, and his representations of women, speak to "difference-in-unity" as central to conceptions of black solidarity across borders.[29] If "what made this black intellectual formation transnational was its vision of a modern black political identity constituted by multiple black nationalities, the belief in black subjects' inherent right to free movement, and the recognition of their perennial desire for a state",[30] then Walrond's writings draw our attention to the pitfalls in "multiple black nationalities", in some consequences "inherent [in the] right to free movement", and the lack of protection when governing bodies (colonial and Panama Canal authorities and, by extension, US national authority) cannot or do not protect their charges. Nonetheless, Walrond's persistent though subtle optimism, despite the pessimistic tones in his life and writing, suggests his desire to "think" differently about intraracial difference and unity.

Walrond was born in British Guiana (now Guyana) to Barbadian parents,[31] and he lived in several anglophone Caribbean countries in addition to Panama, England, France and the United States. These migrations seemed to have made it difficult for critics to "place" Walrond, as can be seen in the myriad ways he continues to be described: the writer has variously been identified as African American, Guyanese, Barbadian, Caribbean, West Indian and black.[32] This collection of adjectives, as well as the locations, identities and discourses each represents, might be understood as a consequence of the "fluidity with which ideas, objects, capital, and people now move across borders and boundaries".[33] However, Walrond's experiences in each place, not to mention his self-described mental "instability", suggest that the fluidity and connection-across-borders to which black transnationalism aspires were difficult for this writer to forge and maintain. Brent Edwards observes: "The level of the international is accessed unevenly by subjects with different historical relations to the nation (for instance, in a collaboration between a US citizen marked by a context of violent racist exclusion, disenfranchisement, and segregation of a minority population, and a French West African citizen marked by a context of colonialism, invasive subjugation of a majority population, and Eurocentric structures of privilege and mobility)."[34] This statement appears particularly applicable to Walrond's lived reality. He experienced regional and racial biases in each place in which he lived. Moving from British Guiana to Barbados and then to Panama to reunite with his father, Walrond "was again an outsider, a foreign-born 'Mudhead' (a term denigrating the natives of British Guiana, which is below sea level) in Barbados and a 'Chombo' (a black West Indian) in Panama", and "despite the prejudice he encountered as a black and as a West Indian (a 'monkey chaser') [in the United States], Walrond experienced his greatest literary success [there]".[35]

One might argue, then, that his difficult migrations affected his emotional state, an interpretation supported by statements he made in letters as well as by his status as a "self-admitted patient" in Roundway Psychiatric Hospital between 11 May 1952 and 5 September 1957.[36] In making these observations, I do not intend to present a simplistic correlation between events in Walrond's extra-literary life and themes in his literary work. Instead, I highlight a relationship between Walrond's troubled migrations, *the ways he described* his mental state and his writing style as signs of his challenges to some representations of black solidarity. I also argue that it is these resonances in his fiction that qualify Walrond as, in the words of Winston James, "among the most distinguished intellectuals of the Renaissance and undoubtedly one of the most gifted and prolific short story writers of his generation".[37]

Attempting to account for his failure to complete research funded by the Guggenheim Foundation, Walrond wrote to Henry Allen Moe, secretary general of the foundation, in 1940, from an address in Wiltshire, England. Walrond explained that "as a depression casualty I have had my ups and downs; *my quest for security in a world in which nothing is stable* led me astray".[38] The effect of being so frequently uprooted[39] and his failed quest for stability can be seen in the form, style and content of Walrond's stories, particularly those collected in *Tropic Death* and others published in *Roundway Review*.[40]

In the December 1952 issue of this publication, Walrond published an autobiographical piece entitled "From British Guiana to Roundway". It is in Walrond's description of Panama that one finds stylistic reflections of his creative writing: "the swamp was full of reeds, machineel [sic], the bone white spectres of dead and leaflessly dying trees. The east wind wafted its exhalations over the town."[41] Curiously, however, an essay written to document the author's movement from his birthplace to the place of his mental recuperation is light on autobiographical detail; instead, Walrond opts for descriptions of the landscapes in which he resided and the kinds of work he performed. Considered in the context of migration and diaspora, this short piece offers insight into Walrond's associations of place and identity. He describes Barbados as "a British possession since 1605; many of its early settlers came from Wiltshire, and it is sometimes called . . . 'Little England in the Caribbean Sea'", and he writes of Panama as a "'plague-spot', one of the worst in the world".[42] Notably, Panama is also a place where about twenty-two thousand men, mostly French, died in the attempt to build a trans-Isthmian canal and whose noxious climate "was occasionally mirrored in the faces of mestizos [whom Walrond] passed in the street on the way to and from school".[43] In his failure to introduce Caribbean migrants into this specific equation of nature and identity, as he does with Europeans and people native to the isthmus, the autobiographer seems to protect the former and himself from the negatives of the Panamanian natural environment. Instead, he associates his Caribbean and migrant-selves with man-made improvement on the isthmus. Working as a junior clerk in "the nerve centre of the public health service", Walrond had a "'birds-eye' view of the measures which had not only made the construction of the canal possible, but had made the Canal Zone one of the healthiest places in Latin America".[44] This is how the author describes his "early formative years".[45]

"From British Guiana to Roundway" casts the author's emigration to New York in a similar vein. Working in an architectural firm as a temporary replacement for a practically irreplaceable "West Indian", Walrond leaves this job to work for a "young English doctor from South Africa".[46] Although this English/South African doctor is fixated on an unstated aspect of Walrond's persona (twice asking the autobiographer's architect-employer, "Where did you get a man like that?"),[47] the doctor hires Walrond and allows him to witness the vitality of the hospital switchboard and to see "something of the kind of patients that were admitted – seamen injured in storms at sea or in cafe brawls on the water-front, stockbrokers . . . an old Irish woman with cancer".[48] After establishing a connection between West Indian migrants, their exemplary work and their participation in altruistic works, the author returns to his moves from birthplace to place of hospitalization: "The jump, for a 'depression casualty' in the years following the Wall Street crash of 1929, is almost frightening. It is as though I'd entered a new world, a compact, almost self-contained community set in surroundings of rare beauty. . . . For myself, I can only say that my experience as a voluntary patient so far has been in keeping with the spirit at large in the Hospital."[49] It is in this way that Walrond writes his mental illness and financial crisis into man-made and triumphant contexts.

Yet the author's pleasant description of health, healthcare and the Roundway Hospital coexists with spectres of victimization ("depression *casualty*") and fear. For the most part, this autobiographical piece reads as an attempt at innocuously packaging a debilitating depression (supported by Walrond's celebration of himself and West Indians at work), but it nonetheless communicates an unease stemming from "the jump" between varied geographical locations and the stated tenuous economic and social climate in them.

♒

Of the ten stories in *Tropic Death*, seven are set in Barbados or Panama. Of the remaining three, one is set in Demerara, another on a ship en route to Jamaica from Honduras and the title story is set in Barbados, aboard a ship and in Panama. Walrond's intricate, rich and oppressive creative vision and his ambivalent view of migration are the threads that connect these stories.[50]

Each story's form (abrupt transitions, choppy language, stark characterizations, bleak landscapes) and themes (people oppressed or victimized in their various locations, suffering from inculcated racism or colourism and problematic migrations, and troubled male/female relations) reflect Walrond's unstable extra-literary world, but his fictional representations offer critiques of the circumstances that shape his characters rather than a judgement of the characters themselves. Despite human and natural adversities, the author's stories reflect the potential in some characters' refusal to be simply defined by nature or circumstance.

"Panama Gold" is a story that captures the range of Walrond's writerly – and personal – concerns. The second story in *Tropic Death* describes protagonist Ella Heath ("a mulatto, with plenty of soft black hair")[51] as a lonely old maid with an intense respect for the land, that which it nurtures, and Bajan folktales and foodways. Readers learn that "all of nature gave flavor to Ella, [and] wrought a magic color in [her] life".[52] With his Panama-derived accoutrements (masculinity and money), Colón Man Poyah (so named because of his work on the Panama Canal) fancies himself a suitable beau; the protagonist, however, rejects him because of his "possessions", namely his materiality, dark skin and handicap. Seemingly a tale about a missed romantic opportunity, "Panama Gold" explores – through contrasting male/female, industrial/agricultural and Barbadian/US associations – the growing conflict between industrial/modern and agricultural economies in Barbados, the benefits – but more significantly – the costs of Panama Money to aspects of the Bajan personality.[53]

In the tension between Poyah and Ella, Walrond manifests the challenges between the pre-modern and the modern, and between prejudices that undermine productive intra-racial relations. Yet in his interpretation of "Panama Gold", Kenneth Ramchand finds a romantic relationship between Ella and Poyah most significant. The critic writes that "the association of Ella with fertility rituals is obviously a celebration of her connections with the earth, but it also looks forward symbolically to the opportunity coming into her life with Mr Poyah".[54] From this perspective, the protagonist's relationship with the Colón Man appears preordained. However, this interpretation can only be sustained if one overlooks details that communicate Walrond's ambivalence about such a union. A critical attempt to marry these characters in fact manifests the *impossibility* of such an outcome, particularly if US industrial and Bajan agricultural traditions – as well as intra-racial unity and heterosexuality – make up its constitutive parts. Given Walrond's allusions to Ella's aggressive independence and Poyah's materialistic masculinity, a "relationship" between the protagonist and the Colón Man is fraught with complication. Ella's characterization further alludes to the author's equivocal vision of the folk. While the author endows her with a love of the land and local folklore, he complicates her representative "folkness" by expressing a spiteful colour prejudice through her. Poyah's arrogant certainty of his attractions (derived from his Panama-derived work and possessions) also undermines his characterization.

Poyah returns to Barbados with enough money to open a shop; however, readers learn that some part of his Panama Money is compensation for a work-related accident. His amputated leg, therefore, confirms the importance of his money: it becomes a part of him as much as the cork that replaces his leg.

In an exchange with Pettit Bruin, Poyah makes known the connection between his damaged body, Panama Money and the canal enterprise. Pontificating, he says:

> "Pay me? Man, yo' should o' see how fas' dey pay me! Pay me fas' enough, indeed! Five hundred pounds! Ev'y blind cent! Man, I wuz ready to sick Nelson heself 'pon dem. At a moment's notice, me an' de council wuz gettin' ready fo' ramsack de Isthmus and shoot up de whole blasted locks! Hell wit' de Canal! We wuz gwine blow up de dam, cut down de wireless station an' break up de gubment house! If dey didn't pay me fo' my foot!"[55]

Through an aggressive pride in his British identity (Poyah let canal authorities "understand quick enough dat [he] wuz a Englishman *and not a bleddy American nigger*"[56]) and the money earned in Panama, Walrond's Colón Man is wholly defined through his relationships with colonial and imperial powers, a self-definition that fosters an animosity towards other African-descended canal workers. Perhaps mirroring the internal conflict between Ella and Poyah (see below), the distinction between the Colón Man from Barbados and black American canal workers is counter-intuitive. By separating his black and colonial self from black Americans, Poyah summarily rejects what could have been a powerful coalition against canal authorities. But such an alliance had to contend with that which divided (or could divide) its members. Though Poyah was able to get his compensation without the aid of US blacks, the similarity to his fraught relationship with Miss Heath – and its ambiguous outcome – suggests that there is potential and value in a complicated process towards union.

Poyah also asserts a masculinity distinguished by his work in the Canal Zone. "I's a man, man" [Poyah] said . . . "I wuz a brakesman in Palama, don't fomembah dat. I wuz de bes' train hooper on de Isthmus!"[57] Announced as Ella walks through his door, Poyah catalogues his attributes to make a positive impression on her. The Colón Man also has an image of Isthmian migration to speak for him because it announces his bravery and desire for self-improvement. Yet despite these distinguishing characteristics, Ella is not impressed. Because "Panama Gold" marks her as uniquely self-contained, much like the black "Englishmen" called to service in Poyah's fight against canal authorities, she does not need external support.

Walrond goes to great lengths to describe Ella's independence and expertise with her crops and animals. Members of her village of Lower Side, however, are preoccupied by the absence of a man in her life. In fact, Lizzie's daughter, Capadosia, harshly criticizes Ella because of it, and loudly enough for Ella to hear: "Capadosia, [cuts] her eyes at [Ella] and [murmurs], 'come complainin' 'pon me – de old hag – why she don't go 'n get sheself a man?'"[58] Contrary to the girl's invective, the protagonist does not seem to want a man. She has, after all, her land and livestock. The author describes Ella as god-like in her ability to reproduce in nature. She splices dissimilar trees and plants, and crossbreeds pigeons and ground doves in order to breed new life. Through these practices, Ella conveys an aggressive fertility. In fact, her desire to create seems quite urgent: "sometimes, unmoved by their genetic dissimilarity, Ella'd use drastic, aggressive methods".[59] Ella's certainty of her ability to breed life on her own is affirmed by the zeal with which she approaches it.

We learn that the protagonist's success with birds and plants extends to different types of animals. The narrator indicates that "sows fared prodigiously at the hands of Ella. She filled huge, fat-stinking troughs of slime for them. Ella's boars grew tusks of flint-like ivory. Vicious, stiff-haired boars who ate up the sow's young, frothed at the mouth at [her dog] Jit's approach, tried to stick their snouts between Ella's legs whenever she ventured in the pen."[60] Continuing, the narrator informs readers that "under Ella's tutelage the one cow she owned streamed milk. From fat luscious udders filled skillet after skillet."[61] Ella is both in line and, because she is single, at odds with the mores of her community: she is tied to and successful on the land and respects local foodways and folklore, but she disregards the community's prescribed definitions of womanhood.

As "Panama Gold" unfolds, Walrond continues to define Ella as at once part of and outside of her community's traditions. As a consequence, a relationship between her and Poyah appears less and less likely; the Colón Man is so certain that his attributes *should* attract Ella that readers are left with little to challenge his conviction. Walrond centres his characterization of Ella around a femaleness defined by independence and connection to nature, a direct challenge to Poyah's kind of masculinity, contingent as it is upon material goods and skills derived through Panama migration.

Ella's concern with Capadosia's remark notwithstanding,[62] the older woman is content with her lifestyle. But if her relationship to her plants and animals is not sufficiently suggestive of this, she could not be any more explicit in her denunciation of the Colón Man's handicap, his colour, worldliness and material possessions. Ella rejects Poyah because she finds his skin too dark, and she expresses this prejudice as a condemnation of the Colón Man's money and possessions. Thus, what might simply be interpreted as an example of intra-racial prejudice in Barbados is tied to the ways that Caribbean workers get access to the materiality and modernization afforded by labour on the Panama Canal.

Upon first seeing Poyah at his shop, Ella says to herself "Gahd, he are black in troot" and "with a stab to the breast, she [notes] the protrudent tip of the cork leg".[63] Poyah thus makes a doubly negative impression on her. This does not, however, prevent him from calling on Ella at her home. When the Colón Man comes courting, Ella's disapproval of him is biting and very specific in its conflation of the Isthmian worker's handicap, colour and materiality. Heath rants:

> 'All dem bag o' flour yo' 'a' got, an' dem silk shut, an' dem gold teets, an' dem Palama hats yo' a spote round heh wid – dem don't frighten me. I is a woman what is usta t'ings. I got me hogs an' me fowls an' me potatoes. *No wooden foot neygah man can frighten me wit' he clothes or he barrels o' cologne . . .*"
>
> Yellow kerchief mopping his brow, he walked off . . . peg step, peg step . . . leaving Ella by the well, gazing with defiance in her being.
>
> "What he t'ink I is, anyhow?"
>
> "Go back an' lahn, go back an' lahn, dat not de way fi' cote."[64]

Ella obviously takes exception to everything that Walrond uses to define Poyah. Indeed, each of the "faults" she lists can be seen as building on the others, forming a structure that the protagonist uses to "unman" him. Confronted with what Ella asserts is the superiority of her work, colour and status, the Colón Man and his Panama Money are utterly lacking. Yet she entreats him to "go back an' lahn" how to court.

Soon after Ella shames Poyah into retreat, his shop catches fire and the protagonist contributes her bucket of water to relief efforts despite her expressed feelings for him. At the scene, she frantically searches for Poyah ("'Where is Missah Poyah, where is Missah Poyah?' Ella screamed"[65]), but all she finds are traces: "A straw valise, label spattered – decker's luggage – an old shirt – one or two stray sacks of split peas – the money canister". These effects underscore the Colón Man's signification of modernity and materiality: the fire reduces him to the sum of his defining Panama parts. Upon learning that Poyah was inside the burning shop, "Ella realized how for nothing was her bucket of water."[66]

The ambiguous ending of "Panama Gold" leaves more questions than answers: Is Ella unable to bring Poyah anything? If she can bring him something, would it be useless or unnecessary? Does she try to bring him her folk self and does it come too late for him? Is Poyah, as a symbol of a particular kind of progress, not viable in a Bajan context? Is Ella, as a perversely fertile and happily single woman, a transgressive female? Is Poyah, wounded but still "masculine" because of his migration, out of place in Barbados? These questions leave readers with a suspicion that, with the Colón Man denigrated and dispatched, Ella nostalgically stands for a past where Bajans were tied more closely to the land. Still, one cannot ignore her prejudices that allow readers to pity the rejected Poyah. The strangeness that characterizes Ella and Poyah's relationship suggests that a union between modern and traditional cultures, between the "superior" Bajan man and the "superior" Bajan woman, might be inevitable but nonetheless fraught with troubles. But readers must contend with Ella's remarks to Poyah's retreating back: "Go back an' lahn, go back an' lahn, dat not de way fi' cote."[67] Perhaps it is not the Panama man's self and what he represents that is at issue, but rather the *way* he represents his romantic interest. Essentially, Ella chastises Poyah because he does not court her properly.

Walrond's ambivalent ending promises neither the maintenance of an idealized Barbadian reality – Ella's aggressive fecundity and prejudices indicate a problematic world view – nor the pure valuelessness of modern progress signified by Poyah's money. What both of these positions do reveal – and what is suggested by the possibility that Poyah might have learned how to approach Ella better – is how intrinsically interconnected these characters are. They define each other – despite the fact that the protagonist seems to find the shopkeeper repulsive. In "Panama Gold", Poyah's self brings this definition/repulsion paradigm about; it is the absence – and potential "presence" – of a man in Ella's life that defines her as unusual and marks the tension in the story.

Walrond deliberately identifies Poyah as male through his work and injury in the Canal Zone, setting up a sequence that begins with Caribbean migration to the Panamanian isthmus. In other words, the author links Barbados's (and the Caribbean's) fraught movement into modernity to a conflicted heterosexual relationship that is constituted by troubling features of Isthmian migration, agricultural traditions, and intra-racial as well as gendered conflicts. Critical attention to the facets of this couple's literal and figurative interactions, considered with Ella's urgent attempt to save Poyah despite her rejection of him, suggests that some kind of relationship between the two is not inherently unthinkable. Though the story ends with Poyah's (likely) death, the fact that Ella's feelings change (or could change if his seduction methods changed) – or that they are not so fixed as to prevent her from coming to his aid – alerts readers to the possibility of realizable coalitions across differences. Signs of "unity in difference" can be seen in other parts of Eric Walrond's oeuvre.

"Tropic Death" opens with a telling statement: "the little boy was overwhelmed at being suddenly projected into a world of such fluid activity".[68] Such a phrase appearing in Walrond's "most autobiographical story"[69] highlights connections between the author's fiction and his description of his feelings in a similar situation ("the jump [from birthplace to psychiatric hospital], for a 'depression casualty' . . . is almost frightening").[70] Adult Walrond, writing as an eight-year-old boy, seems to have remembered childhood feelings as well as imbued the young character with his then lifelong experiences with travel, migration and uprootedness. Yet the story that begins with a bleak tone nonetheless contains glimmers of something else.

Appearing at the end of a collection that shares its title, "Tropic Death" depicts Gerald Bright's pilgrimage with his mother, Sarah, to reunite with her delinquent husband and children's father, Lucian. In meeting and learning about his father, Gerald recalls his life in Barbados and experiences in Panama's streets and tenements. Yet despite grinding poverty, inter- and intra-racial prejudice, infidelity and illness, Gerald's mother evolves in her faith and Gerald demonstrates feelings for his fallible father. Embodied in Gerald Bright, too, are two seemingly contradictory states: he is overwhelmed by chaotic and unfamiliar situations as he prepares to leave Barbados and "he was too unspeakingly concerned over the concurrent miracles of sea and sky" to worry overmuch about his voyage.[71] The ambivalence in the author's word choices – "overwhelmed" and "unspeakingly concerned" – can be interpreted in myriad ways to reflect every point on a continuum of possible feelings. Awed by the views from the ship to the Central American country or diminished by them, swept away by the activity on the docks or fascinated by the novelty, Walrond writes the protagonist of "Tropic Death" indeterminately, perhaps as a single representative of the author's vision of blacks' movements across boundaries.

Gerald has a flashback to Black Rock, Barbados, while on board the packet to Panama and this vision, with its scenes of poverty and disease, resonates with the Panamanian tenement the boy describes later in the story. Yet there is a type of joy in the former that is absent from the latter. The fowls in Black Rock were "dying of the pip and the yaws; the dogs, a rowing, impotent lot; the crops of dry peas and cassava and tannias and eddoes, robbed, before they could feel the pulse of the sun, of their gum or juice".[72] Still,

> the joys, for a boy of eight – a dew-sprayed, toe-searching tramp at sunrise for "touched" fruit dropped in the night by the epicurean bats, almonds, mangoes, golden apples; dreaming of the day when the cocoanut tree planted at a particularly fecund part of the ground would grow big enough to bear fruit; waiting, in the flush of sowing time, for a cart loaded to the brim to roll rhythmically over the jarring stones and spill a potato or yam.[73]

Walrond, however, taints this depiction of a carefree Bajan boyhood: "he'd pluck an ear of corn out of the heap . . . and roast it, and stuff it hot as it was in his tiny pants pocket and then suffer excruciating rheumatic pains in his leg days afterwards".[74] The author directs readers to resist simplistic comparison, for this scene's closing statement prevents us from reducing the story's locations to "good" Barbados and "bad" Panama. Yet one might read Gerald's lingering "excruciating rheumatic pains" as a physical harbinger of the following scene where Sarah decides to travel to Panama to locate her wayward husband – and the effect of this meeting in that place on the young boy.

Gerald Bright wakes up to the sounds, smells and sights of his reunited family's lodgings. "It was seven o'clock", the story reads. "Anger, noise, confusion – a cock's lofty crowing. Opening his eyes, he stood quietly, deciding. . . . Ah, he was not now on the ship. Nor was he at the tailor shop [where his father worked]. This must be – home."[75] In search of his missing mother, Gerald first encounters a "lank, black, cruel-faced woman brewing a cup of hot milk". Readers soon learn that this mother stands in stark contrast to Sarah

Bright; the former berates her boy-child violently: "'Where am I to get it from?' she screamed at him, 'shut up, I say – shut up – before I cuff you – what do I care if you haven't eaten for two days – your stomach burning you – well go to sleep – you been already – well go again – sleep, sleep – it will do you good – it will make you forget you ever had a belly.'"[76] It is impossible to separate this woman's threats from the lack that burns her boy's stomach. Yet into the mouth of this character the author writes poetry: "[W]inds can wake up the dead. Go try – bawl to the winds! But I've got my own song, I've got my own tune."[77] As with his description of Black Rock, Walrond intermingles harsh scenes and language and beauty and, in these lines, a hint at something uplifting despite the deprivation ("but I've got my own song"). And finally, by contrast to this mother/son pair, Walrond offers readers a constant that transverses place. Sarah Bright is the constant that unites in Barbados, on board the ship that carries them to the isthmus, and in Panama: Sarah Bright.

Navigating the cesspool and a "St Thomas virgin with the *peso* in her hand", the protagonist heeds his mother's call: "Come, wash yo' face and drink yo' tea, Gerald, befo' it got cold."[78] The filth and violence of Panama, and the disease and lingering pains of Barbados, are punctuated by the presence of Sarah (as well as by sublime moments Gerald discerns through his travels). Despite the "Spanish boys" in the streets who destroy his toys and call him "*Chumbo*! *Perro*!"[79] and his father who is an adulterer and afflicted with a disease that exiles him to a colony,[80] Gerald's mother grounds Gerald's awesome self. The awful aspects of each place that the boy encounters in "Tropic Death" touch him intimately, yet he is not hardened against his father's pain and eventual exile. Where those with "perfidious souls" seek solace in religion to assuage the effects of their traumatic move from agricultural work in the Caribbean to industrial labour on the Panama Canal,[81] Gerald and women of the Caribbean appear to have broader, though not uncomplicated, options.[82]

Walrond writes that "among the women the transfiguration (from agricultural to canal work) was less brilliant.... The 'drops' and cakes and food and pops vended to the serfs and squatters on insular estates found a husky-throated market at the ends of the pay car lines".[83] The type of work performed by migrants, it appears, is quite significant; plying the markets in the Caribbean or on the Isthmus of Panama cannot remake females' nurturing souls into perfidious ones. Sustained by familiar work and the self it cultivates,

Caribbean women in the Central American country can remain (more or less) intact. Gerald, though male, can discern not only that which can transform the people around him, but also that which affirms their essential or "soulful" selves; enabled, perhaps, by his mother's influence, this young male can perceive his migrations and destinations as complex. Aspects of "home" that travel with migrants, then, can mediate differences/adversities that they encounter in their new place.

That Lucian abandons his family, drinks on his tailoring job, is publically known as an adulterer, and ultimately succumbs to an unnamed illness (most likely leprosy), supports the idea that things accrued in migration can have a negative impact on one's self. Walrond is deliberate in representing Gerald as experiencing this lesson through his mother's perspective on Lucian's degeneration. When Sarah cares for her husband after he has been assaulted for paying too much attention to another man's woman, she only earns his verbal abuse; Gerald's emotional response to his mother's "bruising" is extreme: "all night Gerald was restless, bruised by his mother's sorrow, and unable to rid himself of the hideous nightmares surrounding it".[84] The long-suffering and supportive wife is a familiar literary figure, but the author layers the impact of Sarah's Lucian-generated trials on her young son, and emphasizes the gendered nature of these trials.

Through named and unnamed black and brown male characters in "Tropic Death", Gerald Bright learns lessons of want and deprivation, random violence and anti-black prejudice. Roving gangs of "Spanish boys" or *"pacos"* destroy or steal Gerald's toys and call him derogatory names if he protests. The protagonist learns not to fight back: "To the pirates and urchin gods of Bottle Alley, Gerald was the bait that lured a swarm of felt-hatted *pacos* who kept the alley under sleepless surveillance. It was risky to loiter, play marbles, spin gigs – and there wasn't enough to keep Gerald occupied upstairs. So he hit upon the notion of going at dusk to his father's shop."[85] Seeking an alternative to the unsafe streets, the boy turns to his father's tailoring shop and finds him treating a "red, sore arm" with leeches. Gerald was "stricken dumb" and "uncomprehending [he] patiently waited".[86] Walrond writes Gerald into a position of preparedness, a black boy poised between stasis and incomprehension.

The next stage in the protagonist's evolution returns him to the lessons of his mother. Sarah Bright indoctrinates the youth into her faith, but at church he also learns to embrace diasporic Caribbean subjects living in the space between home and receiving country, former lives lived on the land now contending with a "less elemental, more ephemeral set of chores".[87]

Yet where the labour of male novitiates shows a marked transformation, the modern Caribbean woman in the Canal Zone bought and sold wares as she did at home. Yet Walrond writes Gerald into and between the myriad worlds of men and women, those of Caribbean descent as well as others; tumultuous as it may be, the boy learns to take stock of his worlds and record their variations.

Ultimately, Lucian's home remedies fail and he is institutionalized. And it is at this point that Walrond most clearly articulates Gerald's transformation:

> After they came and got [his father], Gerald began to feel things ever so much more keenly. His vision, too, grew less dim. But a pallor fell on things. In the morning he went to the cesspool to whistle to the canary while the Cholo girl washed it. But as he approached she fled in terror screaming.... The little boy, the seven o'clock one, refused to let him come hear him.... None of the old gang, who'd been willing to elude or defy the *pacos* and foregather down in the alley came any more.[88]

Previously rejected because of his blackness and foreignness, Gerald is now isolated because of his father's illness. The protagonist is pushed and pulled by these overlapping communities, seemingly rendered as powerless as a cork floating in the sea. Nevertheless, Walrond situates the boy and his mother among the members of Sarah's church. It is important to note that every church member is not "a child of the Lord", but they are "firm, solid, lasting"[89] These are the people – complex and fluidly steadfast – who do not reject him.

"Tropic Death" ends ambiguously, with Lucian hospitalized pending transfer to "Palo Seco – dah's de colony", Sarah blessing him, and Gerald in tears: "'E love 'e pappy, ent 'e?"[90]

What readers are left with, then, is a protagonist who sees and records his locations and who is simultaneously part of and alienated from communities. Living within these shifting realities, Gerald is Walrond's modern, black, transnational subject, one who nicely exemplifies a truth of his moment. The author offers Gerald's complicated and imagined self as the point of departure from which readers can theorize transnational possibilities.

Poverty was the primary motivating factor in Walrond's migrations from British Guiana to Barbados to Panama, and – to a lesser extent – to the United States; ethnic, racial, religious, linguistic and cultural differences when living within these locations contributed to what became his durable categorization as "outsider".[91] These circumstances informed his equivocal creative vision of migration generally, and the consequences of such in particular. Walrond's attention to the dangerous environments in which black immigrants found themselves, the regionalism and colourism that characterized their relationships to each other, and the racism that often undermined their sense of themselves as people stand in stark contrast to early views of transnationalism. In identifying these concerns in "Panama Gold" and "Tropic Death", it is clear that Walrond's vision of black transnationalism understood complexities of which his contemporaries (writers of what Michelle Ann Stephens describes as "empire narratives") became aware only after a series of external challenges. If "Caribbean immigrants in North America throughout the twentieth century have been living their lives across borders" and "from early on they found themselves in the basic dilemma of the 'transmigrant', 'confronted with and engaged in the nation building processes of two or more nation-states",[92] perhaps Walrond's experiences in "three or more nation-states" before arriving in North America afforded him insights unavailable to his peers. Believing himself to be excluded from myriad communities, Walrond anticipated difficulties that would impede a Cyril Briggs-ian "black freedom through internationalism".[93] Still, there is something to be said for experiencing interstitial locations. Eric Walrond in the 1920s was primed to think from a reality that Charles Carnegie predicts in 2002, taking difference and complication as a "compass point, we can use it to guide the multifaceted, particular, and hence historical creation of a more liveable human future, although the dimensions, landscape, and qualities of that future are as yet imperceptible".[94]

NOTES

1. See, for example, representations in Michael Thelwell's *The Harder They Come* (New York: Grove, 1994) and Claude McKay's *Banana Bottom* (New York: Harper and Brothers, 1933). See also Elizabeth M. DeLoughrey, Renée K. Gosson and George B. Handley, *Caribbean Literature and the Environment: Between Nature and Culture* (Charlottesville: University of Virginia Press, 2005), 105–6.
2. Henry Louis Gates Jr and Nellie Y. McKay, eds., *The Norton Anthology of African American Literature* (New York: Norton, 1997), 1195. Sterling Brown, in an excerpt from comments published in the *Massachusetts Review* (reproduced on the cover of the 1972 edition of *Tropic Death*), describes the collection as "a brilliantly impressionistic series of portraits of the author's native West Indies". An anonymous reviewer (whose comments are collected in John E. Bassett, ed., *Harlem in Review: Critical Reactions to Black American Writers, 1917–1939* [Selinsgrove, PA: Susquehanna University Press, 1992]) writes that Walrond "is more free of 'race consciousness' than other black writers and writes vividly, though he indulges in a coarseness of realism that scarcely justifies itself". Theophilus Lewis finds that "the stories are vivid portrayals of characters, 'full of bizarre and satanic beauty' but conform to white American notions of the black as 'exotic and pagan' " (*Harlem in Review*, 66).
3. See Michelle Ann Stephens, *Black Empire: The Masculine Global Imaginary of Caribbean Intellectuals in the United States, 1914–1962* (Durham: Duke University Press, 2005). Also, in "Black Transnationalism and the Politics of National Identity: West Indian Intellectuals in Harlem in the Age of War and Revolution" (*American Quarterly* 50, no. 3 [1998]), Stephens cites Cyril Briggs's attempt to launch his ideas about a black international federation at Marcus Garvey's 1921 Universal Negro Improvement Association convention. What Stephens characterizes as Garvey's paranoia – he interpreted "the [African Blood Brotherhood's] plan as an attempt to co-opt his organization with this idea of Federation" (600) – might also be interpreted as a sign of intra-racial problems inherent to the formation of black transnationalism.
4. Charles V. Carnegie, *Postnationalism Prefigured: Caribbean Borderlands* (New Brunswick, NJ: Rutgers University Press, 2002), 19.
5. Stephens, *Black Empire*, 62.
6. Citing Don Robotham's "The Development of a Black Ethnicity in Jamaica", in *Garvey: His Work and Impact*, ed. Rupert Lewis and Patrick Bryan (Trenton, NJ: Africa World Press, 1993), Carnegie writes: "that people coming to New World plantation societies as slaves did not at first view themselves as black or African. The regime of forced labour, which compelled individuals from different social groups to live and work together under arduous conditions, moving

them about indiscriminately between different sites of production, contributed to the erosion of pre-existing loyalties and fostered the emergence of cross-ethnic heroes and loyalties to replace them" (Carnegie 203n15). See also Michelle M. Wright, *Becoming Black: Creating Identity in the African Diaspora* (Durham: Duke University Press, 2004), 1–2.

7. Louis J. Parascandola, introduction to *"Winds Can Wake Up the Dead": An Eric Walrond Reader*, by Eric Walrond; ed. Louis J. Parascandola (Detroit: Wayne State University Press, 1998), 36.
8. Brent Hayes Edwards, *The Practice of Diaspora: Literature, Translation, and the Rise of Black Internationalism* (Cambridge, MA: Harvard University Press, 2003).
9. Ibid., 1–2, 3.
10. Ibid., 4–5.
11. Ibid., 5.
12. Ibid., 12–13.
13. Ibid., 11.
14. Ibid., 12. See also Wright, *Becoming Black*, 2.
15. Wright, *Becoming Black*, 2.
16. Ibid., 3.
17. Ibid.
18. Ibid., 5.
19. Ibid., 5–6.
20. Ibid., 7.
21. Ibid., 12.
22. Ibid., 13; my emphasis. In this same vein, Brent Edwards (*Practice of Diaspora*, 7) writes: "in terms of the cultures of black internationalism between the world wars, one must consider a great variety of texts: fiction, poetry, journalism, criticism, position papers, circulars, manifestos, anthologies, correspondence, surveillance reports".
23. Stephens, *Black Empire*, 4.
24. Ibid., 58.
25. Ibid., 20.
26. Ibid., 59.
27. Eric Walrond, *"Winds Can Wake Up the Dead": An Eric Walrond Reader*, ed. Louis J. Parascandola (Detroit: Wayne State University Press, 1998), 122
28. Stephens, *Black Empire*, 66.
29. See Audre Lorde, "The Transformation of Silence into Language and Action", *Sister Outsider: Essays and Speeches by Audre Lorde* (Freedom, CA: Crossing Press, 1998), 44.
30. Stephens, *Black Empire*, 49.

31. Carl A. Wade and Louis J. Parascandola, "In Search of Asylum: Eric Walrond's *Roundway Review* Writings, 1952–1957", *Journal of Caribbean Studies* 19, nos. 1–2 (2004–5): 21–42.
32. I found this range of descriptors in a Google.com search for "Eric Walrond", 12 December 2009.
33. Stephens, *Black Empire*, 592.
34. Edwards, *Practice of Diaspora*, 7.
35. Wade and Parascandola, "In Search", 23.
36. Ibid., 22; see also 24–25.
37. Winston James, *Holding Aloft the Banner of Ethiopia: Caribbean Radicalism in Early Twentieth-Century America* (London: Verso, 1998), 184.
38. My emphasis; Kenneth Ramchand, "The Writer Who Ran Away: Eric Walrond and *Tropic Death*", *Savacou: Journal of the Caribbean Artists Movement* 2 (September 1970): 74. Walrond planned to use his Guggenheim Fellowship to support research for "a story of the French attempt to construct a canal through Nicaragua", and "a human interest account of the Canal from the arrival of the French on the Isthmus in 1880 to the opening of the Canal in 1914". Though he made his research trip in 1928–29, he never produced the work. See Wade and Parascandola, "In Search", 23, 23n3.
39. Enid E. Bogle, "Eric Walrond", *Fifty Caribbean Writers: A Bio-Bibliographical Critical Sourcebook* (New York: Greenwood Press, 1986), 474.
40. Wade and Parascandola ("In Search", 21) write that "in the mostly migrations [narratives] published in *Roundway Review*, Walrond reimagines colonial and metropolitan landscapes as sites of fragmentation, placelessness and otherness. These, the core themes of his later writings, suggest that migration and its psychological effects on colonized people remained his consuming passion, albeit with some altered perspectives" (29).
41. All references taken from the essay "From British Guiana to Roundway" are from *In Search of Asylum: The Later Writings of Eric Walrond*, ed. Louis J. Parascandola and Carl A. Wade (Gainesville: University Press of Florida, 2011).
42. Ibid. 149.
43. Ibid. 150.
44. Ibid.
45. Ibid.
46. Ibid., 151.
47. Ibid.
48. Ibid., 152.
49. Ibid., 153.
50. "The Wharf Rats", Walrond's most famous story, epitomizes the distinct culture of Caribbean people in the Canal Zone. In highlighting the ethnic, racial and

colour diversity of this population, the author directly confronts narratives that homogenize people from this region amorphously as "blacks" or "West Indians". Eric Walrond, *Tropic Death* (New York: Collier Books, 1972).

51. Walrond, *Tropic Death*, 47.
52. Ibid., 38.
53. For another example of the Colón Man in Walrond's works see the "The Iceman" in *In Search*, 85–90.
54. Ramchand, "Writer", 72.
55. Ibid., 42.
56. Ibid.; my emphasis.
57. Ibid., 44.
58. Ibid., 35.
59. Ibid., 39–40.
60. Ibid., 40.
61. Ibid.
62. Ibid., 35.
63. Ibid., 43.
64. Ibid., 45–46; my emphasis.
65. Ibid., 49.
66. Ibid.
67. Ibid., 46.
68. Ibid., 161.
69. Parascandola, introduction, 28.
70. "From British Guiana to Roundway", in Parascandola and Wade, *In Search*, 153.
71. Walrond, *Tropic Death*, 164.
72. Ibid., 167.
73. Ibid.
74. Ibid.
75. Ibid., 177.
76. Ibid., 177–78.
77. Ibid., 178.
78. Ibid., 180.
79. Ibid., 181.
80. Ibid., 191.
81. Ibid., 187–88.
82. The language of this passage suggests that the move from agricultural to canal work turns former tillers of the soil into treacherous souls: "in the isles of their origin they were the tillers of the soil – the ones to nurture cane, and water sorrel, stew cocoanuts and mix Maube – now theirs was a less elemental, more ephemeral set of chores" (187–88).

83. Ibid., 188.
84. Ibid., 183.
85. Ibid., 185–86.
86. Ibid., 186
87. Ibid., 186–87.
88. Ibid., 188.
89. Ibid., 188–89.
90. Ibid., 191.
91. Wade and Parascandola, "In Search", 23.
92. Stephens, *Black Empire*, 597.
93. Ibid., 598. Briggs (1888–1966) was born in Nevis and was a founder of the radical African Blood Brotherhood.
94. Carnegie, *Postnationalism*, 19.

6

ERIC WALROND AND THE PROLETARIAN ARTS MOVEMENT

MICHAEL NIBLETT

IN THE SECOND VOLUME of his autobiography, *American Hunger* (1977), Richard Wright describes the impact had on him by radical leftist magazines of the 1920s and 1930s:

> I lay on my bed and read the magazines [*International Literature* and *Left Front*] and was amazed to find that there did exist in this world an organized search for the truth of the lives of the oppressed and the isolated. When I had begged bread from the officials, I had wondered dimly if the outcasts could become united in action, thought, and feeling. Now I knew. It was being done in one-sixth of the earth already. The revolutionary words leaped from the printed page and struck me with tremendous force. . . . It was not the economics of Communism, nor the great power of trade unionism, nor the excitement of underground politics that claimed me; my attention was caught by the similarity of the experiences of workers in other lands, by the possibility of uniting scattered but kindred peoples into a whole. . . . [I]t seemed to me that here at last in the realm of revolutionary expression was where Negro experience could find a home, a functioning value and role.[1]

The magazines that so encouraged Wright were part of an international politico-arts movement that emerged in the early to middle decades of the twentieth century. Often referred to as the proletarian arts movement, it drew much of its initial impetus from the world upheaval of 1917 to 1921.[2] As Michael Denning observes:

In the wake of the European slaughter, regimes and empires were challenged: there were revolutions in Czarist Russia and Mexico, brief lived socialist republics in Germany, Hungary and Persia, uprisings against colonialism in Ireland, India and China, and massive strikes in Japan, Italy, Spain, Chile, Brazil and the United States. The "imaginative proximity of social revolution electrified a generation of young writers who came together in a variety of revolutionary and proletarian writers" groups.[3]

Denning goes on to identify three initiatives that were particularly influential: the "formation of the first international writers' association, *Clarté*, in 1919 by Henri Barbusse"; the "emergence of a proletarian culture movement in revolutionary Russia, . . . which soon became known by the abbreviation 'Proletkult'"; and the "Baku conference of 1920, which marked the turn by the Communist inheritors of European socialism to the anticolonial movements in Asia and Africa, generating the powerful alliance of Communism and anticolonialism that was to shape the global decolonisation struggles of the twentieth century".[4]

The proletarian arts movement confronted a world subordinated to the logic of imperialism in the wake of the expansion of colonial conquest in the late nineteenth century, an era characterized, according to Lenin, by "the final partition of the globe – not in the sense that a *new partition* is impossible . . . but in the sense that the colonial policy of the capitalist countries has *completed* the seizure of the unoccupied territories on our planet".[5] Throughout the world-system, writers and artists responded to the social convulsions unleashed by imperialism. For those aligned, even if only loosely, with the proletarian arts movement – and not all were proletarians: as Denning notes with respect to revolutionary novelists, some came from the working classes, others "were the 'talented tenth' of colonized peoples", and still others "were children of bourgeois families and elite schools who had come to the left from the ranks of the modernist avant-gardes".[6] This response took the form of a critical interrogation of the exploitation, inequality, and class- and race-based oppression integral to the dynamics of capital accumulation on a world scale. It is not hard, therefore, to see why it was in the realm of such revolutionary expression that Wright felt he had found a home for African American experience, a home that permitted the articulation of the specificity of the latter at the same time as underscoring its similarities with the "experiences of workers in other lands".

This chapter will examine Eric Walrond's *Tropic Death* in the context of the proletarian arts movement. On the one hand, there are good biographical reasons for doing so: during his time in New York, amid the flowering of the Harlem Renaissance, Walrond became involved in the kinds of magazines that inspired Wright. As Louis Parascandola observes, in the early 1920s Walrond contributed to the leftist periodical *Messenger* and later became "a contributing editor of the communist journal *New Masses* from 1926 to 1930, though he never published in it". Indeed, his links "with radical political movements, albeit apparently without ever officially joining the socialist or communist parties, are not surprising considering his ties with the Harlem Caribbean community, where such prominent personalities as Claude McKay, Cyril Briggs, Grace Campbell, Hubert H. Harrison, Richard B. Moore, and Frank R. Crosswaith belonged to such groups".[7]

On the other hand, it might seem something of a stretch to consider Walrond in terms of proletarian or committed literature when he consistently argued in his essays and reviews that "literature should be judged for its aesthetic quality, not for its political message".[8] His espousal of such arguments, however, tended in the 1920s to be aimed more at the views on art expressed by W.E.B. Du Bois, whose belief that "literature should depict the lives of the 'Talented Tenth', the small group of professional Blacks who would advance the race" contrasted with Walrond's emphasis on displaying "all aspects of Black life, even unfavorable ones".[9] In this regard, *Tropic Death*'s portrayal of the grinding poverty, deprivation and violence surrounding working-class Caribbean peoples suggests strong affinities with the kinds of concerns and motifs found in literature more usually associated with the proletarian arts movement. Indeed, in registering the brutal impact of capitalist modernization in the peripheries of empire, stories such as "Drought" and "Subjection" provide clear grounds for comparison with an array of works produced in the same period in countries similarly subject to colonial or imperial intervention.

One of the defining features of capitalist modernity is its unevenness. As Frederic Jameson has argued (echoing Trotsky's theorization of uneven and combined development), modernity is distinguished by the overlap of the new with the residual – with the pre-existing cultural traditions and social forms it encounters and works upon.[10] Such unevenness is especially marked where societies are subject to direct imperialist intervention and the forcible imposition of capitalist structures onto pre-capitalist modes of production. In such situations it is common for imperialism to deliberately retain or prop up pre-capitalist forms of social authority as a means of maintaining stability and order. The New World plantation system offers an obvious example of this kind of amalgam of the modern and the archaic. The large-scale agriculture of the sugar plantation involved a unity of field and factory and the application of technical features in operations that predated the Industrial Revolution.[11] At the same time, it was dependent upon slave labour and quasi-feudal relations of personal domination.

In *Tropic Death*, Walrond's stories frequently take place against the backdrop of such an uneven development. In "Drought", for instance, we see how archaic modes of domination have persisted long after the abolition of slavery. The quarry at which the black peasant Coggins Rum works is organized, on the one hand, around the use of modern plant equipment, including drills and rock engines, and, on the other, around a plantation-like system of control in which the labourers are overseen by a "driver", a "buckra Johnny – English white".[12] Panama-set stories like "The Wharf Rats" and "Tropic Death", meanwhile, point to continuities between this plantation-based organizational structure and the treatment of labour under US imperialist authority during the building of the Panama Canal. The latter was an extraordinary feat of modern engineering. Yet many of those tasked with its physical construction – "the bulk of the actual brawn for the work was supplied by the dusky peons of those coral isles in the Caribbean ruled by Britain, France and Holland" notes Walrond in "The Wharf Rats" – lived and laboured in circumstances often reminiscent of slavery.[13] The work itself was frequently dehumanizing: "canal authorities perceived West Indian men as little more than living machines", notes Rhonda Frederick.[14] There also existed the threat of violence from white US officials acting in an overseer-like capacity, a threat dramatized by Walrond in "Subjection".

Perhaps the most interesting example of this imbrication of a modern industrial project with older forms of social organization is provided by Walrond's portrayal of the overcrowded quarters in which the labourers are barracked. The "Wharf Rats" describes how "the blacks were herded in boxcar huts buried in the jungles of 'Silver City'; in the murky tenements perilously poised on the narrow banks of Faulke's River; in the low, smelting cabins of Coco Té. The 'Silver Quarters' harbored the inky ones, their wives and pickaninnies".[15] These "boxcar huts", whose inhabitants are treated like cattle ("the blacks were *herded* in"), recall the lodgings of the enslaved on the plantation. But they also evoke the kind of urban tenement buildings that were a common setting for a number of proletarian narratives concerned to delineate the working-class districts of industrialized or newly industrializing towns and cities.[16] Think, for example, of the New York tenements of Michael Gold's *Jews without Money* (1929); or of the cramped Tokyo alleys of Tokunaga Sunao's *Taiyo no nai machi* (*The Sunless Street*) (1929); or of the Port of Spain barrack-yards evoked in the work of Alfred Mendes and C.L.R. James: "Every street in Port-of-Spain could show you examples of the type: a narrow gateway leading into a fairly big yard, on either side of which run long, low buildings, consisting of anything from four to eighteen rooms, each about twelve feet square. In these lived the porters, the prostitutes, cartermen, washerwomen, and domestic servants of the city."[17]

Walrond's depiction of housing conditions in the Canal Zone, however, points up a further form of uneven development that was specific to the organization of labour on the Isthmus of Panama. The terms "Silver City" and "Silver Quarters" refer to the policy of dividing employees into "gold" and "silver" workers. Originally "signifying the currency in which each group was paid, US citizens in gold, non-citizens in silver", by 1908 it had become explicitly linked to race. As Bonham Richardson observes, "'gold' [white staff] and 'silver' [black labourers] payrolls were the euphemism for racial segregation in housing, schools, pay levels, and canteens".[18] A system of wage-labour was in place, therefore, but one compromised by its own two-tier payment structure: for by reintroducing a racial criterion, this structure short-circuited the logic of abstract equivalence upon which wage-labour is based. Indeed, it made visible the inequalities central to the latter, which the objective mechanisms of the market normally obscure. The gold/silver policy thus exemplifies the way in which the demands of imperialist domination deform socio-economic configurations.

The overlap of different realities characteristic of the Canal Zone is also emphasized by Walrond's portrayal of the relationship between the country and the city in his stories set on the isthmus. Consider, for example, "The Palm Porch". Here we move from the opening description of the modern industrial processes employed in digging the canal to an account of the titular establishment, a bordello in Colón run by Miss Buckner. The latter is described as "a lady of poise, charm and caution" to whom clings "an idea of sober reality".[19] Obsessed with whiteness, Miss Buckner's "life is ruled by a rigid code of decorum which dictates that her daughters cannot take up with those she feels are beneath them" – by which she means those with darker skin.[20] She dresses in Victorian-style clothing and when, "of a Sabbath, her hair in oily frills, wearing a silken shawl of cream and red, a dab of vermilion on her mouth, she swept regally down Bolivar Street on the way to the market, maided by the indolent Zuline, she had half the city gaping at the animal wonder of her".[21] The world conjured by this narrative is an urban, bourgeois one, with its particular styles, habits and pretensions. It is clearly very different to the peasant world evoked, say, in "Drought". And yet adjacent to, and overlapping with, Miss Buckner's domain is precisely something like this peasant world. Take, for example, this description of one area of the workers' quarters in "The Wharf Rats":

> As it grew dark, the hewers at the Ditch, exhausted, half-asleep, naked but for wormy singlets, would hum queer creole tunes, play on guitar or piccolo, and jig to the rhythm of the *coombia*. . . . Over smoking pots, on black, death-black nights legends of the bloodiest were recited till they became the essence of a sort of Negro Koran. . . . On the banks of a river beyond Cristobal, Coco Té sheltered a colony of Negroes enslaved to the *obeah*. Near a roundhouse, daubed with smoke and coal ash, a river serenely flowed away and into the guava region, at the eastern tip of Monkey Hill.[22]

Here the communal interaction (so different from Miss Buckner's house, where a "strip of canvas cloth" is put up around the porch to "shut out eyes"),[23] the folk songs, the storytelling and the centrality of obeah are all evocative of a more rural, peasant way of life. Within the enclave of the Canal Zone, then, the country and the city coexist, the former again subject to penetration by capital insofar as those peasant labourers have been converted into a kind of agrarian proletariat by working conditions on the dig.

That the overlap of the modern and the archaic, and of rural features with typically urban ones, is so condensed in the Canal Zone context is a testament to the magnitude and intensity of the project, to its massive transformation of the natural world and its flinging together of advanced engineering and industrial processes with a huge labour force drawn in large part from agricultural/plantation backgrounds. In this connection, I want now to turn to the issue of the production of nature. The latter in fact is integral to all of the phenomena we have touched on above: the spread of capital, the reorganization of the countryside, the relationship between rural and urban areas – all involve or imply in some way the production and reproduction of nature, and, as a corollary to this, the production and reproduction of particular kinds of space. Indeed, the unevenness we have been describing in terms of economic backwardness/modernization can be grasped also in terms of the uneven development of space under capitalism. As Neil Smith points out, this unevenness derives from capitalism's contradictory tendencies towards "the differentiation but simultaneous equalization of the levels and conditions of production. Capital is continually invested in the built environment in order to produce surplus value and expand the basis of capital itself. But equally, capital is continually withdrawn from the built environment so that it can move elsewhere and take advantage of higher profit rates."[24] The constant circulation and immobilization of capital in this way involves the constant production of nature and differentiation of space in a systematic yet highly unequal fashion.

To speak of the production of nature may seem paradoxical. "Nature", observes Smith, "is generally seen as precisely that which cannot be produced; it is the antithesis of human productive activity. In its most immediate appearance, the natural landscape presents itself to us as the material substratum of daily life, the realm of use-values rather than exchange-values." However, he continues, with the "progress of capital accumulation and the expansion of economic development, this material substratum is more and more the product of social production, and the dominant axes of differentiation are increasingly societal in origin. In short, when this immediate appearance of nature is placed in historical context, the development of the material landscape presents itself as a process of production of nature."[25] Nature, then, is always already social: it forms a differentiated unity with human activity. Moreover, its production must be understood as always taking place within a specific mode of production, and in relation to the particular social relations and structures instantiated by the latter. Thus, each reorganization of the environment is also a reorganization of social relations.

Under capitalism, a radical separation is imposed between nature and society. As Marx puts it, what requires explanation is not the unity of "living and active humanity with the natural, inorganic conditions of their metabolic exchange with nature", but rather "the *separation* between these inorganic conditions of existence and this active existence, a separation which is completely posited only in the relation of wage labour and capital".[26] In other words, it is the antagonistic social relationship at the heart of capitalism between the owners of the means of production and those forced by their lack of property to sell their labour that engenders a relation to nature whereby the latter confronts the labourer as an external object. No longer related to the individual as, "so to speak, his extended body", nature appears before him now as *"not-property*, as *alien property*, as *value* for-itself, as capital".[27] This situation has as its precondition the historic process by which that opposition between wage-labour and capital is brought into being: the dissolution of "the various forms in which the worker is a proprietor, or in which the proprietor works", including the dissolution of "the relation to the earth – land and soil – as natural condition of production – to which he relates as to his own inorganic being".[28] The latter is achieved via the expropriation of the worker from the land and the smashing of those older social structures through which the individual related to the earth as a member of a community. The landless wage-labourer now stands as an isolated, "free" agent destined to be reinserted into a social world itself reconstructed as a post-natural assemblage of autonomous zones and processes.

Such changes clearly imply a radical transformation in the environment: a landscape organized around subsistence farming, for example, will look very different to one organized around concentrated property ownership and production for exchange. But they also suggest radical transformations in the physical body and subjectivity of the worker as well as in how space is experienced. By dissolving the worker's relationship to the land and instantiating nature as an extra-social object world, capitalism creates the conditions for the ascendancy of commodity exchange and, as a corollary to this, the emergence of abstract space. The latter stands in opposition to natural space. In pre-capitalist formations, to the extent that nature and society are still grasped as a unity, there is no differentiation between place and society. Where such is the case, "all places are imbued with social meaning [in immediate experience]. There is no abstract space beyond place and no place beyond society. Place and society are fused as a unity."[29] Societies organized in this way "inhabit natural space, meaning quite literally the space created out of natural processes, activities, and forms, social or otherwise".[30] Insofar as capitalism pursues as its historic mission the dissolution of such unities, it strips space of its qualitative distinctions, integrating it into the new world of the market economy as merely quantitative extension. As Smith contends, following Alfred Sohn-Rethel, the "abstraction of space into a concept removed from direct practice is closely connected to the development of commodity exchange. The abstraction from use and from the material aspect of a commodity, which is inherent in the exchange act, provokes the possibility of the abstraction of space from immediate material existence."[31]

Such are the effects of capitalist modernization and the transformation in the production of nature it entails – effects Walrond clearly registers in *Tropic Death*, just as numerous proletarian writers did as they sought to document the brutal remoulding of bodies and landscapes at the exploitative hands of capital. Thus in "Subjection" we witness the reification of a group of labourers subject to the industrial discipline of the Canal Zone: "Toro Point resounded to the noisy rhythm of picks swung by gnarled black hands. Sun-baked rock stones flew to dust, to powder. In flashing unison rippling muscle glittered to the task of planning a mound of rocky earth dredged up on the barren seashore."[32] As Frederick observes, the narrative's atomization of the men's bodies into motor reflexes suggests their reduction to little more than "moving parts in a pulverizing machine".[33] "The Palm Porch", meanwhile, opens with a description of a rock engine "crushing stone, shooting up rivers of steam and signaling the frontier's rebirth. Opposite, there was proof . . . of the gradual death and destruction of the frontier post. Black men behind wheelbarrows . . . emptied the sand rock into the maw of a mixing machine. More black men . . . formed a line which caught the mortar pouring into the rear organ of the omnivorous monster."[34]

The narrative conveys a sense of the relentlessness of the construction project, its production of nature initiating the continual "death" and "rebirth" of the frontier. The transmutation of the cement mixer into a wild creature not only underscores the project's insatiable thirst for land and bodies, but also implies the naturalization of this particular form of the labour process. Here the labourers relate to the means of production as to something alien to them and over which they have no control.

Something similar is evident in "Drought", where the production of nature revolves around the quarry at which Coggins Rum works:

> The whistle blew for eleven o'clock. Throats parched, grim, sun-crazed blacks cutting stone on the white burning hillside dropped with a clang the hot, dust-powdered drills and flew up over the rugged edges of the horizon to descent into a dry, waterless gut. Hunger ... pressed on folk ... wrenching themselves free from the lure of the white earth. Helter-skelter dark, brilliant, black faces of West Indian peasants moved along, in pain – the stiff tails of blue denim coats, the hobble of chigger-cracked heels, the rhythm of the stride ... dissipating into the sun-stuffed void the radiant forces of the incline.[35]

The transformation of the hillside under the dominion of colonial capital engenders the land as an object to the labourers, one that confronts them as an external enemy bent on intensifying their suffering. The emphasis on the whiteness of the parched environment underscores the social dimension of this produced nature, its organization in line with the economic imperatives of the white elite at the expense of the needs of the black peasants. Simultaneously, we see how the alienation of the land has as its corollary the production of the workers as isolated individuals, units of energy to be driven "[h]elter- skelter" across the quarry. Coggins Rum is reduced to "a black animate dot" on the road,[36] his name (which recalls "one of the island's major commodities"[37]) bespeaking the reification of his subjectivity.

More generally, the story makes tangible the savaging of the peasants' bodies under these conditions. An element of the grotesque enters as we move from the hobbling stride of the workers evoked in the above passage to Coggins's stubbing of his toe on the white marl road: "He paused, and gathered up the blind member. . . . A curve of flesh began to peel from it. Pree-pree-pree. As if it were frying. Frying flesh. The nail jerked out of place, hot, bright blood began to stream from it. Around the spot white marl dust clung in grainy cakes. Now, red, new blood squirted – spread over the whole toe – and the dust became crimson."[38] Once home, his wife takes care of the damaged flesh with a pair of scissors: "Zip! Onion-colored slip of skin fluttered to the floor. Rattah Grinah, the half-dead dog, cold dribbling from his glassy blue eyes on to his freckled nose, moved inanimately towards it."[39] There is something nauseating about this scene with its peeling, bloody flesh and the half-starved dog looking to eat it. The motif of bodies suffering under the onslaught of the landscape climaxes with the death of Coggins's daughter Beryl. To combat her hunger, the girl has been eating the stony dust from the ground, poisoning herself. Her death points to the harshness of the natural world, but more especially to the iniquities of the colonial system responsible for placing her in such a situation in the first place (something emphasized by the way Beryl's eating of dirt recalls one of the means by which the enslaved would commit suicide on the plantation).

The theme of bodily horror introduced in Walrond's work is one that reappears in a succession of proletarian narratives. As Heather Bowen-Struyk notes, Hiroshi Aramata has argued that "proletarian literature is a kind of horror literature".[40] Bowen-Struyk cites two stories by Korean proletarian writers which bear out this point: Ch'oe So-hae's "The Death of Pak Tol" (1925) and Chang Hyok-chu's "Hell of the Starving" (1932). Both are set in colonial Korea during the Japanese occupation (Japan annexed Korea in 1910, exercising colonial rule until 1945), and both register, as Samuel Perry puts it, "the violent shock with which a primarily agricultural Korean society confronts capitalism".[41] Thus in "Hell of the Starving", in a twist reminiscent of the fate of Walrond's Beryl, a malnourished boy is given a meal of steamed grain by his mother after the colonial authorities distribute "relief-aid" to the starving in the form of free millet. In a brutal irony, the meal causes intestinal failure in the boy, whose stomach has become unaccustomed to food, and he dies. In "The Death of Pak Tol", meanwhile, a young child is "fed spoiled fish by his desperately poor and uneducated mother, who then runs off to a local doctor when the boy falls ill. The doctor refuses to give the woman medicine on credit, and, when the boy finally dies, the mother goes insane, seeking a gruesome revenge on the doctor by eating his face off."[42]

I want to turn now to Walrond's story "Panama Gold", in order to consider further the opposition between natural and abstract space mentioned earlier. Set in rural Barbados, the story revolves around Ella Heath, a lonely "old maid" with "an intense respect for Barbadian folktales and foodways, as well as the land and that which it nurtures".[43] Ella tends to a flourishing plot that provides her with a level of self-sufficiency. Into her life comes Mr Poyah, returned from Panama where he lost a leg on the canal dig. Thanks to the compensation he received for his accident and the relatively high rates of remuneration on the isthmus as compared to the Caribbean islands, Poyah is able to open up a shop and considers himself a suitor for Ella.[44] His entry into the village can be read in terms of the penetration of industrial capital into an agricultural setting. Rich, propertied and not afraid to show it, Poyah embodies the kind of reconstructed subjectivity produced under the aegis of modern industry and the cash nexus. His mutilated, rebuilt corporeality (his missing leg has been replaced by an artificial one) points to capitalism's consumption and remoulding of working-class bodies, while his appearance in Ella's domain indicates the threat this particular kind of modernization represents to her way of life, her self-sufficiency.

Indeed, in terms of the production of nature, the world Ella has created through her labours is clearly marked as antithetical to that which has engendered Poyah's "modernized" body. We noted earlier how capitalism entails the separation of nature from human activity and its positing as an external object world. With regard to Ella's plot, however, the unity of the natural and human worlds is still intact:

> The wind tossed the lanky guava tree. Scudding popcorn – white, yellow, crimson pink guava buds blew upon the ground. Forwards and backwards the wind tossed the guava tree. It shook buds and blossoms on the ground – moist, unforked, ground – on Ella Heath's lap, in her black, plenteous hair, in the water she was drawing from the well. Guava buds fell in Ella's bucket, and she liked it. They gave flavor to the water. All of nature gave flavor to Ella, wrought a magic color in Ella's life.[45]

In this lush environment, Ella retains a felt connection to the landscape. Nature here still forms, to borrow Marx's phrase, her "extended body"; it has yet to be reified as merely an object. As a corollary to this, it is clear too that we are still in the realm of natural space: "Inexhaustible stems of green sprang up around Ella's domain. It'd take five years to mature, but she had planted a cocoanut tree on the northern-most wing of the cabin. Half an acre of land, but it was no trifling stake. Inch by inch green overspread it. Corn, okras, gunga peas, eddoes, *tannias*, tomatoes – in such a world Ella moved."[46] Ella's plot forms a self-contained world, a qualitatively distinct, concrete place opposed to the undifferentiated plane of sheer quantitative extension that defines abstract space.

This implied confrontation between natural and abstract space – that is, between a subsistence peasant economy and the world of market capitalism – can be understood as symbolized by Ella's refusal of the materialistic Poyah. Her reply to his entreaties that she is not frightened is an assertion of independence in the face of the commodity culture he represents. Another factor in Ella's rejection of Poyah, however, is her prejudice against both his dark colour (Ella herself is a mulatto) and his disability, such sentiments pointing to the retrograde features of the kind of enclosed, peasant life Ella leads. In this connection, the fact that the idea of a relationship between Ella and Poyah is raised in the text, and that at the end of the narrative there is some suggestion of reconciliation insofar as she tries to help when his shop is burning, indicates that what in fact we have here is not a straightforward rejection of modernity as such.

Crucially, the modernization process does have certain progressive effects. In the context of the Panama Canal dig, the impact on Caribbean labourers included more than just the suffering imposed by industrial working practices. Many of them had their first encounter with trade unionism in Panama, subsequently taking this experience back to their home countries, where the growing union movement in places such as Jamaica and Trinidad in the 1930s and 1940s would help pave the way for independence.[47] Poyah might be bragging when he tells a local in Barbados how he fought for compensation for his leg – "Hell wit' de Canal! We wuz gwine blow up de dam, cut down de wireless station an' breck up de gubment house! If dey didn't pay me fo' my foot!"[48] – but his attitude emphasizes how workers were radicalized on the isthmus, their consciousnesses raised to the possibility of asserting their collective rights.

It is this progressive element in the experience of capitalist modernity that Poyah might bring to Ella. If it could be melded with her rejection of commodity culture, her independence and her sensuous connection (via non-alienated labour) to the materiality of the land, then the basis is there for the construction of a different kind of modernity to that which marks Poyah's body, one beyond the limits of capital and the rule of exchange value. In other words, this would be a modernity organized around the needs and practices of the poor and the labouring classes. This utopian possibility is embedded in the portrayal of Ella's agricultural labours, the impulse to remake the world figured in the fecund vegetation of her land, her own association with fertility rituals and the way she constantly rejuvenates the world of her plot with new combinations of species: "As if she were an immemorial lark, Ella experimented with the green froth of the earth. One day she was grafting a pine and breadfruit. Standing, 'jooking' a foreign stalk in – tamarind, star apple, almond – and strapping it into the gummy gash dug in the tree's side."[49] One might read this figuratively as implying that for the potential for collective renewal symbolized in the plot to be brought to fruition, some new kind of social combination is needed also. And so it is that one can argue that just as Ella's loneliness could perhaps be solved by Poyah, so figuratively the union of certain aspects of the modernity he embodies with the self-sufficiency and folk life she represents might provide the grounds for that flowering of a genuinely alternative, non-capitalist modernity.

However, such a union proves abortive in the story. Poyah is, as it were, completely overcome by modernity: there seems no possibility of isolating the progressive elements associated with the latter from its negative effects. When his shop catches alight Ella searches frantically for him, but all she finds are his "straw valise, label spattered – deckers' luggage – an old shirt – one or two stray sacks of split peas – the money canister".[50] As Frederick observes, these remains "underscore Poyah's signification of US industry and material goods: the fire reduces the Colón Man to the sum of his (Western) parts".[51]

Several other stories in *Tropic Death* contain intimations of utopian promise which likewise appear unable to cohere into fully articulated expressions of social transformation, instead remaining constrained by capitalist reification. As with Ella's plot, these utopian impulses are connected to the eruption of nature, to the recrudescence of lush vegetation within the otherwise flat, alienated landscape engendered by colonialism and imperialism. In "Subjection", for example, amid the squalor of the Canal Zone, the protagonist Ballet glimpses "a vision of buxom green cocoa palms spread like a crescent – from the old rickety wooden houses walled behind the preserves of the quarantine station all the way past the cabins of the fishing folk and dinky bathhouses for the blacks to the unseemly array of garbage at the dump".[52] Similarly, in "Tropic Death", there erupts an hallucinatory spectacle of verdant nature that transforms the air of misery and agitated claustrophobia that hangs over the dilapidated workers' shacks: "On that galvanized roof the sun bristled. . . . It was a fluid, lustrous sun. It created a Garden of the roof. It recaptured the essence of that first jungle scene. Upward, on one the roof's hills spread the leaves of banyan tree. Fruit – mellow, hanging, tempting – peeped from between the foliage of coffee and mango and pear."[53] In both instances, however, the prospect of renewal associated with such visions remains more symbolic than real: the possibility of fulfilling a utopian potential in terms of the radical transformation of social relations is never really given concrete expression.

This clearly is one way in which Walrond's work differs from the narrative tendencies of much proletarian literature, where the emphasis is often precisely on the realization of such potential through the raising of revolutionary consciousness and active resistance to capitalist exploitation. The strike narrative, for example, as Denning observes, "becomes, not surprisingly, a core element in these works"; and if "the strike is often defeated, it is because it stands as a figure for a promised revolution".[54] We do not have such moments of explicit social and political confrontation in Walrond's writing. Undoubtedly, at least part of the reason is his desire to avoid producing fiction with an overt political message. Nevertheless, I want to end by suggesting that Walrond's stories in *Tropic Death* do offer their own kind of utopian compensation for the alienation and brutalities they document. This is to be found in the literary style of his narratives, and is of a paradoxical hue.

Fredric Jameson argues that even as the increasing reification of the lifeworld under capitalism imposes the break-up of traditional unities and social forms, at the same time "these now isolated broken bits and pieces of the older unities acquire a certain autonomy of their own, a semi-autonomous coherence which, not merely a reflex of capitalist reification and rationalization, also in some measure serves to compensate for the dehumanisation of experience reification brings with it, and to rectify the otherwise intolerable effects of the new process".[55] He gives sight as an example, suggesting that as the latter becomes a separate activity it acquires new objects that are themselves the products of a process of abstraction and rationalization. The experience of the concrete is stripped of such attributes as colour, spatial depth and texture, which in their turn are reified as autonomous properties. In that autonomy, however, they acquire an intensity that can provide a kind of compensatory gratification for what has been lost through reification. This process, suggests Jameson, is reflected in the history of artistic forms. Thus, modernism in visual art – the triumph of the "autonomy of the visual ... in abstract expressionism" – is to be associated with the reification which is its precondition; but one must also recognize "the Utopian vocation of the newly reified sense, the mission of the heightened and autonomous language of color to restore at least a symbolic experience of libidinal gratification to a world drained of it, a world of extension, gray and merely quantifiable".[56]

Walrond's prose, I want to argue, can be grasped in a similar way, its style both a register of the reification and fragmentation imposed by capitalism and a source of utopian compensation by way of its descriptive intensity and imagistic power. Take this fairly typical passage from "Drought":

> Yesterday, at noon . . . a roasting sun smote Coggins. Liquid . . . fluid . . . drought. Solder. Heat and juice of fruit . . . juice of roasting *cashews*.
>
> It whelmed Coggins. The dry season was at its height. Praying to the Lord to send rain, black peons gathered on the rumps of breadfruit or cherry trees in abject supplication. . . .
>
> The sun had robbed the land of its juice, squeezed it dry. Star apples, sugar apples, husks, transparent on the dry sleepy trees. Savagely prowling through the orchards blackbirds stopped at nothing. . . . Turtle doves rifled the pods of green peas and purple beans and even the indigestible Brazilian *bonavis*. Potato vines, yellow as the leaves of autumn, severed from their roots by the pressure of the sun, stood on the ground, the wind's eager prey. Undug, stemless – peanuts, carrots – seeking balm, relief, the caress of a passing wind, shot dead unflustered eyes up through sun-etched cracks in the hard, brittle soil. The sugar corn went to the birds. Ripening prematurely, breadfruits fell swiftly on the hard naked earth, half ripe, good only for fritters. . . . Fell in spatters . . . and the hungry dogs, elbowing the children, lapped up the yellow-mellow fruit.[57]

Here, the short, punchy sentences and broken, occasionally disjointed syntax reflect the reifying impact of modernization. The detailed description of the environment and its flora and fauna constructs the reader as an eye penetrating and enumerating the scene, this emphasis on the visual is the narrative correlative to the atomization of the body under capital. Yet the subsequent intensity of perception and the vivid, effulgent quality this gives to the prose offers utopian recompense for the fragmentation and desiccation of the colonized life-world. Even as it depicts the life-draining ferocity of a drought exacerbated by the colonialist-driven overwork of the land, the narrative provides a form of sensory gratification through its own richness, vibrancy and imagistic excess. In other words, the degradation evoked in the story's content is compensated for by the stylistic plenitude of the writing.

This would seem altogether appropriate for a writer Kenneth Ramchand described as one of the great stylists of the Harlem Renaissance.[58] And it is the utopian promise embedded in his style that takes Walrond closer to the utopianism of many of the works commonly thought of as proletarian literature. While Walrond was always suspicious of fiction with an avowedly political purpose, the way in which *Tropic Death* registers the impact of imperialism and capitalist modernization across the Caribbean and its surrounding rimlands, especially with regard to the production of nature, chimes with the efforts of many of his contemporaries in the proletarian arts movement. In the peripheries of empire the penetration of capital reorganized the landscape, disarticulated pre-existing social formations, frequently propped up archaic modes of domination, and reprogrammed and reproduced bodies for life and work in the increasingly reified world of market capitalism. In stories like "Drought" and "Subjection" Walrond emphasizes the brutality and devastation these transformations entailed. But in a story such as "Panama Gold" he also offers us the possibility of an alternative social order grounded in a sensuous connection to the land and its produce, organized around non-alienated labour, and resistant to the imperialist logic of global capital.

NOTES

1. Richard Wright, *American Hunger* (New York: Harper and Row, 1977), 62–64.
2. Several other slogans were used to designate the literary work associated with this movement, including "proletarian literature", "neorealism", and "progressive", "engaged", or "committed" writing. See Michael Denning, *Culture in the Age of Three Worlds* (London: Verso, 2004), 52.
3. Ibid., 57.
4. Ibid.
5. V.I. Lenin, *Imperialism, the Highest Stage of Capitalism*, in *Essential Works of Lenin: What Is to be Done? and Other Writings*, ed. Henry M. Christman (New York: Dover, 1987), 227.
6. Denning, *Culture*, 59.
7. Louis J. Parascandola, introduction to *"Winds Can Wake Up the Dead": An Eric Walrond Reader*, by Eric Walrond; ed. Louis J. Parascandola (Detroit: Wayne State University Press, 1998), 18.
8. Ibid., 16.
9. Ibid., 18.
10. Frederic Jameson, *Postmodernism, or The Cultural Logic of Late Capitalism* (New York: Verso, 1991), 307.
11. Sidney Mintz, "Enduring Substances, Trying Theories: The Caribbean Region as Oikoumene", *Journal of the Royal Anthropological Institute* 2, no. 2 (June 1996): 295.

12. Eric Walrond, *"Winds Can Wake Up the Dead": An Eric Walrond Reader*, ed. Louis J. Parascandola (Detroit: Wayne State University Press, 1998), 189.
13. Ibid., 210.
14. Rhonda Denise Frederick, "Mythographies of Panamá Canal Migrations: Eric Walrond's *Tropic Death*", in *Marginal Migrations: The Circulation of Cultures within the Caribbean*, ed. Shalini Puri (Oxford: Macmillan, 2003), 57.
15. Walrond, *"Winds"*, 210.
16. See also Denning (*Culture*, 66), who, in mapping the common modes, forms, and genres of the proletarian novel, observes that one "formal option was to represent the tenement, the crowded and chaotic collective households of urban workers which spilled out into the streets of the proletarian quarter".
17. C.L.R. James, "Triumph", in *The Oxford Book of Caribbean Short Stories*, eds. Stewart Brown and John Wickham (Oxford: Oxford University Press, 1999), 35.
18. Bonham C. Richardson, *The Caribbean in the Wider World, 1492–1992: A Regional Geography* (Cambridge: Cambridge University Press, 1992), 82.
19. Walrond, *"Winds"*, 224.
20. Parascandola, introduction, 27.
21. Walrond, *"Winds"*, 225.
22. Ibid., 210–11.
23. Ibid., 224.
24. Neil Smith, *Uneven Development: Nature, Capital, and the Production of Space* (Athens: University of Georgia Press, 2008), 6.
25. Ibid., 49–50.
26. Karl Marx, *Grundrisse: Foundations of the Critique of Political Economy*, trans. Martin Nicolaus (London: Penguin and New Left Review, 1973), 489.
27. Ibid., 491, 498.
28. Ibid., 497.
29. Smith, *Uneven Development*, 107.
30. Ibid.
31. Ibid., 102.
32. Eric Walrond, *Tropic Death* (New York: Collier Books, 1972), 99–100.
33. Frederick, "Mythographies", 57.
34. Walrond, *"Winds"*, 222.
35. Ibid., 189.
36. Ibid.
37. Parascandola, introduction, 26.
38. Walrond, *"Winds"*, 191.
39. Ibid.
40. Heather Bowen-Struyk, "Guest Editor's Introduction: Proletarian Arts in East Asia", *Positions: East Asia Cultures Critique* 14, no. 2 (2006): 258.

41. Samuel Perry, "Korean as Proletarian: Ethnicity and Identity in Chang Hyok-chu's 'Hell of the Starving'", *Positions: East Asian Critique*, 14, no. 2 (2006): 295.
42. Ibid.
43. Frederick, "Mythographies", 62.
44. On the money sent or brought back from Panama by Caribbean migrants, see Richardson, *Caribbean*, 139.
45. Walrond, *Tropic Death*, 38.
46. Ibid., 39.
47. See Rhonda Cobham, "The Background", in *West Indian Literature*, 2nd ed., ed. Bruce King (London: Macmillan Education, 1995), 14. See too, on the unionization of the canal labourers, Michael L. Conniff, *Black Labor on a White Canal: Panama, 1904–1981* (Pittsburgh: University of Pittsburgh Press, 1985), 45–74.
48. Ibid., 42.
49. Ibid., 39.
50. Ibid., 49
51. Frederick, "Mythographies", 68.
52. Walrond, *Tropic Death*, 108–9.
53. Walrond, "Winds", 266.
54. Denning, *Culture*, 66.
55. Fredric Jameson, *The Political Unconscious* (New York: Routledge, 2002), 48.
56. Ibid.
57. Walrond, "Winds", 192.
58. Kenneth Ramchand, "The Writer Who Ran Away: Eric Walrond and *Tropic Death*", *Savacou: Journal of the Caribbean Artists Movement* 2 (September 1970): 68.

PART 3

BIOGRAPHICAL SKETCHES

7

ERIC WALROND AND THE DYNAMICS OF WHITE PATRONAGE DURING THE HARLEM RENAISSANCE

CARL A. WADE, ROBERT BONE AND
LOUIS J. PARASCANDOLA

> White capital and influence were crucial, and the white presence, at least in the early years, hovered over the New Negro world of art and literature like a benevolent censor, politely but pervasively setting the outer limits of its creative boundaries.
> —David Levering Lewis, *When Harlem Was in Vogue*

MUCH ATTENTION HAS BEEN paid to the many complex relations between white patrons and the leading artists of the Harlem Renaissance, the possible influence of financial and other types of sponsorship provided by these patrons on the representation of African American culture, and even on the direction of the movement itself. For African American novelist Zora Neale Hurston, these Lost Generation "Negrotarians", as she christened white benefactors, fell into different categories: the earnest humanitarians with sincere interest in the work and careers of black artists, and those who, in David Levering Lewis's words "were drawn to Harlem . . . because it seemed to answer a need for personal nourishment and to confirm their vision of cultural salvation coming from the margins of civilization".[1] Ralph D. Story puts it this way: "For the Harlem Renaissance writers and painters, once they agreed to a patron-artist relationship – especially a financial one – it seemed to obligate them to produce a certain kind of product that would meet the patron(s)' approval. Hence, it is difficult to imagine just what kind of art might have been produced had not the artists been under such covert pressure to please their supporters."[2]

For Marcus Garvey, the influence of such patronage accounted for what he considered the denigrating treatment of black culture in Harlem Renaissance texts such as Claude McKay's *Home to Harlem* (1928). In a severe and unsympathetic review of this novel (as well as, among other texts, Eric Walrond's *Tropic Death*), Garvey alleged that "the white people have these Negroes to write the kind of stuff that they desire to feed their public with so that the Negro can still be regarded as a monkey or some imbecilic creature".[3] In his judgement, *Home to Harlem* was a "veritable libel" against the Negro and writers like Walrond and McKay little more than "literary prostitutes" who had "done damaging harm to the morals and reputation of the black race". He adds, "Whenever authors of the Negro race write good literature for publication the white publishers refuse to publish it, but wherever the Negro is sufficiently known to attract attention he is advised to write in the way that the white man wants."[4]

In the view of many, no relationships more clearly exemplified this type of arrangement than those involving "Godmother" Charlotte Osgood Mason and her protégées, Hurston, Langston Hughes, Alain Locke and the painter Aaron Douglas; it is generally agreed Mason's financial support came at the price of control over these artists' work. Larnell Dunkley Jr referred to Mason as "a prime example of a patron who had specific ideas about African American art, particularly as it pertained to primitivism or folk culture".[5] She wanted the work of her protégées to reflect those modernist notions that, according to Leighten "embraced a deeply romanticized view of African culture (conflating many cultures into one), and considered Africa the embodiment of humankind in a precivilized state, preferring to mystify rather than examine its presumed idol-worship and violent rituals".[6] Though such perceptions, Patricia Leighten adds, "self-consciously subverted colonial stereotypes, both of the right and the left", these "subversive revisions remained implicated in the prejudices they sought to expose".[7] This is a view echoed by Robert Bone, who argues in *Down Home* that although the modernist writers "abandoned the image of the Negro as contented slave, or as ravisher of white womanhood", they replaced this "with a subtler if no less racist caricature":[8] the primitive. Thus, for many scholars the great paradox created by white patronage in the Harlem Renaissance is that, as Jurgen Henreichs proposes, it restricted black artists to racialized themes based on myopic constructs of blackness rather than encouraging them to transcend traditional limitations. "It becomes evident", Henreichs contends, "in the fact that the most conscious endeavors to embrace African based identities returned to long-standing stereotypes. Thus white patronage actually hindered the very development of cultural self-determination that it sought to encourage."[9]

Patrons like Mason therefore presented their African American beneficiaries with a dilemma since, in Dunkley's words, these artists were torn between their need to write about their own experiences "while negotiating the demands placed on them by philanthropic sponsors who had their own agenda for the artistic future of the 'New Negro' in modern society".[10] However, as Story and others note, so powerful was the influence of the patrons that the representation of African American culture and the entire movement itself may not have been the same in its absence.

George Hutchinson, diverging somewhat from what he characterizes as "reductive readings", asserts that "a study of the Harlem Renaissance must inevitably deal with the issue of interracial dynamics".[11] His primary thesis is that the Harlem movement was essentially a synergy between modernism and black vernacular culture, that both black and white intellectuals were integral to the shaping of the Renaissance, which was itself part of a much broader cultural development.

While the contributions of many sponsors such as Mason, Joel and Arthur Spingarn, William E. Harmon, and Fannie Hurst have been explored, at least two important associations that illustrate sharply contrasting dimensions of white patronage during the Renaissance and after still remain to be examined.[12] These involve Guyanese-born author Eric Walrond, and author and translator Edna Worthley Underwood on the one hand, and Walrond and Henry Allen Moe, the first secretary of the Guggenheim Foundation, on the other. Walrond's liminal status as an outsider twice removed, who as a black West Indian immigrant experienced ostracism from both African American and white Americans alike, doubtless made him even more dependent on patronage than his black American counterparts.

The alliance between Walrond and Underwood was mutually beneficial in that Walrond penned reviews of Underwood's novel *The Penitent* (1922) while she used her influence with editors to place his writings in important white-owned publications. However, the association differed in some ways from the typical partnership where, as we have seen, white patrons offered financial support in exchange for certain control over black artists' work. Instead, Underwood peddled her influence in exchange for favourable publicity from Walrond. But the places where she promoted his works often played into the same so-called primitivist impulse that "Negrotarian" patrons such as Mason favoured. Clearly, Underwood, the older, more established author, tried to nudge the fledgling author into writing strictly within the limited frame of his Caribbean experience.

Since Underwood has essentially been lost to modern readers, it is necessary to trace some of her background. She was a preacher's daughter, born in Maine in 1873, but she grew up in Kansas. In 1897, she married a jeweller, Earl Underwood, but bored with her provincial life, she began to write: poetry, fiction and translations. She took a keen interest in languages, eventually training herself to read more than a dozen foreign tongues. Still feeling stifled by life on the prairie, she persuaded her husband to transfer his business to New York where, in 1912, at the age of forty, her sustained publishing career began. It was as a translator that she excelled, being among the first to translate the Spanish and Portuguese poets of South America for her English-speaking audiences.[13]

Underwood was part of a literary movement profoundly rooted in American provincial life. "The Revolt from the Village", as literary historians have called it, encompassed such Midwestern writers as Edgar Lee Masters, Sherwood Anderson, Sinclair Lewis and Theodore Dreiser, and such books as *Spoon River Anthology* (1915), *Winesburg, Ohio* (1919), *Main Street* (1922) and *An American Tragedy* (1925) respectively.[14] These authors, fleeing from the sterility of Midwestern towns, established enclaves in Chicago and New York which became the centres of early modernism. It was precisely the narrowness of small-town life that prompted them to seek first metropolitan and then cosmopolitan perspectives, in what Robert Bone, referring to the modernist movement in general, characterizes as a "gesture of revulsion from a decadent civilization and an effort to restore the waning vitality of Western art through a return to primitive sources", in other words, "a quest for a simpler, purer and more elemental mode of life".[15] Indeed, Underwood confirms this judgement with her observation that "emotion is dying so rapidly that the art of the future must come from the colored races".[16]

It was not through any of the literary luminaries from her circle, however, that Underwood first encountered Walrond in the summer of 1922 while he was working for Marcus Garvey's newspaper *Negro World*. Instead, it was through her "secretary, Amanda Reed, a colored girl of ability and intelligence".[17] Walrond told Underwood of his troubles gaining employment, as well-documented in such sketches as "On Being Black" and "On Being a Domestic", despite his considerable journalistic experience both in Panama and America.[18]

After helping Walrond secure some assistance from the numbers banker – and black patron – Casper Holstein, Underwood encouraged Walrond to write and especially to "rewrite again and again".[19] Underwood relates that Walrond "wrote diligently for months just as I had suggested, bringing the stories to me one after the other. When I thought they were sufficiently ripe and ready to give to the public I told him it might be possible, using these stories as proof, for him to win a Guggenheim Fellowship [he did in 1928] and for him to go up for it at once, make immediately his application."[20] Underwood's assistance, however, did not stop there. The most intriguing part of the story, in fact, is how she went about helping to secure Walrond's fame and how he returned the favour.

From the fall of 1922 to the spring of 1925, she served as Walrond's agent. In a letter dated 19 September 1922, he thanks her for her "wonderful interest [in his career] and generosity".[21] It was she who introduced him, in his role as journalist, to the pages of the *New Republic*, the New York Times' *Current History* and *Forbes' Magazine*. And it was also she who introduced him, as a short story writer, to readers of *Smart Set*, *Success Magazine* and *Argosy All-Story Weekly*.

The nature of their business arrangement is suggested in a letter dated 24 February 1923, from Underwood to Robert H. Davis, editor of the pulp fiction journal *Argosy All-Story Weekly* (which published such authors as Edgar Rice Burroughs of Tarzan fame). Although Davis stated that he could not publish the Walrond material she sent him, he was very encouraging about the young author, and he did, in fact, eventually accept "The Stolen Necklace" and "The Silver King", which Walrond himself described as "two disgusting 'darky' stories". Nevertheless, the publication of these narratives provided him with an opportunity to develop his apprentice writing, hone his craft and expose his work to a popular audience. Walrond speaks of his interview with the nameless editor, clearly Davis, who was in possession of "a mound of manuscript someone [Underwood] had kindly sent him". From Davis, Walrond learned, though he "was not aware of it . . . the scent of the American mind", for which he was grateful.[22] Later, Walrond would also be indebted to Davis for writing a favourable recommendation on his behalf for a Guggenheim award.

Perhaps Underwood's greatest assistance, however, came while he was working for *Opportunity* magazine. She wrote to Charles S. Johnson, the journal's editor, informing him of "her anticipation of a 'new epoch in the history of American letters' wherein a 'new race differently endowed' will be looked to increasingly for art 'because joy – its mainspring – is dying so rapidly in the Great Caucasian Race' ".[23] When Johnson helped arrange the famous Civic Club dinner with Howard University professor Alain Locke on 21 March 1924, bringing together a bevy of publishers and young black artists, Underwood and Walrond were among the guests. Undoubtedly, she used her influence to help get his story "The Palm Porch" included in Locke's ground-breaking anthology *The New Negro* (1925). She was also a judge of *Opportunity*'s 1925 contest for poems and stories written by black authors, while casting her vote for Walrond's story, "The Voodoo's Revenge", the third-prize winner.[24] In her letter of support for the story, she described the author as "the black Kipling",[25] a dubious distinction indeed.

In exchange for using her influence on his behalf, Underwood expected Walrond's help in promoting her forthcoming novel, *The Penitent*, a tale of the Russian author Pushkin, among a potential black readership. This much can be said without conjecture: that a prepublication notice appeared in *Negro World* of 26 August 1922 – unsigned, but probably written by Underwood herself. Walrond mentioned the book in his *Negro World* column from 4 November 1922, and there is an unsigned article, almost certainly by Walrond, entitled "Poushkin [sic] and Dumas" in *Negro World* (21 October 1922). Most important, he also wrote a lengthy favourable review of the novel for this issue, not only urging readers to get the book but also describing Underwood as "a poet and novelist of classic charm" and "a translator and literary critic of international distinction".[26]

The review focuses initially on the African ancestry of Pushkin, whose great-grandfather on his mother's side was a black slave of Peter the Great; and then on the impact of the French Revolution on the Russian autocracy during the reign of Alexander I. The poet Pushkin, as portrayed by Underwood, became a central icon in the storyteller's pantheon of heroes. His African ancestry made him emotionally accessible to the West Indian, his revolutionary politics appealed to Walrond's Promethean instincts, and his dedication to his craft represented an ideal towards which the young novice had pledged himself to strive. Above all, the tragic life of Pushkin touched on the sensitive issue of marginality. For after his banishment by the czar, Pushkin wandered through the world as an outcast, thrust from favour on the ground of his revolutionary principles. An Ishmael of sorts, he became in Walrond's imagination an emblem of the exiled artist – a terrestrial version, if you will, of the Flying Dutchman.[27]

Walrond continued to work on Underwood's behalf while employed by *Opportunity*. He helped arrange for a review of *The Penitent* to appear in the October 1923 issue. In addition, in February, March and April of 1924, *Opportunity* also published three instalments of her translation from the Russian of an unfinished manuscript by Pushkin on the subject of his African ancestry.

Although their arrangement benefited both parties, it was one which Walrond could not tolerate. While Underwood's control of his writing and life was less intrusive than that of patrons such as Mason, who made Hurston account for every penny she spent, it was still too much for him to abide. He was one of the most iconoclastic, fiercely independent of all the New Negroes. Earlier, for example, he had rejected Garveyism because of its emphasis on "propaganda over art" – a perspective that would also distance him from W.E.B. Du Bois and the "Talented Tenth" school.[28] When Walrond approached Underwood to discuss his project about the digging of the Panama Canal – almost certainly "The Big Ditch" – her recommendation to him was that "you should go back to your people – your race – in the tropics and be one of them".[29] This echoed the advice given to prospective writers among Underwood's *West Indian Review* audience: to answer the "race-call" of Africa, "an Africa . . . rich in song, rich in emotion", without which "no art of any kind can be".[30] Writing in this journal, Underwood repeatedly highlighted and promoted the expression and celebration of a racial sensibility – some angst peculiar to people of African ancestry – in the work of Nicolás Guillén and his contemporaries,[31] in preference to their subversive political and social discourses. Instead, Walrond heeded the advice of others and "took the first boat for Paris"[32] to participate in what he considered the broader Modernist movement.

Underwood wanted Walrond to write only of his life in the context of the tropics. As he appeared to grow more distant from this world and its anxieties, she thought that he had lost his creative instincts. Underwood, who paradoxically often took a cosmopolitan view of the world despite her provincial upbringing, translating the writings of various lands such as Russia, Haiti, Egypt and Japan, nevertheless wanted to restrict Walrond to one corner of the globe viewed from a limited perspective. Such racialized thinking was not unusual with many of the white patrons such as Mason who wanted their charges to avoid social protest and adopt exclusively primitivist perspectives.[33] This essentialism often led to fierce resistance on the part of black writers, perhaps most palpably manifesting itself in Hurston's essay "The Pet Negro System".[34]

Walrond ignored Underwood's advice because he abhorred any philosophy that he considered doctrinaire. Inevitably, as he became more closely involved with different political, social and literary causes, he became disenchanted with the dogma that frequently accompanied them. Walrond maintained that the black artist is best served by keeping an independent mind rather than slavishly following any specific ideology – especially one rooted in racial stereotypes, however well-intentioned.

Even after their partnership had ended, Underwood "kept track of him . . . during all the years",[35] and lamented that "he did not write any more at all".[36] She soon realized her mistake and learned that he had produced additional texts, in spite of a lengthy stay in the American Hospital in Paris suffering from appendicitis. When she became associated with *West Indian Review*, she called on her old client again, reprinting several of the late little-known pieces he published in English journals and one new sketch, the delightful dialect piece "Morning in Colon" (August 1940).[37] In these narratives, set in Central America, with a focus on Caribbean life, and often utilizing dialect, Underwood undoubtedly recognized flashes of the old Walrond. It is unfortunate that she probably was not aware of the dozen or so pieces that he would eventually publish in *Roundway Review*, the journal of Roundway Hospital, England, where he was a voluntary patient from 1952 to 1957.[38] With her assistance, perhaps some of these writings might have been published sooner and helped rescue him from his artistic silence. And had this been the case, her own untimely literary demise might have been averted.

Underwood was indisputably a catalyst for Walrond's professional growth, as she doubtless had been for countless amateur writers in the diaspora through her translations of and articles on the literature from the francophone, hispanophone and anglophone Caribbean in *West Indian Review*.[39] With her wide range of contacts in the literary world, she was able to initiate Walrond's American orientation and make it a reality. With her belief in cosmopolitanism, she expanded his horizons and drew him in the direction of her own aesthetic. On the other hand, she reinforced his own romantic tendencies, introducing him to such writers as Pierre Loti and Lafcadio Hearn.[40] Moreover, like so many white patrons of the Harlem Renaissance, she threatened to imprison him, however inadvertently, within her own conception of Modernist black writing, predicated as it was, on essentialist constructs of race.

Walrond's relationship with Henry Allen Moe, secretary of the Guggenheim Foundation, began when he applied for a fellowship in 1927. By contrast, this relationship shows little of the tension, conflict and ambivalence of that with Underwood, and is characteristic of many of the unions between black writers and white patrons of the era. It is important to consider, however, that, unlike Underwood and the majority of white patrons, Moe was representing a philanthropic organization rather than acting in a personal and private capacity.

Born in 1894, Henry Allen Moe is widely remembered as a humanist and philanthropist whose career and interests brought him into contact with a number of individuals from diverse backgrounds. He graduated in 1916 from Hamline University in his home state, Minnesota, before assuming duties as a reporter with *St Paul Dispatch and Pioneer Press*. After a stint in the US Navy in the First World War during which he sustained serious injuries, Moe was awarded a Rhodes Scholarship to further his studies at Oxford University, England. Admitted to the Bar in 1923, he assisted in the development of the plan for the establishment of the Guggenheim Foundation, later becoming its first secretary (chief executive officer), a post that he retained until 1963. In addition to his formal duties, Moe held several important positions with prominent national and private philanthropic institutions and those devoted to the promotion of the arts, such as the American Philosophical Association, the National Endowment for the Humanities – of which he was the first director – and the Museum of Modern Art. Many awards are named after him in tribute to his public service. In addition, the American Philosophical Association records that Moe is "remembered for his dedication to helping artists and fellows pursue their work.... [He] brought a personal touch to his work. Moe remembered former fellows and their work, often remaining in contact with them for years, and encouraged them to think of the Guggenheim as their 'intellectual home', always allowing time to see them when they returned to the foundation."[41]

Such sympathies may account for Moe's public service and explain his compassionate, even avuncular, relationship with Walrond, who was a mere four years his junior. His public service extended to others such as Hurston (herself a Guggenheim Fellow),[42] who dedicated her most famous text, *Their Eyes Were Watching God* (1937), to the secretary and whose letters repeatedly extol his generosity, support, sympathy and understanding.[43] Walrond's relationship with Moe survived for almost forty years – nevertheless punctuated by periods of long silence that coincided with the writer's own mysterious disappearances from the limelight – and persisted even when the writer's hopes of fulfilling his obligations to Moe and the foundation had long vanished.

Throughout his association with Walrond, Moe's actions transcended the formal responsibilities of the scrupulous and efficient chief executive assisting the young writer to negotiate and comply with the conditions of the Guggenheim award to embrace those of literary agent, advocate and, to all intents and purposes, patron. It appears that he took a sincere interest in Walrond's work and desired the best for the young writer. As far as can be determined, Moe did not advance any obvious personal agenda or attempt to influence the artistic product, respecting always the writer's prerogative and province, unlike Underwood and other patrons. It is likely too that Moe used his considerable influence as an officer of the foundation to Walrond's advantage, especially when the latter applied for a renewal of the fellowship and on other occasions. Although the extension was granted for six months and not the full year that Walrond requested, it did provide him with a financial lifeline at a difficult point of his career. Moe was careful to explain, in a letter dated 8 March 1929, that the Guggenheim's decision on the request was no reflection on his (Walrond's) standing with the foundation but, rather, of its financial difficulties. Correspondence from March and April of 1928 also implies that Moe may have smoothed over some uncertainties in Walrond's letter of request for renewal.

Furthermore, the condition that the period of extension should be spent in Europe may have been in compliance with Walrond's stated request or influenced by Moe's recognition of and concern for the writer's considerable talent and an understanding of the difficulties that such artists – especially those with Walrond's known proclivities for revelry – could encounter in the heady environment of the Harlem Renaissance. If in specifying that the grant was not available for work in the United States (8 March 1928) Moe was seeking to protect his charge from the distracting influences of New York City, he failed to recognize – unlike Underwood – that Harlem existed in Paris as well.[44]

One example of the lengths Moe went to on Walrond's behalf is seen when, on 17 September 1931, he sent a letter about the manuscript of the ill-fated and mysterious "The Big Ditch" to Frederick Hitchcock of Century Company publishers. Although he had not read the entire work, Moe stated that what he had read seemed "extremely interesting" and ought to be considered for publication. Whether the secretary intervened upon Walrond's entreaty cannot be determined in the absence of any supporting documentation. In any event, judging from what we know about Walrond's non-fiction work about the Panama Canal – as evidenced by "The Second Battle" published in fifteen instalments in *Roundway Review* (April 1956–July 1957) – and the difficulty "The Big Ditch" experienced at the hands of editors in the late 1920s, it would seem reasonable to conclude that Moe's assessment of the merits of the work was somewhat exaggerated. His admission that he had not completely read the text might also be evidence of Walrond's tendency to utilize uninteresting facts and details in his historical writing about this episode. In any event, at the publishers' invitation, Moe forwarded the manuscript on 21 September 1931, after which it disappears from history and becomes one of Walrond's most painful sources of regret and disillusionment. The publication of "The Big Ditch", its defects notwithstanding, could have transformed the writer's literary career and perhaps his entire life.[45]

In 1940 and again in 1942, during a period of Walrond's mysterious disappearance from the literary and social limelight, Moe wrote to Eric's mother, Ruth Ellen Ambrozine Walrond, in Brooklyn, New York, inquiring about her son's whereabouts, for reasons that are not known.[46] Since Walrond's formal relationship with the Guggenheim Foundation had long since ended, the reader is left to speculate whether Moe was acting out of genuine interest in the writer, a gesture that supports the American Philosophical Association's view of his camaraderie with past Guggenheim Fellows.

In his correspondence with the secretary, Walrond, for his part, is deferential and respectful, faithfully documenting his movements, activities and achievements. This is true especially in relation to his journey to Central America and the Caribbean in fulfilment of the terms of the first award. Moreover, his reports from almost every port of call create the impression that he had come to regard Moe not simply as an administrator, but also as a friend and confidant. One recognizes in Walrond's letters a sincere appreciation for Moe's interventions, support and assistance – especially the expeditiousness and care of his arrangements for the disbursement of the Guggenheim funding.

In addition, the writer's reappearances often coincide with an accounting for his absence and silence in the form of lists of stories published in England and Europe – especially in *Roundway Review* – that accompanied his correspondence to Moe in June 1949, September 1953 and August 1954. The letters may also be construed as pleas for recognition and validation as well as proof that his life was not totally wasted and misspent and that Moe's trust in him was not misplaced and unmerited. It is noticeable too that Walrond, perhaps out of embarrassment, does not disclose his medical condition or place of residence (Roundway Hospital) during this period until a letter dated 9 October 1954, and only then in response to Moe's pointed query about how he could be reached.

This impression that he had disappointed Moe, and proved himself unworthy of his support and trust through his own failure to fulfil his obligations to the foundation, is poignantly communicated in a letter to the secretary dated 11 June 1960, which also expresses determination "to try somehow to get on with some of my own, long neglected work". Walrond adds, "in spite of age and years of silence I have not lost sight of my objectives, or the high aims with which I set out as a Guggenheim Fellow such a long time ago".[47] At the same time, his reference to the stability, sense of purpose and belonging engendered by his relationship with the Guggenheim family is evidence of another, important dimension of the value of his long association with Henry Allen Moe to his life and work.

Nevertheless, there is a suggestion that Moe's patience and confidence in Walrond may have been exhausted by the writer's failure to honour his contractual obligations, and understandably so. The occasion was Walrond's application for a Rosenwald Fellowship in 1940. No less a person than Charles S. Johnson, the former editor of *Opportunity*, in a letter to Ethel Ray Williams dated 3 January 1940 expresses scepticism about Walrond's chances, owing partly to Moe's membership on the fellowship committee. Johnson, who had encouraged Walrond to apply but was himself a member of this committee and therefore ineligible to serve as one of his referees, had two concerns. The first was that the committee had customarily limited its grants to African Americans residing in the United States and Southern whites. "The other concern", he writes, "is that another member of the committee is Henry Moe of the Guggenheim Foundation".[48] While he did not elaborate, Johnson was clearly hinting that Walrond's failure to fulfil the terms of his Guggenheim award would cost him the support of the influential secretary of the foundation on this occasion, which it apparently did, since the application was not successful. In all probability, it was this disappointment that accounts for the apologetic tone of Walrond's correspondence to the secretary during the next twenty years. Moe's apparent decision, however, does not invalidate his claim to be regarded – albeit in a limited sense – as one of the humanitarian patrons of the Harlem Renaissance, as defined by Hurston. Instead, it may be viewed as a pragmatic, even understandable reaction after his many years of generosity.

Dunkley, reflecting on the relationship between the white patrons and black artists, concludes, as do Story, Lewis and others, that "it is not clear if the Harlem Renaissance could have flourished without assistance from or access to white power and money. . . . Without the presence and influence of white patronage, the Harlem Renaissance, as it is known today, may not have existed."[49] Eric Walrond's contrasting literary relationships with Edna Worthley Underwood and Henry Allen Moe exemplify both the restrictive and liberating possibilities of these unions, and affirm, in some ways, the often complex dynamics of race in the Harlem Renaissance.

ACKNOWLEDGEMENTS

A shorter version of this article is forthcoming in the *Langston Hughes Review* 24–25 (2010–11).

NOTES

1. David Levering Lewis, *When Harlem Was in Vogue* (New York: Vintage Books, 1982), 99.
2. Ralph D. Story, "Patronage and the Harlem Renaissance: You Get What You Pay For", *CLA Journal* 32, no. 3 (1989): 289.
3. Marcus Garvey, "'Home to Harlem' Claude McKay's Damaging Book Should Earn Wholesale Condemnation of Negroes", in *"Look for Me All Around You": Anglophone Immigrants in the Harlem Renaissance.* ed. Louis J. Parascandola (Detroit: Wayne State University Press, 2005), 95.
4. Ibid.
5. Larnell Dunkley Jr, "White Patronage", in *Encyclopedia of the Harlem Renaissance*, ed. Cary D. Wintz and Paul Finkelman (New York: Routledge, 2004), 1254.
6. For more on Mason, see Robert Hemenway, *Zora Neale Hurston: A Literary Biography* (Chicago: University of Illinois Press, 1977), and Valerie Boyd, *Wrapped in Rainbows: The Life of Zora Neale Hurston* (New York: Scribner, 2004).
7. Patricia Leighten, "The White Peril and L'Art Negre: Picasso, Primitivism, and Anti-Colonialism", *Art Bulletin* 72, no. 4 (December 1990): 610.
8. Robert Bone, *Down Home: Origins of the Afro-American Short Story* (New York: Columbia University Press, 1988), 125.
9. Jurgens Henreichs, "Primitivism", in *Encyclopedia of the Harlem Renaissance*, ed. Cary Wintz and Paul Finkelman (New York and London: Routledge, 2004), 2:993. For further discussion on primitivism in art and literature, see Kimberly Pinder, ed., *Race-ing Art History: Critical Readings in Race and Art History* (New York: Routledge, 2002); Susanna Pavloska, *Modern Primitives: Race and Language in Gertrude Stein, Ernest Hemingway, and Zora Neale Hurston* (New York: Garland, 2000); Lisa Rado, "Primitivism, Modernism and Matriarchy", in *Modernism, Gender, and Culture: A Critical Studies Approach*, ed. Lisa Rado, 283–300 (New York: Garland, 1997).
10. Dunkley Jr, "White Patronage", 1253.
11. George Hutchinson, *The Harlem Renaissance in Black and White* (Cambridge, MA: Belknap Press, 1995), 15.
12. For a discussion of other similar associations of this time, see Robert C. Hart, "Black-White Literary Relations in the Harlem Renaissance", *American Literature* 44, no. 4 (January 1973): 612–28.

13. Underwood served as unofficial literary editor to *West Indian Review*, founded in Jamaica by the English expatriate Esther Chapman in 1934. She wrote many articles on every facet of Caribbean literary expression from the earliest times to the modern era under the heading "West Indian Literature". These essays were later released in book form in 1935. See Carl A. Wade, "Re-Imagining a Community: *West Indian Review*, 1934–1940", *Wadabagei: A Journal of the Caribbean and Its Diasporas* 11, no. 3 (2009): 3–27. For more on her life and career, see Carol Ward Craine, *Mrs Underwood: Linguist, Littérateuse* (Fort Hays, KS: Kansas State College, 1965).
14. See for example, Carl Van Doren, "The Revolt from the Village", *Contemporary American Novelists, 1900–1920* (New York: Macmillan, 1922), and Anthony Channell Hilfer, *Revolt from the Village, 1911–1930* (Chapel Hill: University of North Carolina Press, 1969).
15. Bone, *Down Home*, 126.
16. Edna Worthley Underwood, "West Indian Literature: Negro Poets", *West Indian Review* (September 1935): 40.
17. Edna Worthley Underwood, "West Indian Literature: Some Negro Poets of Panama", *West Indian Review* (March 1936): 37.
18. See Eric Walrond, *"Winds Can Wake Up the Dead": An Eric Walrond Reader*, ed. Louis J. Parascandola (Detroit: Wayne State University Press, 1998).
19. Holstein, a native of the Virgin Islands, helped finance the *Opportunity* awards for writers and was considered by David Levering Lewis one of the notables fostering the Harlem Renaissance, a black patron of African American expressive arts in his own right. Walrond dedicated the first edition of *Tropic Death* to him. Holstein, an early supporter of Garvey's Universal Negro Improvement Association, also wrote several articles on the condition of Virgin Islanders, including one highly critical of the United States' management of the islands. See Casper Holstein, "The Virgin Islands" *Opportunity* 3, no. 34 (October 1925): 304–6.
20. Underwood, "Some Negro Poets", 37.
21. Four letters from Walrond to Underwood are located in the Edna Worthley Underwood Collection at Pittsburg State University in Pittsburg, Kansas. Thanks to James Davis of Brooklyn College for pointing this out to us and to librarian Janette Mauk for making this material available.
22. Eric Walrond, "Adventures in Misunderstanding: A Personal Experience", *World Tomorrow* (April 1926): 111. The Davis letter is in a private collection.
23. Letter quoted in Lewis, *Harlem*, 115.
24. Underwood, "Some Negro Poets", 36, 37.
25. Edna Worthley Underwood, letter to Charles S. Johnson, 15 March 1925. Located in the Charles S. Johnson file, Fisk University, Box 61, Folder 4.

26. Eric Walrond, "'The Penitent' Shows Alexander Pushkin, Russia's Great Negro Poet, Was Influenced by Shelley", *Negro World* (21 October 1922): 3.
27. This is similar to Edouard Glissant's theory of errantry set forth in *The Poetics of Relation*, trans. Betsy Wing (Ann Arbor: University of Michigan Press, 1977), 11–17.
28. See, for example, "The New Negro Faces America" and "Imperator Africanus: Marcus Garvey: Menace or Promise" both in Walrond, *"Winds"*.
29. Underwood, "Some Negro Poets", 37.
30. Underwood, "Negro Poets", 39.
31. Wade, "Re-Imagining", 3–27.
32. Underwood, "Some Negro Poets", 37.
33. Bone points to what he considers a "fundamental contradiction" in Walrond's early work. "On the one hand, he adopts the myth of primitivism and works within its terms. Influenced by the writings of [Pierre] Loti (1850–1923) and [Lafcadio] Hearn (1850–1904), and encouraged by the climate of the times, he explores the theme of atavism in its various ramifications. On the other hand, in his secret heart he endorses the missionary point of view. He believes in racial progress up the evolutionary level into some ineffable White Heaven. In consequence, he cannot really bring himself to celebrate the primitive. *Tropic Death* is in fact the veiled confession of a colonized black that he cannot return to his primitive sources" (*Down Home*, 202–3).
34. See Zora Neale Hurston, *I Love Myself When I Am Laughing . . . and Then Again When I Am Looking Mean and Impressive: A Zora Neale Hurston Reader*, ed. Alice Walker and Mary Helen Washington, 156–62 (New York: Feminist Press, 1979).
35. Underwood, "Some Negro Poets", 57.
36. Underwood, "Negro Poets", 37.
37. See Walrond, *"Winds"*, 310–14.
38. For more on these pieces and Walrond's hospitalization, see Carl A. Wade and Louis J. Parascandola, "In Search of Asylum: Eric Walrond's *Roundway Review* Writings, 1952–1957", *Journal of Caribbean Studies* 19 , nos. 1 and 2 (2004–5): 21–42.
39. Wade, "Re-Imagining", 3–27.
40. See Bone, *Down Home*, 185–94. See also the anonymous essay (almost certainly by Walrond) "Of Lafcadio Hearn" *Negro World* (3 June 1922): 4.
41. The Henry Allen Moe papers, 1920–1975, are lodged at the American Philosophical Society, Philadelphia. We are indebted to the society's website (www.amphilsoc.org) for much of this information on Henry Moe. In time, Moe's designation would change from secretary to secretary general (1937–1961; president, 1961–1963; president emeritus, 1970–1975). Among the many awards given in his honour are the Henry Allen Moe Prize in Humanities awarded by the American Philosophical Society; the Henry Allen Moe Prize for Catalogs

of Distinction in the Arts, awarded by the New York Historical Association; the Dr Henry Allen Moe Award for Nursing Excellence, presented by Bassett Health Care, Cooperstown, New York (Moe was chairman of the board). Moe's text, *The Power of Freedom in Human Affairs* (Philadelphia: American Philosophical Society, 1977) was published posthumously.

42. Underwood, "Some Negro Poets", 36.
43. Zora Neale Hurston's correspondence with Moe is also illustrative of this type of partnership, unlike that which she endured with Mason. Her letters to Moe are often informal, even coquettish; in one she refers to him as "busha", a Jamaican Creole name for a (white) overseer, to which Moe replies that the fellows are the real "bushas". She writes to him not only about grant-related activities but of other experiences, in Jamaica and elsewhere. On no occasion is Moe shown to be more understanding than when Hurston is robbed in Jamaica of her cash and letter of credit from the Guggenheim Foundation. Apart from protecting the foundation's funds, Moe ensures that Hurston receives replacement finances, and offers words of solace to the embarrassed and humiliated writer. "Don't feel so sad," Moe writes, "and don't be so apologetic. The first day I ever had a letter of credit I lost it; but I was lucky and I got it back again. So I don't myself feel at all superior to anyone who had such a document stolen" (3 May 1936). There are also solicitous comments about her health, and complimentary observations on her work in other letters. The correspondence between Moe and Walrond, and Hurston respectively, was made available courtesy of the Guggenheim Foundation.
44. The story is often told that Walrond frittered his time and his award money in Europe, achieving little of substance during this period. See, for example, Michel Fabre, *From Harlem to Paris: Black American Writers in France, 1840–1980* (Urbana: University of Illinois Press, 1991), 138–39.
45. Walrond submitted a trade dummy of "The Big Ditch" in support of his application for a Guggenheim Fellowship. He wrote to Moe on 17 December 1927 explaining that serialization of the manuscript had not yet been possible owing to dissatisfaction on the part of editors. Even though there is even a reference to the work as a published text, complete with price and page numbers (Elizabeth Lay Green, *The Negro in American Literature: An Outline for Individual and Group Study* [Chapel Hill: University of North Carolina Press, 1928], 50–53, 68), there can be no question, especially when we read Walrond's correspondence from 1960, that "The Big Ditch" was never published. Underwood confirms this with her report that "New York papers were now advertising briskly his great novel about Panama and the Big Ditch as forthcoming. But it did not materialise" ("Some Negro Poets", 37) According to a letter signed by Donald S. Freide, vice president of Boni and Liveright, dated 27 January 1927, Walrond was con-

tracted to that firm to publish this text subtitled "A Romantic History of the Panama Canal". This work is not to be confused with "The Second Battle", although the latter is clearly a variant of "The Big Ditch".

46. On both occasions, Ruth Walrond stated that she had no idea how her son could be contacted.
47. Kenneth Ramchand, "The Writer Who Ran Away: Eric Walrond and *Tropic Death*", *Savacou: Journal of the Caribbean Artists Movement* 2 (September 1970): 75.
48. Charles Johnson's letters to Ethel Ray Williams (formerly Nance) are housed in the Bancroft Library, University of California, Berkeley.
49. Dunkley Jr, "White Patronage", 1253.

8

A PRISM SO STRANGE
The Biography of Eric Walrond

JAMES DAVIS

MY INTEREST IN ERIC WALROND was sparked by an odd discrepancy between what I had read about him in histories of the Harlem Renaissance and a document I came across in the Columbia University special collections library. I was researching the publicity practices of Boni and Liveright Publishers on behalf of their African American authors, of which Walrond was one. The others, Jesse Fauset and Jean Toomer, were better known than Walrond, about whom I knew only that he had not published another book after *Tropic Death* in 1926. But there in Boni and Liveright's fall 1928 catalogue was "The Big Ditch", Walrond's history of the Panama Canal. Could the scholars have missed this? Of course not. Walrond's failure to publish "The Big Ditch" was corroborated by several critics. What was the nature then of the mistake that led to its inclusion in the 1928 publicity materials? Had Walrond rescinded the manuscript? Had Horace Liveright decided to publish it sight unseen, as he was known to do, and then voided the contract after the catalogue had gone to press? The idiosyncratic stories in *Tropic Death* had made me curious about Walrond, but this mystery piqued my interest. I began to play detective. The more closely I looked into existing accounts of Walrond's life and work, the more glaring the gaps in the record appeared, inviting further investigation.

It quickly became clear that I was not alone in observing that Walrond's work was worth reconsidering. But the number of scholars making the observation far surpassed those actually doing the reconsidering. Forty years ago, Kenneth Ramchand, author of a foundational study, *The West Indian Novel and*

Its Background, wrote the first sustained scholarly article about Walrond in the Jamaican journal *Savacou*, calling him "one of the most imaginative and technically accomplished writers ever to come out of these [Caribbean] islands".[1] But it took almost thirty years for another article on Walrond to appear in a scholarly journal.[2] The intervening years saw a dramatic reassessment of the Harlem Renaissance, including studies that brought once obscure figures to light (such as Zora Neale Hurston, Jean Toomer and Nella Larsen) and reinterpreted established ones (such as Claude McKay, Langston Hughes and James Weldon Johnson). Walrond was not among those rediscovered, despite regular references to his prominence and talent.[3]

What also became clear was how ill-fitting was the one-hit-wonder label that had affixed itself to Walrond. In fact, he was much more than *Tropic Death*. Even if we confine ourselves to his time in New York, it is clear that he was at the centre, socially and institutionally, of the Harlem Renaissance. He was associate editor at *Negro World*, the journal of the Universal Negro Improvement Association. Disillusioned with Garveyism, he left to work as business manager at *Opportunity*, the journal of the National Urban League. These two journals were, along with the National Association for the Advancement of Colored People's *Crisis*, among the highest circulating black periodicals in the country and, particularly in *Opportunity*'s case, were vital to advancing literature and the arts. He soon began placing work in mainstream venues such as *Vanity Fair*, *Forbes*, *New Republic* and *Smart Set*. His close friends included the poets Countee Cullen and Gwendolyn Bennett, the painter Aaron Douglas, and Carl Van Vechten, the white author of the controversial *Nigger Heaven*. But in fact he knew everyone. "Anyone who ever met him remembered him", said Ethel Ray Nance, a friend and colleague at *Opportunity*. "[H]e may not have been six feet, [but] you would think of him as being tall. . . . He was of slight build, had flashing eyes, [and] his face was very alert and very alive. . . . He was very pleasant, but as soon as he entered the room you knew he was there."[4] Shirley Graham, the writer who would later marry W.E.B. Du Bois, was an early admirer of Walrond, whom she described as "handsome as a Greek god, done in ebony".[5] He had married a Jamaican woman, Edith Cadogan, soon after arriving in New York. Three years and three daughters later, he packed them off on a steamer to Kingston and had nothing more to do with them. He had entered a new universe.

In the two years after the publication of *Tropic Death*, Walrond's career took off. He guest edited a special Caribbean issue of *Opportunity*, placed a story in the inaugural issue of the *American Caravan*, an annual anthology that included leading modernist writers, secured a $1,000 advance for a second book with Boni and Liveright, and won three prestigious competitions: a Harmon Foundation Award "for Excellence in Literary Achievement by a Negro", a Zona Gale Scholarship to study creative writing at the University of Wisconsin, and a Guggenheim Fellowship to conduct research in the Caribbean. Of the first 168 recipients of the Guggenheim award, only three were black: Countee Cullen, Walter White and Eric Walrond. When asked by the Harmon Foundation "why you endorse this candidate for this award", Donald Friede, vice-president at Boni and Liveright, wrote, "Because I believe him to be *the* outstanding Negro prose writer of this country, and because I believe that his work will in time place him among the important writers in America – both Negro and white."[6] Robert Herrick, writing in the *New Republic*, saw "no discernible reason why the creator of *Tropic Death* should not go much farther in this field, which he has quite to himself, the sense of which is all in his blood, its color and its human complexity".[7] These were major accolades for someone who a few years earlier held a clerical position in a downtown Manhattan hospital, commuting from a West Indian enclave in Bedford-Stuyvesant.

All of which begged the question, Why hadn't a biography been written? The closest approximation was the introduction to Louis Parascandola's *"Winds Can Wake Up the Dead": An Eric Walrond Reader*.[8] Extensively researched, Parascandola's essay marked a major advance beyond the woefully incomplete accounts of Walrond's career that appeared in critical accounts and reference texts. Each paragraph contained in condensed form kernels of entire chapters that deserved to be developed. But Parascandola also indicated why a proper biography had not yet been written and indeed perhaps *could* not be written.

One factor was the problem that Walrond's status as an immigrant to and then expatriate from the United States posed to what was seen with some justification as a story about African Americans. As a West Indian, Walrond has not fit neatly into the dominant Harlem Renaissance historiography, which revolves around a nationalist narrative of rural, Southern folk coming north in the Great Migration and consolidating the social and institutional basis for new intellectual, political and artistic movements among black Americans.

This narrative has always accommodated certain versions of internationalism – the education of W.E.B. Du Bois in a German university, Claude McKay's sojourns in Russia, France and Morocco, and the summers that Harlem figures occasionally spent in Paris, for example. And of course Africa has been an important presence in this historiography, but mainly as a muse or an abstract problem. The role of Caribbean émigrés in Harlem's cultural ferment, though well documented, did not factor significantly in the mainstream scholarship.[9] On one side of the 1920s, Walrond's origins – Barbadian by way of British Guiana and Panama – presented complications for the nationalist narrative; on the other side, his departure from the United States in 1929 and subsequent decline in productivity effectively relegated him to the margins of this narrative.

Certain practical obstacles also militated against a biography. Walrond left little documentation of his life beyond his published work. Because he died in obscurity, few efforts were made to preserve or collect the extant material. What remains is scattered in far-flung special collections, in the files of the foundations from which he received support, in the papers of W.W. Norton Publishers, which bought Boni and Liveright, and in a few brittle binders in the possession of one of Walrond's daughters. Even an intrepid researcher finds, in synthesizing these materials, that the gaps and silences that remain represent long stretches of time. A plausible narrative can withstand only so much speculation; when the trail of letters, telegrams, unpublished manuscripts and datebooks grows cold, as it often does in Walrond's case, one makes do with the correspondence of his friends and associates, and even then one is compelled to concede that the record is incomplete, perhaps irrevocably so.

Nevertheless, the late Robert Bone, professor of English at Columbia University and author of such pioneering studies as *The Negro Novel in America* and *Down Home: Origins of the Afro-American Short Story*,[10] thought Walrond worthy of biographical treatment and set to work on one in the early 1980s. Bone compiled a thorough bibliography of Walrond's many journalistic writings, ranging from the prominent to the obscure, and drafted several chapters that especially illuminate Walrond's family background and early years, eventually securing a contract for the book with Harvard University Press.[11] At a critical point in this process, however, Bone confronted another of the obstacles to the production of a Walrond biography: the fraught relationship of the descendants to his legacy. Frank Stewart, Walrond's grandson, was Bone's collaborator and conducted extensive research. Though they shared a commitment to recovering Walrond for posterity, Stewart was family while Bone was a scholar; their investments in the project differed. Because his grandfather had deserted his family, Stewart knew Walrond only through his published writing and through the accounts of his mother and aunts, which were, at best, conflicted.[12] Perhaps it is not surprising, then, given the emotionally charged nature of the project, that the planned biography never appeared. In large part, however, it has been through the kind cooperation and encouragement of Frank Stewart's mother, Dorothy, her daughter Joan and Dorothea Bone, Robert Bone's wife, that Louis Parascandola and his sometime collaborator, Carl A. Wade of the University of the West Indies, have managed to build on the work that Bone and Stewart began three decades ago. As Joan Stewart observes, "It is a time to heal."[13]

If it was the detective work of historical recovery that first provoked my interest in Walrond, what sustained it was the potent combination of intellectual issues his career raises. These are issues that have animated recent scholarship in transnational American studies and are distinct from the concerns of previous generations of scholars. For Bone, as for other critics of his generation, the story of Walrond's career is one of unfulfilled talent, a story of interesting, poignant failure, but failure nonetheless. The analysis runs along two basic lines: one, that Walrond never recovered from his father's desertion of the family, a childhood trauma he continually worked through but never resolved in his fiction or his life; the other, that a multiple transplanted intellectual in exile such as Walrond is by definition a fragmented subject without a cultural identity or path to self-knowledge. Certainly, there is evidence to support this analysis in Walrond's case, not the least of which is Walrond's own account of his preoccupations, goals and anxieties. However, our current critical moment allows us to examine the presuppositions underwriting this analysis and pose alternatives.

Locating such determinative effects in the trauma of the absent father, for example, however forcefully it bore on Walrond's mind and imagination, flattens a great deal of the complexity of his career into a mechanical Freudian psychodrama.[14] Casting Walrond as psychologically damaged, this analysis presupposes a "whole" or "well" individual subject for whom the Freudian family romance operates more favourably. The second line of analysis presupposes something similar but at the level of the social rather than the individual. Though plenty of expatriate writers have struggled with feelings of alienation and cultural displacement, we make a fetish of national identity if we ignore the ways in which writers have also managed to affiliate themselves transnationally or the ways in which cultures – the forms and traditions writers adopt and adapt – tend to transgress national borders. It is indisputable that Walrond's successive relocations were profoundly unsettling, but national identity and the stability of cultural traditions attending it are no guarantees of a whole, undamaged selfhood that is the precondition for great writing.

Particularly in the case of the Caribbean, observers from Stuart Hall to Edouard Glissant to Michelle Stephens have argued that the "identity" of this region is characterized precisely by the *tension* between the struggle for national sovereignty and the compulsory internationalism of empire, the slave trade and the diasporic movement of people within and from the region.[15] Would Eric Walrond's cultural identity have remained intact had he stayed in his birthplace of British Guiana? Perhaps he could then be claimed as the literary forebear of Edgar Mittelholzer, Jan Carew and Wilson Harris, though it is difficult to imagine careers more productively contaminated by multiple national affiliations than these. What happens when we look to someplace like British Guiana for the elements of the stable cultural identity that would sustain self-knowledge and nurture individual talent? The Guianese intellectual A.J. Seymour posed exactly this exercise for himself in a 1949 review of T.S. Eliot's *Notes toward a Definition of Culture* in one of the first literary journals in the Caribbean, *Kyk-over-Al*. Having rehearsed Eliot's list of the signal features of English culture, Seymour slyly challenged the hierarchy implicit in Eliot's assertion of the integrity and significance of English culture:

> The list Eliot offered in the book prompted me with a gleam of mischief to match it from Guiana and to suggest our culture in Guiana has the sun and malaria, and August sports and Kaieteur, and black pudding and souse and pepperpot and qwehqweh dances and Tadgah; and sugar, the Sea Wall and little white wooden houses standing on stilts out of flood water, and crowded matinees and porknockers.[16]

Even if we take Seymour to be strictly in earnest, to be claiming that Guianese culture is as distinctive and extensive as anything England offers, we must acknowledge the splendidly hybrid quality of his list – the juxtaposition of "souse and pepperpot and qwehqweh dances", for example, marking out lexically the multivalent strains that "distinguish" Guianese culture. Indeed, from the perspective of non-Caribbean observers, British Guiana's culture has seemed quite hopelessly illegible and incoherent. In his 1957 account *British Guiana: The Land of Six Peoples*, the English diplomat Michael Swan speculated: "It would take, I imagine, half the lifetime of a social anthropologist to define the structure of Georgetown society accurately; to plot the relationship between the various peoples, the Chinese, Indians, Negroes, coloured people, high coloured people, British and Portuguese, not to mention the results of miscegenation between all, would require the subtlety of a Guianese Proust."[17]

Had Eric Walrond remained at home, perhaps we would have had our Guianese Proust, recognizably situated in a national tradition that cultivated his individual talent. But I would suggest that our desire to identify the sources of Walrond's struggles – literary and psychological – need not make recourse to reductive notions of national identity. Moreover, recent developments in post-colonial studies allow us to re-examine a conventional trope of the Caribbean intellectual as stuck in a debilitating bind, caught between the Scylla of Victorian English gentility and the Charybdis of African primitivism. To be sure, a great deal of pressure was exerted on Caribbean intellectuals to fashion themselves after English gentlemen. As Belinda Edmondson has argued, "For nonwhite, non-English men to make the case for self-government, they [had to] state their case as gentlemen, which means they [had to], in essence be 'made' into Englishmen."[18] Nevertheless, observers have been too willing to cast these figures as cultural schizophrenics, confused or even paralysed to inaction by the appeals of conflicting cultural forces – white civilization and the pre-modernity of the Negro – ostensibly locked in an inexorable antagonism.[19] Reassessing Walrond's career requires that we unpack the shopworn figure of the tragic colonial intellectual.

For Bone, Walrond's writing is Gothic, and the reason he went Gothic was "to express the primitive and atavistic features of his heritage":

> Underlying Walrond's whole career is the tragic dilemma of the black Englishman. A British colonial by birth and early education, he remained throughout his life what the French would call an *évolué*. That is the inner logic of his successive moves . . . the outward and visible emblems of a spiritual journey: the

> black Briton's pilgrimage to Westminster. Walrond's life and work reveal the secret longing of the colonized black for whiteness, enlightenment, gentility, metropolitan sophistication, and similar marks of cultural "salvation". At the same time, Walrond's traumatic exposure to American racism drove him back upon his blackness. Recoiling from a civilization that was capable of such injustice, he turned in self-defence to the myth of primitivism. . . . He employed [the Gothic] to express that part of his personality which remained resistant to the white man's culture: the black, African, pagan, ungovernable, unassimilable, or in a word demonic self that stubbornly refused to be "redeemed". Walrond's excursion into demonism brings him to the brink of the abyss. Like Kurtz he journeys to the heart of darkness only to recoil from the horror.[20]

Bone identifies Walrond as a Gothic writer who equates the repressive Freudian superego with white civilization and the always incompletely repressed id with black barbarism. The Gothic characterization may be granted, but as an account of either Walrond's life or his fiction the rest is far too schematic.[21] The chain of signifiers – "black, African, pagan, ungovernable, unassimilable, or in a word demonic" – rarely operates without disruption or inversion in Walrond's work.[22] Bone's account strains under the weight of its own reified categories: "It is on the rock of primitivism that Walrond's art eventually founders. In the end his anglicized sensibility prevents him from mounting a convincing demonstration of his chosen myth."[23]

Walrond's art does occasionally founder, but not on the rock of primitivism. He maintained throughout his career a healthy scepticism towards the mythology of white civilization; the binaries on which this discourse rests – European reason and African unreason chief among them – simply did not survive his experiences in a series of racially diverse societies. As traumatic as his confrontation with US racism was, it was preceded by his intimate acquaintance with racial segregation in the Panama Canal Zone and with the forms of violence perpetrated by or in the name of European civilization in the West Indies. If he "recoiled from a civilization that was capable of such injustice", he had been doing so long before arriving in the United States and had formed a nuanced, critical perspective on Anglo-European cultures. If his "traumatic exposure to racism drove him back upon his blackness", it was a blackness he had embraced long before coming to the United States, and it did not resemble a cartoonish heathen in a Conradian jungle.[24] With Walrond, as with other twentieth-century Caribbean intellectuals, our analytical framework must be alert to agency not just abjection, to negotiation not just surrender.[25]

In fact, Walrond was as alert as any observer of his time to the extraordinary complexity of African diaspora experience. One of the most compelling reasons to tell his story, it seemed to me, was the larger story about intra-racial differences onto which it opens. In an important sense his biography is about the tension between notions of racial identity and community, on one hand, and the differences, on the other hand, in ethnicity, class, religion and language that cut across race but are subsumed and obscured by categories such as those Walrond negotiated: *black, Negro, coloured*. Above all else, Walrond's writing is concerned with staging this tension, with clarifying the importance of both impulses, examining the hidden injuries this tension produces and the inner resources it requires, but refusing to resolve it. His biography, I felt, was a story not about the West Indies, Panama, Harlem, France or England, but about their relation to one another, filaments in the fabric of the twentieth-century Caribbean diaspora.

The other story that I felt Walrond's story would allow me to tell is of the fitful transition from traditional forms of colonialism, such as the English form he grew up with in the Caribbean, to the distinctively modern form of neo-colonialism that the Panama Canal represented. The US practice of "colonialism without colonies", as some critics call it, effectively took over where the declining European powers left off, improving on its errors in public relations and in orchestrating the interests of the state, corporations, investors and workers. As Michelle Stephens has noted, Walrond

> understood, as early as the 1920s, what it meant to say that the Caribbean was, in modernity, an American sea. The presence of the United States as an economic force in the Caribbean, and a political force in the world at the beginning of the twentieth century, meant a story of economic and cultural integration between the United States and the Caribbean as early as the 1920s. This is a story that has yet to be fully told in the fields of African American, Caribbean or American literature.[26]

The complexity of competing colonialisms found early, incisive expression in Walrond's writing. In fact, he spent much of his life after 1928 trying to complete the book, "The Big Ditch", that would use the case of Panama to illuminate the conditions and implications of these geopolitical shifts.

Although these stories about intra-racial difference and colonial history remained central to my understanding of Walrond's career, as my research continued I became more familiar with Walrond as a person, and these stories had to be made to accommodate the full human dimensions of his tumultuous life. It became impossible to think of him as simply the repository of a particular set of ideas, the producer of certain kinds of texts, or the representative of certain categories: the West Indian, the exile, the black intellectual, the struggling writer. This level of abstraction, though comfortable for the scholar, was not sustainable after having visited, for example, the New Jersey home of Walrond's only surviving daughter and poring over her father's papers while her advanced age and illness prevented her even from meeting my eye, much less discussing her father. Nor did my abstractions survive the conversations I had with his former neighbours from the 1940s in the English town of Bradford on Avon. Perhaps it was because they were unaware that he had been a decorated writer in New York that their recollections tended towards the quotidian. For them, Walrond was an eccentric but quiet presence. The only black man in a town of four thousand residents, he kept mainly to himself, they told me, engaging in polite conversation, playing with the rabbits and chickens that the children of Ivy Terrace kept in their yards, and disappearing for stretches of time so long, they said, that they suspected he was involved in "the war effort". Even Colón, Panama, I found so redolent today of the anxious poverty about which Walrond wrote that Bottle Alley and the six-story tenement into which his mother moved the family in 1911 became, in my mind, more than mere conventions of the Caribbean "street novel". The distinctive individuality that emerges in the course of reconstructing a life challenges the biographer to integrate the academic with the human dimensions of the subject. One informs the other, and they keep each other honest.

Another aspect of Walrond's life whose significance I was slow to appreciate was his struggle with depression. Initially it seemed like a discrete event (Walrond admitted himself for treatment to the Roundway Hospital from 1952 to 1957) that was of little importance to his career outside of these years. I may have minimized his depression because the archetype of the modern writer (who among them was not emotionally tormented?) prevented me from making careful distinctions. I was unaware of how prevalent mental illness was among this generation's Caribbean writers in exile; my research led me to other prominent instances. Most of all, I failed to grasp how depression operates, the extent to which it fundamentally informs and deforms experience. The novelist William Styron wrote, "Depression is a disorder of mood, so mysteriously painful and elusive in the way it becomes known to the self . . . as to verge close to being beyond description . . . . The pain of severe depression is quite unimaginable to those who have not suffered it."[27] The more I learned about Walrond's life, the clearer it became that he was more or less continually managing his condition, that it was not an ancillary topic, not a local irruption into an otherwise stable psyche.[28] It affected his work all along, to varying degrees. This is not to say simply that all – or any – of his fiction reveals "symptoms of depression". Rather, he was almost always writing along the seams where the discourse of racial *grievance* meets the discourse of racial *grief*.[29] In my view, Walrond wrote fiction because the discourse of racial grievance to which he initially turned – Garvey's militant nationalism, the National Urban League's integrationist sociology – were inadequate to fully expressing racial grief, which was for Walrond the primary arena of struggle.

We should recall here the poem "Incident", which Countee Cullen dedicated to Walrond, his friend and colleague at *Opportunity*. Having been called "nigger" by a white boy his own age, the speaker concludes,

> I saw the whole of Baltimore
> From May until December;
> Of all the things that happened there,
> That's all that I remember.[30]

It is among Cullen's most directly confrontational poems, but it is important not to miss its dramatization of the production of racial grief as something inexpressible in the register of grievance. Like the speaker in "Incident", the most biographical of Walrond's work exhibits a profound racial melancholia, which Ann Anlin Cheng has identified as both "a *sign* of rejection and a psychic *strategy* in response to that rejection".[31] More than documenting racial slights and insults, his work is concerned with the management of the grief that ensues. As James Baldwin would later write about "the rage of the disesteemed", Walrond knew that racial grief "can only with difficulty, and never entirely, be brought under the domination of the intelligence and is therefore not susceptible to any arguments whatever"; that it "cannot be hidden, it can only be dissembled".[32] Walrond also knew that a materialist account of history had to reckon with the affective dimension of experience – or as Baldwin put it, that "rage, so generally discounted, so little understood even among the people whose daily bread it is, is one of the things that makes history".[33]

In close connection to the question of depression, it has been necessary to reframe the rhetoric of failure attending Walrond's career. His letters indicate that he was more aware than anyone of his failure to fulfil the expectations he had created in New York. The biographer, confronted with regular hand-wringing and furrowed brows throughout the critical commentary and the primary documents, has a few different options. One option, which I pursued first, is to reject the failure label outright. I analysed the writing he'd done after Harlem and developed what I still think is a good case for its significance.[34] But there remains something indisputable about his dramatic decline in productivity and the uneven quality of much of his later work. I realized that his failures could not simply be denied by calling them successes by another set of standards or chalking them up to rotten luck. But what I also realized is that failure can be as significant and as revealing as success, that it ought to be handled imaginatively and resourcefully. Thus, even if the latter half of his career failed by any reasonable measure to fulfil the promise of the former, we ought to better grasp the conditions of possibility for such a failure, not only in terms of Walrond's own life but also in terms of the institutions of English publishing in the 1930s to 1950s.

Was it possible for black West Indian writers – writers whose work was marked by their blackness or their West Indianness – to get published at this time? Yes, it was. But one need only look to V.S. Naipaul, the most commercially successful West Indian expatriate writer, to understand how assiduously even the most gifted had to work to place their writing, and how common was failure among them. Despite his freshly minted degree from Oxford and his relentless determination, Naipaul struggled to get anything in print and suffered a nervous breakdown in 1952. Without the support and encouragement of his English wife, Naipaul claims, he would have taken his own life. Two years later, still without much to show for himself, he narrowly averted another crisis. "I felt all my old nervous breakdown insensibly overpowering me & making the world dark & unreal", he wrote to his wife, "I know you don't believe in breakdowns; but take my word – What happens is this: one's life is so unsatisfactory, so terribly insecure, so haunted by fear & doubt & sense of failure – that the mind in a clever beastly way removes attention from these truths so hard to swallow, and fixes it on an alien dread." Naipaul's biographer says that "the breakthrough without which he would have gone on sinking" came a few weeks later in the form of a job offer from the BBC, a three-month contract to host the radio programme *Caribbean Voices*. "That saved my life really," Naipaul recalled, "I was living more or less at the limit of despair."[35]

Thus, to the stories I set out to tell – the dramas of intra-racial difference and the uneven transition from traditional to modern forms of colonialism – I was compelled to add these other stories about the complexities of depression and the rhetoric of failure haunting Walrond's career. A visit to London prompted further reflection on the position – geographically and temporally – from which we evaluate success and failure. I had been studying the black anticolonial activists and writers in 1930s England and was deeply impressed with them: with the movements they had launched, with the shrewdness of their analysis of the "colour bar" in England and colonial policies abroad, with their advances in bringing about the end of empire.[36] I expected that my research in London would deepen my understanding and confirm my admiration. It did. What I did not expect was how forcefully London *itself* would change my perspective on these developments about which I had been reading. I had spent a fair amount of time in London but had never been to Parliament. Visiting Parliament – walking its hallowed halls and sitting in on the morning session at the House of Commons – confronted me in a way that no reading ever could with the imposing authority of the English state. Everything about the place conspired to produce a profound sense of unassailable tradition, from the architecture and the paintings to the bearing of the clerks and the performances of the members of Parliament themselves. "We are English", they seemed to say, "We bend to no one. It has always been thus, and always will be. We welcome you: witness the grandeur and soundness with which we govern, the greatest system in human history." It seemed to me that Parliament communicated something very different from, say, Capitol Hill, the White House or the palace at Versailles. It embodied in every fibre and polite gesture a quality of impenetrable certainty and self-assurance, of being beyond reproach, of having endured all and enlisted the best and the brightest in the maintenance of its vision for humanity.

This was the enormous construct, the imposing physical and ideological edifice of the state against which a congeries of loosely affiliated pan-Africanists and anticolonials arrayed themselves in the 1930s. Recalling this, my first thought was how silly I had been to imagine them as important. They had assumed proportions in my imagination that now seemed absurdly exaggerated – as though anyone could really touch this state, match wits with it, force concessions from it. My next thought, however, was quite different, for I realized that it was precisely this unassailability that made their efforts so audacious. Confronted with the massive, concentrated authority of the English state, with government buildings the size of entire villages in their home countries, with a discursive rhetoric of impervious superiority and a visual rhetoric to match it, these expatriates and colonial subjects somehow remained undaunted and resolved, month in and month out, to take on the whole elaborate apparatus. I left with a new appreciation for the sheer audacity of their efforts and the results they yielded. In post-colonial studies we are so accustomed to the David and Goliath battle between colonial subjects and colonial authority, so invested in the narrative that produces David's triumph as the inevitable conclusion, that we lose sight of the unlikelihood, even the imprudence, of his having taken up arms to begin with.

Finally, I sought to resist the tendency among North American scholars to cast the Caribbean as an undifferentiated mass of islands and to identify the specificity of Panama. Seven of the ten stories in *Tropic Death* are set there, as is much of his other fiction and of course his ill-fated history, "The Big Ditch". Introducing himself to readers of *Success Magazine*, a New York pulp, in 1924 Walrond wrote,

> I am spiritually a native of Panama. I owe the sincerest kind of allegiance to it.
> For –
> I grew up there.
> I went to school there.
> I began working there.
> I had my first struggles there.
> I had my first – and possibly my only – love affair there.
> I studied and played truant – I rambled and roamed and adventured – all there.[37]

Predictably, the canal looms as large in Panamanian cultural history as in its geography. However, this history is highly contested and one key site of struggle in the effort to frame it is the presence and role of Afro-Caribbean nationals. Because they mainly supplied the manual labour rather than the engineering skills employed in the canal construction – the brawn to back the North Americans' brains, as the story goes – the Afro-Caribbean nationals who migrated to Panama by the tens of thousands have a tenuous place in the mythology of the canal.[38] In the triumphalist narrative that prevailed for most of the twentieth century, they worked (and in many cases died) for the noble cause of uniting the seas, enhancing global trade and securing the hemisphere against unwanted military incursions. In the countervailing narrative of US neo-imperialism that has emerged in the past thirty years, they are pawns in a hegemonic struggle among nations in the global north. Neither narrative does justice to the complexity of the experience of Afro-Caribbean nationals in the region or affords them historical agency. Rhonda Frederick addresses this when she writes of "Colón Men" (as the Panamanian migrants were known throughout the West Indies) that they "participated in an exploitative project, but they learned more than victimization": "[T]hey used their work experiences to revise the ways exploitation defined them. . . . [T]hey were not limited by the views of their supervisors; they possessed their own agendas, ones that contested their officially denigrated bodies and labor. This reclamation manifested as their revised vision of themselves. Examples of Colón Men's social existence complicate the view of these men as slaves to economic trends or passive victims of railroad and canal officials."[39] In some instances, Walrond's work seems to reinforce the portrayal of Afro-Caribbean nationals in Panama as victims (for example, *Tropic Death*'s "Subjection" and "The Wharf Rats"). But as a whole, his work throws into relief the tremendous linguistic and cultural complexity Panama represented: West Indian lives conducted in a newly independent Latin American country under occupation by North Americans enforcing racial segregation.

When I visited Colón my cabdriver, Rigó, was, like many Afro-Panamanians of his generation, the grandchild of a canal builder. When I told him about the project that brought me to Panama, I was not surprised that he did not recognize the name Eric Walrond. Despite his having been among the earliest chroniclers of black life on the isthmus, Walrond is unknown outside of specialized academic circles in Panama because he published in North

America in English. What surprised me, however, was Rigó's unfamiliarity with the canal construction era more broadly. He was not an uneducated man, having left Colón to attend high school in Panama City. But he had not heard of the "silver roll" and "gold roll", the racially differentiated practices for compensation that extended into all arenas of social life in the Canal Zone, from housing to employment to education. He said his grandparents had emigrated from Barbados, but he did not know from which area, nor had he ever been there himself. When I showed him my copy of *Tropic Death* and read a passage about Colón's "Bottle Alley", he was vaguely interested but conceded that he could not make it very far in such a book because his reading ability in English was limited. His schooling had been exclusively in Spanish, as is the case with almost all Panamanians, so although he was raised in an English-speaking home of Barbadians and often spoke English with his fellow West Indians in Colón, the *lingua franca* in his community was Panamanian Spanish. This points to one of the many ironies of Afro-Caribbean history on the Isthmus of Panama. The backlash against the US occupation that mounted throughout the nationalist period of the 1960s to 1980s involved the assertion of *latinidad* in the face of North American hegemony. As Spanish was revived as the official resurgent language of a country in which power had spoken in Yankee English, an unintended casualty was the residual English of the relatively powerless Afro-Panamanians. Efforts are being made to preserve the bicultural and bilingual quality of Afro-Panamanian life, as are efforts to recognize the signal achievement of West Indians in Panamanian history and their influence on Panamanian culture. They must contend with both the force of historical amnesia and with a highly stratified social structure in which Afro-Panamanians are disproportionately represented in a large urban underclass, conferring a stigma on blackness. Even the indigenous people of the isthmus have, despite their difference from Latin Americans and their extreme poverty, been more successfully embraced by the public rhetoric of contemporary Panamanian nationalism than Afro-Panamanians. For the first time in the history of the national census in Panama (begun in 1911) the 2010 census asks residents, "Does someone in this house regard him/herself as Negro (Black) or of African descent?"

Thus, not only is this an opportune time to re-evaluate the career of Eric Walrond for the fields of African American studies and British post-colonial studies, it is also an opportune time to revisit his work – or to introduce it, as the case may be – in relation to Caribbean studies. But rather than claim his work and legacy for one or another of these nationally or regionally defined fields, we should be alert to their failure in each case to account fully for the significance of his career. As with Walrond's own writing, these are productive failures, compelling us to reflect on the construction of our cultural histories, their various parochialisms, and the opportunities they present for thinking more rigorously and comparatively about cultures of the Afro-Caribbean diaspora.

NOTES

1. Kenneth Ramchand, "The Writer Who Ran Away: Eric Walrond and *Tropic Death*", *Savacou: Journal of the Caribbean Artists Movement* 2 (September 1970): 75.
2. Carl A. Wade, "African American Aesthetics and the Short Fiction of Eric Walrond", *CLA Journal* 42, no. 4 (June 1999): 403–29.
3. Sterling Brown recalled, "Eric Walrond was tremendous", and "his *Tropic Death* was really quite a book. *Tropic Death* and *Cane* were the brilliant high marks in fiction" of the movement. Charles Rowell, " 'Let Me Be with Old Jazzbo': An Interview with Sterling A. Brown", *Callaloo* 14, no. 4 (1991): 811. David Levering Lewis described *Tropic Death* as "one of the truly avant-garde literary experiments of the Harlem Renaissance, a prism so strange and many-sided" that even the chariest critics "saw its iridescence" (*When Harlem Was in Vogue* [New York: Vintage Books, 1982], 189). Robert Bone called *Tropic Death* "a notable achievement of the Harlem Renaissance . . . to be particularly treasured by American Negroes of West Indian descent as a pioneer attempt to grapple with" their heritage (*Down Home: Origins of the Afro-American Short Story* [New York: Columbia University Press, 1988], 203). Sandra Pouchet Pacquet included Walrond alongside Mary Prince, Mrs Seacole, George Campbell, Claude McKay and C.L.R. James, as "among those whose literary accomplishments helped establish (along with the oral literature of the folk) a basis for the emergence in the 1950s of a West Indian literary tradition" ("West Indian Autobiography", *Black American Literature Forum* 24, no. 2 [Summer 1990]: 359). George Hutchinson wrote that Walrond "deserves considerable further scrutiny, particularly in the current wave of interest in the cultural history of the 'Black Atlantic' " ("Review of *'Winds Can Wake Up the Dead': An Eric Walrond Reader*", *Resources for American Literary Study* 26, no. 1 [2000]: 134). Louis Parascandola, responsible for major advances in scholarship on Walrond, noted, "He is especially impor-

tant for his depiction of Black immigrant life during the 1920s, a subject that has not yet received the attention it deserves" (introduction to *"Winds Can Wake Up the Dead": An Eric Walrond Reader,* by Eric Walrond; ed Louis J. Parascandola, [Detroit: Wayne State University Press, 1998], 11).
4. Ethel Ray Nance interviewed by Ann Allen Shockley (1970). Charles S. Johnson Collection, Fisk University Library.
5. Gerald Horne, *Race Woman: The Lives of Shirley Graham Du Bois* (New York: New York University Press, 2000), 105.
6. Donald Friede correspondence, 31 August 1927, Box 51, Harmon Foundation, Inc., Records, Library of Congress.
7. Robert Herrick, review of *Tropic Death, New Republic,* 10 November 1926, 332.
8. Parascandola, introduction.
9. Typically, the West Indian background of Harlem Renaissance figures has been treated as "an incidental fact of biography", as Michelle Stephens writes, "relevant at most in terms of how their ethnicity shaped their individual projects as writers in the United States. Their Caribbean American ethnicity is much less often recognized as the embodiment of historical forces bringing the Caribbean and the United States into contact during the period of the Harlem Renaissance itself" ("Eric Walrond's *Tropic Death* and the Discontents of American Modernity", in *Prospero's Isles: The Presence of the Caribbean in the American Imaginary,* ed. Dianne Accaria-Zavala and Rudolfo Popelnik [London: Macmillan, 2004], 168).
10. Robert Bone, *The Negro Novel in America* (1958; rev. ed. New Haven: Yale University Press, 1965) and *Down Home.*
11. Correspondence between Bone and Harvard University Press is in the personal collection of Louis Parascandola.
12. A decade later, while living in Japan, Stewart published a long essay in the scholarly journal of a university with which he was affiliated. Frank E.L. Stewart, "Eric Walrond, *Tropic Death,* and the Predicament of the Colonial Expatriate Writer", *Studies in the Humanities and Sciences* (Hiroshima Shudo University) 38, no. 2 (1997): 29–88. Stewart's personal investment in framing his grandfather's life story is evident: "Early in his life, Walrond lost something which he tried to transform and replace with words. But words could not replace the estrangement he had experienced when a youth, and then the pain and disillusionment of a failed marriage. Nor would words relieve the guilt that would come to burden and haunt Walrond's life in his latter years. He had abandoned a young, loving and devoted wife just when she needed him most – when she was pregnant. . . . Walrond had sacrificed wife and family in the name of a 'Muse', as his youngest daughter described it, that lead [sic] him away from the most important things in life, things he was never able to recover or restore, less [sic] of all

redeem. He would never be able to atone for depriving his daughters of their father when they were children, girls, young women and mothers: Decades, formative years, entire young lives passed away in silence and indifference from their father. He deprived Edith's life of happiness. He was responsible for plunging her into long years of tears and bitterness, of cutting and wounding her so deeply, she never healed" (80).

13. Louis J. Parascandola and Carl A. Wade, eds., *In Search of Asylum: The Later Writings of Eric Walrond* (Gainesville: University Press of Florida, 2011), xi.

14. In Bone's view, "an absconding, improvident, and debauched father whose life ended in defeat and failure" was "the agent responsible for the earliest and undoubtedly most painful of [Walrond's] uprooting" (*Down Home*, 176). He continues, "Walrond's father, as his son perceives him, is a negative model or antiself: a grim warning of the fate in store for those who succumb to the lushness of the tropics. Walrond's father, in a word, is a backslider. To his son, he represents *blackness unredeemed* (which is to say, un-English). On the social plane, the father's indolence and irresponsibility threaten to declass his son, forcing him to live in hell (the Bottle Alley of his stories). On the psychological plane, he embodies his son's feelings of inferiority. For Walrond's fear of backsliding is at bottom a fear of failure. His father is an emblem of the worthlessness from which he flees, with the help of his mother, into white-collar respectability" (177–78).

15. See Stuart Hall, "Subjects in History: Making Diasporic Identities", *The House That Race Built*, ed. Wahneema Lubiano, 289–300 (New York: Vintage, 1998); Edouard Glissant, *Caribbean Discourse: Selected Essays* (Charlottesville: University of Virginia Press, 1999); Michelle Stephens, *Black Empire: The Masculine Global Imaginary of Caribbean Intellectuals in the United States, 1914–1962* (Durham: Duke University Press, 2005).

16. A.J. Seymour, "T.S. Eliot's *Notes toward a Definition of Culture*", *Kyk-over-Al* (June 1949): 33.

17. Quoted in Brackette Williams, *Stains on My Name, War in My Veins: Guyana and the Politics of Cultural Struggle* (Durham: Duke University Press, 1991), 131.

18. Belinda Edmondson, *Making Men: Gender, Literary Authority, and Women's Writing in Caribbean Narrative* (Durham: Duke University Press, 1999), 5.

19. V.S. Naipaul furnished one of the most familiar accounts of the disabling predicament of Caribbean writers in *The Middle Passage* (London: André Deutsch, 1962), in which he declared the Caribbean without history and thus uninteresting, if not uninhabitable, for the novelist. By contrast, consider the alternative conception C.L.R. James presents in *Beyond a Boundary* (London: Stanley Paul and Co., 1963), which identifies in no uncertain terms the profound effect of English culture on James's boyhood in Trinidad (the same island on

which Naipaul grew up) but with equal vividness depicts the generative and unpredictable ways in which "native" (Trinidadian) and "foreign" (English) cultural traditions informed and inflected one another.

20. Bone, *Down Home*, 173–74.
21. For a more materialist and in my view compelling account of the Gothic in Caribbean fiction, see chapter 4 ("Gothic Americas") in Joan Dayan, *Haiti, History, and the Gods* (Berkeley: University of California Press, 1995).
22. I tend to agree with Michelle Stephens's characterization instead: "Many modernists would turn to the Caribbean and Africa for fetishes of the primitive that they hoped would help animate their own creative work. Walrond attempted to counter these exoticized images of the Caribbean with a grimmer, materialist reality" ("Walrond's *Tropic Death*", 169).
23. Bone, *Down Home*, 174.
24. George Hutchinson claims that Walrond's "point of view . . . looks back at that of 'Heart of Darkness' from the other side of the 'veil', almost exactly inverting Conrad's perspective and blurring his stark white/black duality" (*The Harlem Renaissance in Black and White* [Cambridge, MA: Harvard University Press, 1997], 409).
25. The terms here are borrowed from Ann Anlin Cheng, introduction to *The Melancholy of Race: Psychoanalysis, Assimilation, and Hidden Grief* (Oxford: Oxford University Press, 2000), 17. Robert Reid-Pharr writes similarly of the value in challenging some of our most cherished narratives about African American history in order to restore the agency of actual African Americans, whose blackness has come to stand for a version of static, inert subjectivity, history's products rather than history's producers. See Robert Reid-Pharr, *Once You Go Black: Choice, Desire, and the Black American Intellectual* (New York: New York University Press, 2007).
26. Stephens, "Eric Walrond's *Tropic Death*", 175–76.
27. William Styron, *Darkness Visible: A Memoir of Madness* (New York: Vintage, 1990).
28. A few examples will have to suffice. As early as May 1924, Walrond wrote to Alain Locke, "Things have not been so very well with me and I have been in a pretty melancholy state for the past week. . . . I am in one of my old shifting, restless, nervous moods." In January of the following year, he lamented to Locke, "So far I have not been able to get away – and the result is a state of anxiety, melancholy, and depression", putting him in a "high-strung, unnatural, morbid, discontented state of mind". He goes on to say, "There is really a self, a side of me, I think, that is not bad, not undesirable, but as fate would have it, this side has been for some time submerged by the harsh rulings of life" (Alain Locke Papers, Moorland Springarn Research Center, Howard University, Box 164-91, folder 38). Others in whom he confided about his struggle with depres-

sion prior to committing himself in 1952 included Shirley Graham (Du Bois), to whom he wrote from southern France in 1931, and Henry Allen Moe, secretary of the Guggenheim Foundation.

29. Cheng writes, "The vocabulary of grievance (and its implied logic of comparability and compensation) that constitutes so much of American political discourse has ironically deflected attention away from a serious look at the more immaterial, unquantifiable repository of public and private grief that has gone into the making of the so-called minority subject" (*Melancholy*, 6).
30. Countee Cullen, "Incident", in *My Soul's High Song: The Collected Writings of Countee Cullen, Voice of the Harlem Renaissance*, ed. Gerald Lyn Early (New York: Doubleday, 1991), 90.
31. Cheng, *Melancholy*, 20.
32. James Baldwin, *Notes of a Native Son* (Boston: Beacon Press, 1955), 165.
33. Ibid.
34. James Davis, "Anticolonial on the River Avon: Eric Walrond's Black British Writing" (paper presented at the American Studies Association conference, October 2006). Excellent accounts of Walrond's post-Harlem writing appear in the introduction to Wade and Parascandola, *In Search of Asylum*, and in Carl A. Wade and Louis J. Parascandola, "In Search of Asylum: Eric Walrond's *Roundway Review* Writings, 1952–1957", *Journal of Caribbean Studies* 19, nos. 1 and 2 (2004–5): 21–42.
35. See chapter 8 ("They Want Me to Know My Place") in Patrick French, *The World Is What It Is: The Authorized Biography of V.S. Naipaul* (New York: Alfred A. Knopf, 2008).
36. These included the League of Coloured Peoples, the International African Service Bureau and the West African Students Bureau.
37. Reprinted in Eric Walrond, *"Winds Can Wake Up the Dead": An Eric Walrond Reader*, ed. Louis J. Parascandola (Detroit: Wayne State University Press, 1997), 333.
38. From Barbados alone, where Walrond's family lived before migrating to Panama during the canal construction, roughly twenty thousand workers signed contracts with the US government. And as historian Julie Greene notes, "Probably at least that many more went to work in Panama without a contract, many of them wives or children of contract laborers" (Julie Greene, *The Canal Builders: Making America's Empire at the Panama Canal* [New York: Penguin, 2009], 30).
39. Rhonda Frederick, *"Colón Man a Come": Mythographies of Panamá Canal Migration* (Lanham, MD: Lexington Books, 2005), 43.

9

A WEST INDIAN GROWS IN BROOKLYN
The Early American Experiences of Eric Walrond

LOUIS J. PARASCANDOLA AND
JAMES DAVIS

WHEN ERIC WALROND FIRST came to New York City in 1918, he lived not in Manhattan, but with his aunt and uncle in Brooklyn. His initial move to Brooklyn was like that of many newly arrived Caribbean immigrants to the United States. "Between 1900 and 1920 at least 28,000 foreign-born Negroes, mainly from the West Indies, migrated to the Empire State."[1] More specifically, they came to New York City – particularly Manhattan and to a lesser, but still important, extent Brooklyn. In fact, by "1930, 11,266 of New York City's 54,754 foreign-born Negroes resided in Brooklyn. This constituted the largest black immigrant community in the country outside Harlem."[2] Walrond's Brooklyn years from 1918 to 1923 marked a crucial transitional period for him, one allowing a passage from his life in the Caribbean to an immersion into African American culture. His experiences during these years are documented in his early journalism in the Garveyite *Brooklyn and Long Island Informer* and *Negro World* and such fictional works as "Cynthia Goes to the Prom" and "Miss Kenny's Marriage", and especially the more mature and reflective "Success Story".[3] All three stories express Walrond's initiation into and eventual chafing at the confines of life in Brooklyn, particularly in the restrictive West Indian community.

Walrond's links to the Brooklyn West Indian community took root shortly after his arrival in America. Initially, he lived with his aunt and uncle, Julia and Charles Nichols, for several months in the Bedford-Stuyvesant area, then home to Poles, Italians and Jews as well as a growing number of blacks, including many Caribbean immigrants. The Nichols were staunch members of the Plymouth Brethren. The church was the family's means to keep a connection to both their West Indian and British heritage. It was also a way to maintain an air of middle-class respectability in their new land, a vital concern for many immigrants.

Walrond's early years in Brooklyn were marked by his inability to find what he felt was a suitable job as a journalist. Although he had been a reporter for two years for the *Panama Star and Herald*, a leading Latin American paper, Walrond was unable to gain employment in this field in the United States and was forced to take up menial positions such as being a domestic or a dishwasher. However, his pride and ambition would not allow him to keep such positions for long. After being denied newspaper jobs in white- and African American–controlled papers, it is perhaps not surprising that Walrond turned to the Caribbean community. He soon secured a position with the Brooklyn-based Garveyite publication *Weekly Review*, where he was invited to join the staff on a part-time basis as an associate editor. No copies of the paper are extant, but Garvey scholar Robert Hill describes it as "a new Negro journal devoted to commerce, politics, news, industry, and economics".[4]

When the enterprise folded after a few issues, Walrond joined the *Brooklyn and Long Island Informer*, a weekly that appeared from June 1920 to January 1922. Incorporated in Jamaica, Queens, with Walrond as magazine editor, the *Informer* was inspired by the principles of Garveyism, stressing racial pride and black business enterprise in its editorial and advertising policies. Practising their own version of black capitalism, the editors were part-time owners as well as working journalists. For the twenty-two-year-old Walrond, who was on the verge of being married, the venture was a risky one. However, staking his future on the black West Indian community, he decided to become a full-time newspaperman. Having gained a foothold in Garvey's Caribbean-focused world in the fall of 1921, Walrond joined the Jamaican leader's flagstaff journal, *Negro World*, where he worked as an editor for two years.[5]

After breaking with Garvey, Walrond joined *Opportunity*, the journal of the integrationist National Urban League. Here he helped initiate the use of fictional writing within the periodical. One of these early stories was his own "Cynthia Goes to the Prom". Cynthia, a high school senior, is popular at her school in East New York, Brooklyn. She "was a favorite . . . at a school where Irish, Jew, Italian, Anglo-Saxon mixed". Cynthia views the world through a non-racial lens, ignoring racial problems other family members encountered. Her older sister, for example, "was balked in her attempts to get the job she had prepared herself for – that of teaching French in a high school". Even worse, her father, "a compositor who was born in the West Indies . . . never had a steady job the twenty-two years he has been in America".[6] The father tries to make Cynthia more racially conscious, attempting to get her to read coloured newspapers, but she ignores him. "I can't see the sense of it, this race-conscious business. I can't see it."[7]

Cynthia wants to go to the prom even though there had been racial tensions at an earlier one. Her assertion that race does not matter is indicative of many newly arrived West Indian immigrants (though she herself was born in the United States), who believe they will be judged on their merits rather than their race. Despite the colourism and class consciousness that existed in their native lands, they were unprepared for the highly racialized strata that existed in America. She maintains that her popularity at school will ensure her success in other social settings with whites. Her high school prom, an initiation into adulthood for many American youths though not nearly as important a marker in the Caribbean, is her attempt to become fully accepted not only into adulthood but also American society. Significantly, the prom is held in the McAlpin Hotel, an opulent midtown Manhattan hotel, fairly recently opened in 1912. At the time of its opening, the twenty-five-storey hotel was the largest hotel in the world. However, as in other Walrond pieces, such as "Vignettes of the Dusk", the immigrant is rebuffed. Interestingly, she is rejected at a dance, where there would be white boys present. The possible sexual danger she and other black girls pose to white America is clear. She gets her first sense of trouble when the "white-haired orderly" eyes the "gowned Cleopatras" (an obvious racial reference) with suspicion and is reluctant to give them entrance. After discussing the matter with his boss, who tells him to admit them because they are just "kids", and presumably not a threat, the "white"-faced man wordlessly points a finger at the elevator.

Once inside, the rude treatment continues. The face of the white woman in charge of the cloak room "barked" at them, and she tells the girls there are no hooks though "a whole row of vacant hooks" was clearly visible.[8] With some of the steely calm of those who would later integrate segregated venues during the civil rights movement, they remain despite their mistreatment. Things worsen as the white girls, including ones who had encouraged the black girls to attend the prom, now, under peer pressure, ignore their friends. The prom has also turned into a racial initiation for them, reinforcing rigid segregated norms that "friendship" with blacks cannot extend beyond the school building. As the black students leave, the nameless narrator (perhaps Walrond himself) asks Cynthia, as they cross the Brooklyn Bridge (from Manhattan), "What do you think of social equality now?" After Cynthia's awakening to American racism, she remarks, defiantly, "Not much, I tell you one thing, though – whenever I get a chance I'm going to these affairs. They've got to get used to us! They must!"[9]

This story is reflective of the militant spirit of many Caribbean immigrants. As has been pointed out by many observers, such as Winston James, West Indian immigrants were often leading figures in radical political movements in America. It was, in fact, such a widespread belief that Kelly Miller, conservative dean of Howard University, stated that by definition, a Negro radical is "an *over*-educated West Indian without a job".[10] Cynthia may well be on her way to becoming one of these radicals.

"Miss Kenny's Marriage" is also, like "Cynthia Goes to the Prom", an initiation tale, this time of black Southern migrants trying to fit into the black Northern elite. Its theme, as Robert Bone points out, is "the pretender brought low".[11] Miss Kenny has been in Brooklyn for three years since she migrated from the South. She sets up her hairdressing salon on "unfashionable" Atlantic Avenue. She is filled with pride in her "Beauty Parlor", and refuses to advertise because she thinks it is beneath her: "There ain't none of the nigger in me, honey."[12] Yet, in reality, she "embodies various forms of pretentiousness: linguistic, cultural, and social".[13] Walrond seems to take an almost sadistic pleasure in ridiculing her: "Miss Kenny hadn't any charm or beauty at all. Persons in the know would look at the tar tumbling down the temples of her bronze face and retreat in terror."[14] The forty-eight-year-old woman maintains that the way to advance is through hard work and obtaining money and status, trying to gain acceptance by marrying a young attorney, Elias Ramsey (he is twenty-five), who was "born and bred in Brooklyn". However, the "uppity, ignorant, arrogant", Ramsey easily deceives Miss Kenny. Three months after their marriage, he chloroforms her and runs off with her fortune, over nine thousand dollars.

Though Miss Kenny is a victim, it is hard to be too sympathetic with her because she had been so class-conscious herself, even allowing only Elias to address her by her first name, Catherine. Miss Kenny is another example of succumbing, as does a character in "Vignettes of the Dusk", to a sort of "vanilla temptation", striving to go beyond your place. Even at the end, unlike Cynthia, she has no epiphany. Her final words in the story are, "I wonder where I can find him."[15] We are left to ponder whether she wants Elias back just to recover her money or because she is still taken in by him. Walrond seems to take no pity on this grown woman who is undone by her own pretensions and foolishness.

Both "Cynthia Goes to the Prom" and "Miss Kenny's Marriage" deal to varying degrees with characters who fail to gain acceptance into new societies. Walrond is not, however, advocating just accepting one's position. Cynthia learns there are differences between races but whites have to be forced to accept a larger vision of America. She no longer holds the naïve belief that America is a raceless society, but she will not accept a subordinate status. The younger woman, with an immigrant background, embodies the forceful New Negro. Miss Kenny, on the other hand, does not fully learn her lesson. The older, Southern-born woman, is more reflective of the old Negro.

Walrond had hoped to publish "a short story of about 3,500 words in length which deals with life in the West Indian Negro slum quarter of Brooklyn NY" as early as 1939 in the English literary journal *New Writing*.[16] This piece would eventually become the six-part "Success Story" published in *Roundway Review*. This lengthy tale would be Walrond's fullest embodiment of his Brooklyn years. In many ways, "Success Story" exemplifies Caribbean diaspora writing. It masquerades as a traditional US immigration narrative but turns out to be more complex. It is difficult to fix geographically: though the setting is New York, the story continually exceeds this frame, alternating between a narrative present in Brooklyn and the remembered past in Barbados and Panama during the canal construction. Thematically, it seems fairly conventional: the protagonist moves from a rural to an urban setting, from a religious to a secular society, and from a communal identity to an individual identity – all common tropes in US immigrant literature. But the story departs from the straightforward narrative teleology that is characteristic of this genre. Its formal complexity produces an alternative account of migration, diasporic rather than linear, the protagonist's Caribbean past continually erupting into the narrative present. Moreover, Walrond set the story in Brooklyn but published it in postwar England, during the birth pangs of the *Windrush* era[17] that would challenge English national identity. Thus the story suggests the constitutive tensions in early attempts such as this to write the Afro-Caribbean diaspora. Since Brooklyn is said to be home to the largest number of West Indians outside of Kingston, Jamaica, "Success Story" is an important, relatively undiscovered account of this community's emergence.

The plot of "Success Story" hews closely to Walrond's own life. Jim Prout, the twenty-year-old protagonist, arrives on the front stoop of his Aunt Josephine's house in the Brooklyn neighbourhood of Bedford-Stuyvesant, fresh off the boat from Panama, where he had moved as a child from Barbados. Josephine and her large, church-going family live in a shabby tenement, a clothesline in the front room, the front door swinging on one hinge, and "an assortment of rugs, mattresses and bed-linen" hung out the windows.[18] The story follows Jim's efforts to get his bearings in his new surroundings and escape these squalid conditions by finding a decent job and becoming self-sufficient. After several frustrating weeks, he is hired as a clerk in an import-export firm in Manhattan. In moving out he has also moved up: he will receive a salary, be called "mister", operate sophisticated office machinery, conduct business with far-flung offices, and give instructions to secretaries in pink blouses and white corduroy skirts. We are meant to understand that his persistence and ambition have paid off. A week earlier, his cousin Timothy Cumberbatch told Jim he could get him a job as an elevator operator. When Jim demurred, saying he was still waiting "for the kind of job I want", Timothy had told Aunt Josephine, "That guy takes the cake . . . Why, he must be nuts to think he can get the kind of job he had in Panama in this country. Running an elevator ain't good enough for him, huh? Well, you wait till the cold weather sets in. He will come crawling, you wait and see."[19] Jim's success, then, is that he beats the odds: rather than operating an elevator he winds up riding one to his nineteenth floor office in a Manhattan skyscraper, where he succeeds in landing a job with a soap company.

The story does not end simply with the protagonist's triumphant rise to the nineteenth floor but with a heated exchange between his new boss, Mr Runck, and a colleague, Mr Palmer. The last lines of the story are: " 'I see,' said Mr Palmer, 'that you've got a nigger in your department.' Mr Runck took the cigar out of his mouth. 'He is not a nigger,' he growled with a glint in his blue eyes. 'He is a foreigner.' "[20] What is at stake in Runck's distinction? Palmer is meant to sound racist, of course, in his willingness to disparage Jim's blackness. But it also illustrates an important sub-operation of that racism, a collapse of differences in ethnicity and national origin. The exchange underscores the violence of the binary logic of race in the United States. And it raises critical questions about immigration, questions that tend to be overlooked in traditional studies of so-called white ethnics in the American melting pot. Where have Afro-Caribbean immigrants stood in relation to mainstream US culture and in relation to the African Americans whose presence has defined blackness in the United States? How have they understood their cultural identity, and how have others determined their place for them? By insisting that Jim is a foreigner, is Runck denying that Jim is black or is he insisting on a more expansive definition of blackness, one that is not reducible to the African Americans invoked in Palmer's slur?

Walrond was among the shrewdest analysts of these questions of race in the 1920s, and the questions acquired urgency as immigration to New York City from the West Indies grew exponentially after the turn of the century. In Harlem alone, which was just becoming a black community, some forty thousand immigrants of African descent settled between 1900 and 1930; most of them were from former British colonies in the Caribbean.[21] Their presence is obscured by the two major demographic shifts of the time: massive immigration from southern and eastern Europe and the so-called Great Migration of African Americans from the rural US South to the industrial North. But issues of Afro-Caribbean identity, community and acculturation were vigorously discussed. The most prominent catalysts may have been West Indian radical intellectuals, but the terms of the discussion were hammered out in beauty parlours and barbershops, nightclubs and church basements, around the kitchen table and in the pages of New York's many black-owned periodicals. Even the black establishment journals were attentive. W.E.B. Du Bois speculated about the prospects for racial solidarity between African Americans and West Indians in the journal of the National Association for the Advancement of Colored People, *Crisis* (1920); W.A. Domingo extolled the Caribbean immigrants' contributions to American society in "Gift of the Black Tropics", represented in Alain Locke's anthology *The New Negro* (1925); and *Opportunity* magazine devoted a special issue, largely assembled by Walrond, to promoting mutual understanding between African Americans and West Indians (1926).

If "Success Story" seems to resolve the question of the West Indian's status in the United States in its closing paragraph – Jim is not a "nigger", he is a "foreigner" – the rest of the story works to complicate this opposition and requires us to read the ending much more equivocally. Jim's Aunt Josephine speaks like the Barbadian that she is, much to her children's chagrin. To them, her dialect reveals her cultural backwardness and refusal to embrace America.

> "And how is Beatrice, no?" [Josephine asks Jim,] "How is yo' mahmie when you left she? I ain't see she for so long."
> "Hear that Nimta?" Hyacinth whispered aloud.
> Nimta stamped her foot. "Can't you say 'mother', mother?" she demanded.
> Aunt Josephine paled. Her lips trembled. . . .
> "Why all-you don't let me alone, no?" she cried, stomping round on the children, "Why unna don't stop persecuting me, no?"
> Hyacinth started to giggle.
> "Aren't you ever going to speak properly, mother?" cried Nimta, "You are in America now, not in Barbados, don't say 'unna'."
> "Go along, unna pack o good-for-nothings," retorted Aunt Josephine, "Mock unna murrah!"
> "Oh dear," sighed Nimta wearily, "If it isn't 'mahmie' it is 'murrah'."[22]

However, Josephine is an expert on American culture compared to her newly arrived nephew. "You know Jim," she said, "in America we does eat three square meals a day, not like in the West Indies. No bread and tea 'pon a morning, but a big breakfast."[23] "Let me show you how you must sleep in America", she adds.

> I always does have to show the new [ones]. . . . You mustn't think you does sleep in America the same as in the West Indies. No, bo. . . . You must not lay down 'pon the sheets, but betwixt them. That is the secret. And you must never forget to do that wherever you da-go. You must not let anyone think you just come. You must remember that in America everything is different, even sleeping.[24]

As Aunt Josephine claims, everything *is* different in America, and Jim is soon confronted with the most significant difference of all: the difference his colour makes in limiting his employment prospects, despite his professional qualifications. In this respect it becomes clear that, contrary to Aunt Josephine's wisdom, there may be an advantage to "let[ting] anyone think you just come". How else is he to distinguish himself from the rest of the Negro race, that monolithic, blunt instrument that is constantly used against him in his quest for respectable employment? He must accustom himself to the rumble of the elevated train outside his window, accustom himself to the "quality" white folks of Brooklyn – nothing like the "poor buckra" of Bridgetown, Josephine tells him, and accustom himself to big city life, "the anonymous mass of which he had now become a part".[25] But must he also capitulate to the system that would make a Negro out of him?

For object lessons, he need look no farther than his own American family. His cousin Timothy, described as "tall, slim, and black" like the protagonist and roughly the same age, is a foil to Jim's character. He "had been born in Barbados", Walrond writes, "but the outward manifestations of his powers of adaptation were so impressive Jim had found it difficult to believe Timothy had spent only ten of his twenty-one years in Brooklyn".[26] He throws around American expressions like "For crying out loud, fella!" and "It's a copper-bottom cinch!"[27] When he catches Jim daydreaming, Timothy says, "Buck up, boy, you ain't down in the jungles now. You can't git nowheres going all moony like a-so."[28] But what his Americanization has also yielded is complacency with his second-class citizenship. "Did I tell you about the new bathing suit I got?" he asks another cousin. "Boy, it's a honey! Wait till you see it. It's got a big yellow oval on the chest, some lodge sign or other, I guess. . . . Guy up in Six 'D' gave it to me, the sporty guy what got the meat ball stand at Far Rockaway. *You* know. All it's got is a hole in the leg, down here. Why I can fix that myself."[29] Admiring Timothy's pluck, Jim is nevertheless scandalized by his contentment with a life of second-hand, castoff possibilities. If, as Timothy says, Jim "must be nuts to think he can get the kind of job he had in Panama" over here, Jim's persistence is a repudiation of the brutal alchemy of race that has set the limits of Timothy's aspirations.

The elder generation of West Indian men led lives of endless toil and domestic strife. Josephine's husband, William Seafort, "hardly saw [his children] except on Sunday afternoons – his one half-day off" each week from a job "in the pantry of a well-to-do family on Brooklyn Heights", a job which "began early in the morning and often did not finish until after midnight".[30] He calls his schedule "lamentable because he did not wish his children to get out of hand", which they continually do.[31] Timothy's father, Amos, with whom he lived, had been known back home as "an up and coming go-getter": "Amos Cumberbatch from Carrington Village in Barbados? Man, he is rugged, rugged!" In Brooklyn "he was caretaker and janitor for a string of apartment houses in Flatbush", "a wheezy little dynamo of a man [who] strode from house to house tending the boilers, shaking down and building up the fires, and wheeling out the ash cans". What's more he "had put every member of his family to work": "One sister was just big enough to push a pram along Ocean Parkway in the afternoons; the other one, too big for anything so light as nurse-maiding, was at nineteen a full-blown general houseworker. She cooked, washed, and ironed for a family of eight persons." Timothy "tended to the switchboard" in the apartment complex, while his mother "armed with mop and pail, kept the tiles all the way up to the top floor nice and clean". Even the little brother, "who was in the fourth grade, ran errands after school for the local trades people". And for all this, Jim observes, the Cumberbatches lived in a "low-ceilinged basement" apartment "so dark [that] the electric lights had to be kept burning all day long. The air, never free of coal gas, was almost unbreathable."[32] Hence Jim's scepticism when Timothy offers him vocational counselling. "Listen fellah!" Timothy says, "You don't seem to realise that you is in America. Don't nobody wait for jobs in America. You goes out arter 'em and grabs 'em."[33] But Jim won't grab if that means manual labour or joining the ranks of the black servant-class, the people he calls "ebony flunkeys, resplendent in blue uniforms trimmed with gold braid [who] moved with stately pomp" through the hallways of Manhattan office buildings.[34]

He does not wish to believe his skin colour disqualifies him from the positions he is seeking, but his experiences leave him no alternative:

> How many times during those three weeks Jim had not had, from the window of an "El" train, a close-up of the white and gilt dome of the Borough Hall? Or skirted, still on the "El," the West Indian slums of Third Avenue on the long ride out to South Brooklyn? . . . Or tramped – dusty, footsore, and weary – the sidewalks along the endlessly "El"-shaded length of Brooklyn's Broadway? Yet no matter how early Jim had gotten up in the morning to answer the "Help Wanted" advertisements in the *New York World* he never seemed to have got up early enough. Someone was always there ahead of him. Or maybe he did not have the required kind of experience. Or maybe they wanted a woman. Once or twice – at the foreman's shed of a building contractor – he had been definitely looked at askance (there was no mistaking it). . . . He had become accustomed to being bowed out with a promise that he would be sent for should an opening occur.[35]

The "triumph" of "Success Story", then, is predicated on Jim's foreignness, on the claim it allows his boss to make that he is "not a nigger". It is a logic that is reinforced by the ethnic marking of Jim's new colleagues. They are Latinos with surnames like Guzman, Alejandro and Jimenez, or, in the case of John Gonzaga, the "son of a pushcart pedlar in 'Little Italy'".[36] Taking his place alongside them, Jim removes himself symbolically and materially from the Afro-Caribbean community, a community whose assimilation to African American life appears fitful but inexorable. The story's ending comes to seem bitterly ironic. In what sense is it a "success story" that Jim has circumvented the racial logic of segregation-era New York? His success merely underscores the false choice faced by others in his position: *either* black *or* an immigrant, a "nigger" or a "foreigner".

Brooklyn's immigrant history is legendary. In the mythology of New York, the borough is the springboard for working-class Jews, Italians, Russians, Irish, and more recently for Arabs, Asians and Latinos, all sacrificing for their children, working and "going without" so later generations have better. New York's black immigrants, many of whom are West Indian, challenge this narrative; their experiences are cross-cut by different processes of racialization, and Walrond's story represents an early and incisive example of this challenge. Moreover, it places Brooklyn squarely on a map that has been dominated by Harlem. Walrond calls our attention to a different cultural action and location, to Brooklyn's place not only as a site of white ethnic acculturation but also as a West Indian community whose challenges and opportunities differed from their neighbours.[37] In the first half of the century, many West Indians still preferred Brooklyn to Harlem. Walrond notes in "Success Story", "It would be such a relief to [Jim's mother] and such a comfort in her loneliness to know that he had followed her advice not to go up to Harlem (' . . . that sink of iniquity? Avoid it like you would the plague, boy') and had chosen instead to stay with the Seaforts beneath the tall spires of the City of Churches."[38]

By 1924, there had been significant changes in Walrond's life in America. He was disenchanted with Garvey and was in the process of leaving *Negro World*. He had a literary agent, Edna Worthley Underwood, and had begun publishing with mainstream periodicals. He began attending classes at the College of the City of New York and cast his lot as an aspiring writer. He also had separated from his Jamaican wife and essentially abandoned his three young daughters. He had even, in 1922, taken the dramatic step of embarking on one (and possibly two) runs aboard the banana boat steamer SS *Turrialba* from New Orleans to the Caribbean, Central and South America. Amid all these changes, it is not surprising that he wanted a change in his living space as well. He longed for a complete break from his previous life, which is marked by his move from Brooklyn to Harlem. While the move from one borough to another might not seem so large, in reality his move to Harlem represented a seismic shift, marking his move towards African American culture and the New Negro movement. Significantly, in his essay "The New Negro Faces America",[39] he would say "[t]he American negro of today believes intensely in America".[40] He was looking away from the West Indies and plunging into black America. His transitional West Indian years were over. He had outgrown his immigrant status and was ready to take his place at the centre of the Harlem Renaissance. But this initial experience had proven a necessary incubus that would lead to the next five years, while in Harlem, which would be the most creative period of his life, culminating in the publication of *Tropic Death* in 1926. His passage into this society is presaged by "Cynthia Goes to the Prom", "Miss Kenny's Marriage" and "Success Story". Yet, ironically, his difficulty both fully accepting and being accepted by this world is also reflected in the stories. By 1928, Walrond realized he could not fit into African American life and he would leave the United States never to live there again. His struggle to find a place would remain a lifelong journey.[41]

NOTES

1. Seth M. Scheiner, *Negro Mecca: A History of the Negro in New York City, 1865–1920* (New York: New York University Press, 1965), 8.
2. Harold X. Connolly, *A Ghetto Grows in Brooklyn* (New York: New York University Press, 1977), 76.
3. "Cynthia Goes to the Prom", *Opportunity* (November 1923); "Miss Kenny's Marriage", *Smart Set* (September 1923); "Success Story" (6 parts), *Roundway Review* February–June 1954.
4. Robert Hill, ed., *The Marcus Garvey and Universal Negro Improvement Association Papers* (Berkeley: University of California Press, 1983), 2:181.
5. For more on the Garvey-Walrond relationship at this time, see Robert Bone

and Louis J. Parascandola, "An Ellis Island of the Soul: Eric Walrond and the Turbulent Passage from Garveyite to New Negro", *Afro-Americans in New York Life and History* 34, no. 2 (July 2010): 34–53.

6. Eric Walrond, "Cynthia Goes to the Prom", in *The Opportunity Reader Stories, Poetry, and Essays from the Urban League's* Opportunity *Magazine*, ed. Sondra Kathryn Wilson (New York: Modern Library, 1999), 204–5.
7. Ibid., 205.
8. Ibid., 206.
9. Ibid., 207.
10. Quoted in Winston James, *Holding Aloft the Banner of Ethiopia: Caribbean Radicalism in Early Twentieth-Century America* (London: Verso, 1998), 2.
11. Robert A. Bone, *Down Home: A History of Afro-American Short Fiction from Its Beginning to the End of the Harlem Renaissance* (New York: Putnam, 1975), 182.
12. Eric Walrond, *"Winds Can Wake Up the Dead": An Eric Walrond Reader*, ed. Louis J. Parascandola (Detroit: Wayne State University Press, 1998), 153.
13. Bone, *Down Home*, 182.
14. Walrond, *"Winds"*, 154.
15. Ibid., 160.
16. Letter to John Lehmann, 14 July 1939, Walrond Papers held in private collection.
17. The ship *Empire Windrush* arrived in the United Kingdom on 22 June 1948 carrying 492 Jamaican passengers, heralding the beginning of a wave of Caribbean migration to England that would last until the mid-1960s.
18. Eric Walrond, "Success Story", *Roundway Review* (February–June 1954). Reprinted in *In Search of Asylum: The Later Writings of Eric Walrond*, ed. Louis J. Parascandola and Carl A. Wade (Gainesville: University Press of Florida, 2011), 105. All references are to this edition.
19. Ibid., 132.
20. Ibid., 139.
21. Irma Watkins-Owens, *Blood Relatives: Caribbean Immigrants and the Harlem Community, 1900–1930* (Bloomington: Indiana University Press, 1996), 1.
22. Walrond, "Success Story", 108.
23. Ibid., 117.
24. Ibid., 121.
25. Ibid., 122, 131.
26. Ibid., 129.
27. Ibid., 129, 131.
28. Ibid., 129.
29. Ibid., 132.
30. Ibid., 127.
31. Ibid.

32. Ibid., 129–30.
33. Ibid., 132.
34. Ibid., 131.
35. Ibid., 130.
36. Ibid., 137.
37. Other significant Caribbean-born Harlem Renaissance figures who lived in Brooklyn include bibliophile Arturo/Arthur Schomburg, playwright Eulalie Spence and author Claude McKay.
38. Walrond, "Success Story", 118.
39. "The New Negro Faces America", *Current History,* February 1923.
40. Walrond, *"Winds",* 112.
41. Walrond's move from Brooklyn would not be his last association with the borough, however. When he returned to the United States in 1931, his only visit to the United States, he visited his parents who lived on Herkimer Street, in Brooklyn. He had come full circle. Thanks to Robert Bone for his thoughts on this final paragraph.

10

EXILE ON MAIN STREET
Eric Walrond and Garveyism in Great Britain in the 1930s

CARL PEDERSEN

IN LATE 1934, MARCUS GARVEY transferred the headquarters of his once-powerful organization, the Universal Negro Improvement Association (UNIA), from his homeland Jamaica to London. As Garvey explained in the first British issue of his magazine, *Black Man*, the move to London reflected the status of the city as "the central city of the world, not only from a European point of view, but from the point of view of Negro interest".¹ On a more personal level, the transfer of UNIA headquarters to London can also be viewed as Garvey's final attempt to regain some of the influence he had once had before his deportation from the United States to Jamaica in 1927 for mail fraud, following a vitriolic campaign against him by his many detractors. He had returned to Jamaica, determined to continue his work there. During his six years in Jamaica, he had published a journal, *New Jamaican*, and formed a political party and a labour organization. Just before leaving for England he stopped publication of *New Jamaican* and launched what he hoped would be a worthy successor to *Negro World*. The decision to call his new publication *Black Man* no doubt reflected this desire to abandon his focus on Jamaican politics.² He clearly yearned for a larger stage on which to revive "the great movement of the UNIA under new and honest leadership so that we may continue the battle for African redemption and for the development of the Negro race", as he put it in the first editorial of *Black Man*.³

A few years earlier, another lesser-known Afro-Caribbean man, Eric Walrond, had also settled in England. After the critical success of his collection of short stories, *Tropic Death*, Walrond was awarded a Guggenheim Fellowship, which took him to Europe. Once there, he published very little for the next decade. However, in 1936, Walrond began writing for *Black Man*. His sudden appearance in the pages of Garvey's last publication is remarkable. His return to publication and the renewal of his association with Garvey, which bordered on hostility in the 1920s, can contribute to a reassessment of his legacy. Walrond served as associate editor for *Negro World* from 1922 to 1924. However, from looking at the articles Walrond wrote for *Negro World*, it is clear that he saw himself in the role of journalist and literary critic rather than as a propagandist for Garveyism. Indeed, as early as 1922, he was complaining in the pages of Henry Ford's publication that African American writers were turning away from an examination of black folk-life in favour of propagandistic tracts.[4] The Chekhovian impressionism of *Tropic Death* was ample testimony to Walrond's opposition to the kind of writing advocated by Garvey. When Walrond finally did offer an assessment of the Garvey movement, the tone was anything but flattering. In two articles, "The New Negro Faces America", published in *Current History* in February 1923, and "Imperator Africanus, Marcus Garvey: Menace or Promise?", published in the *Independent* in January 1925, he focused on the development of black leadership in the United States. For Walrond, the problem facing the New Negro was the lack of a broad-based organization with leaders attuned to African American race consciousness and recognition of their place in the modern world. In Walrond's opinion, Booker T. Washington was out of step with the times, W.E.B. Du Bois was too elitist to be sensitive to the aspirations of the "masses" and Garvey was, simply, a "megalomaniac". Recognizing Garvey's achievement in forging an organization of uprooted Southern blacks and immigrant Afro-Caribbean nationals, Walrond nevertheless repudiated the psychological panacea of the back-to-Africa movement and roundly criticized Garvey's various business dealings. In short, Garvey emerged from these articles as someone having the potential for being a true leader of African Americans, but who regrettably squandered this potential on "fairy dreams" of African repatriation and grandiose schemes of black enterprise in the United States.[5]

It is worth noting that both men came from similar backgrounds and in their early lives followed the classic pattern of the West Indian intellectual of constant physical and psychological displacement. In his meditation on the reasons for the involuntary exile of West Indian writers in Great Britain, the Barbadian novelist George Lamming insisted that "[t]he exile is a universal figure", in the sense that a characteristic feature of modernism is displacement and involvement in events beyond our control. This universal sense of exile is complicated in the case of the colonized resident in the land of the colonizer. Lamming went so far as to suggest that it would perhaps be preferable for West Indians to study in countries other than England, where his or her development would not constantly be hampered by memory or history.[6]

The notion that the colonized can attain no true understanding of the colonizer country because of its idealization and cannot connect with the reality of Caribbean life because of its implicit denigration by the prerogatives of the mother country is relevant to an examination of the relationship between Walrond and Garvey. Both came from the English-speaking Caribbean and took a peripatetic route before arriving in the United States. Unlike Walrond, however, Garvey had been to England from 1912 to 1914 before coming to the United States in 1916. As Michelle Stephens has argued, Garvey's politics underscored the diasporic nature of the black imagined community he attempted to establish during his time in the United States.[7] His early experience of travel outside his island home reinforced this global consciousness of black solidarity. Winston James notes that "wide travel contributed . . . to the radicalization of Caribbeans before their arrival in the United States. . . . It is easier for those who have travelled than for those who have not, to develop a Pan-African consciousness."[8] Garvey and Walrond's similar experience of travel in the Caribbean and Latin America would no doubt contribute to bringing them together in New York in the 1920s. Walrond felt a sense of community in the Garvey movement that was later replaced by disillusion over Garvey's business ventures and political missteps.[9]

Garvey's first experience in England is important in examining his intellectual development, for it was there he was exposed to currents of thought that, taken together, make up the amalgam of ideas known as Garveyism. His trip to England in 1912 was his initial contact with the colonizing power, the centre of the empire, an entirely different world from the provincial Jamaica he had left. Garvey attended sessions in the House of Commons and professed his fondness for England even after having heard debates on the future of the colonies under British rule. This part of Garvey's experience fits the classic pattern of the innocent colonial, dazzled by the size and strength of a supposedly superior culture, which had attained a level of political power and advanced economic development that he had only read about in schoolbooks in Jamaica.

However, Garvey's time in England was not restricted to listening to parliamentary debates. He contacted the editor of *African Times and Orient Review*, Duse Mohamed Ali, a Sudanese-Egyptian, who opened Garvey's mind to pan-Africanism and introduced him to African history. In his first published article, "The British West Indies in the Mirror of Civilization", in *African Times and Orient Review* in October 1913, Garvey looked to the West Indies in light of his new-found knowledge. In his admiration for the achievements of the British Empire and his discovery of the rich past of Africa he saw the future of the Caribbean as one in which "the people who inhabit that portion of the Western Hemisphere will be the instruments of uniting a scattered race who, before the close of many centuries, will found an Empire on which the sun shall shine as ceaselessly as it shines on the Empire of the North today".[10] Finally, it was on the boat bound for England that Garvey first read Booker T. Washington's *Up From Slavery*. Washington's narrative of his rise to black leadership from his childhood in slavery, combined with Garvey's restless search to see if the injustices he had seen committed towards blacks in Jamaica were an anomaly or just one facet in the international exploitation of Africans at home or in the diaspora, affected his own future. As he put it, "my doom – if I may so call it – of being a race leader dawned upon me in London".[11]

Because he first came to England in the 1930s, Walrond's world view was shaped not so much by any obeisance to the imperial centre, but rather by the effects of the displacement of Afro-Caribbean nationals caused by the American intervention in the region, crystallized for him in the construction of the Panama Canal. Walrond wrote tellingly of the consequences of the canal for the Caribbean basin in *Tropic Death*, where "a rock engine was crushing stone, shooting up rivers of steam and signalling the frontier's rebirth".[12] Walrond's preoccupation with the cultural and psychological effects of dislocation undoubtedly drew him to Garvey's UNIA movement and its efforts to promote a supra-nationalist solidarity between all people of African origin. Several of Walrond's articles from the 1920s also focused on black migration from the rural South to the urban North, a theme he would return to in the one short story he published in *Black Man*, "A Fugitive from Dixie".

While Walrond's sensitivity to displacement and alienation attracted him to Garvey's message of unification, the key to his initial break with Garveyism can be found in his scepticism towards Garvey's blueprint for African solidarity. Clearly, in Walrond's view, Garvey was simply replacing the myth of the British Empire with an ahistorical notion of a future African Empire. Both standards were unattainable and, in the case of the back-to-Africa movement, only served to compound the psychological damage inflicted on West Indians, who by virtue of their colonization had lost touch with the reality of their own experience. However, unlike V.S. Naipaul, who took the invalidation of the Caribbean experience at face value and looked at the region as essentially being outside of history (summed up in the infamous passage from his Caribbean travelogue *The Middle Passage*, in which he writes that "History is built around achievement and creation; and nothing was created in the West Indies"),[13] Walrond in *Tropic Death* attempted, in part through his experimentation with language, to create this reality.

Walrond's efforts to chart the effects of technological and military intervention on Caribbean culture in *Tropic Death* and his avowed intention to write about the folk-life of the region in the late 1920s in the spirit of Zora Neale Hurston set him against Garveyite notions of the inevitable rise and fall of great civilizations. This conflict, never overtly articulated, probably contributed to the split between Garvey and Walrond in the 1920s and would inform their brief association in the pages of *Black Man* in the 1930s.

The decline of Garveyism after the failure of the Black Star Line and Garvey's deportation to Jamaica in 1927 contributed to the rise of other pan-African movements, most of which were centred in London. In the 1920s, the Comintern had attempted, unsuccessfully, to recruit the UNIA for the Communist cause, recognizing, as Otto Huiswood, a West Indian delegate to the fourth Comintern congress, observed, that the movement had a "rebel rank and file element".[14] Comintern support for black self-determination led to the formation of groups like the Negro International, with its organ, *Negro Worker*, under the editorship of George Padmore from Trinidad. However, the reorientation of Comintern policy in the mid-1930s resulted in neglect of colonial issues, and, in the wake of the Italian invasion of Ethiopia (or Abyssinia, as it was then known), Padmore joined the International African Friends of Abyssinia along with C.L.R. James, Jomo Kenyatta and Garvey's first wife, Amy Ashwood Garvey. In 1925, the West African Students' Union, representing students from British West Africa, and calling for a federation of the four colonies under African rule, was formed. In 1931, the League of

Coloured Peoples, under the leadership of the Jamaican Harold Arundel Moody, was established. A moderate, multi-racial organization committed to welfare and social work, it sought influence among the black seamen residing in Great Britain. Garvey initially supported the West African Students' Union but parted company with it in 1935 over the organization's support for the performances of Paul Robeson, which Garvey felt were degrading to blacks. Not surprisingly, given his fierce opposition to Communism in the 1920s, Garvey immediately came into conflict with the more radical James and Padmore. James's assessment of Garvey in his book *A History of Negro Revolt*, published in 1938, paralleled, to some extent, that of Walrond in the 1920s. Dismissing Garvey's dream of a return to Africa as "pitiable rubbish" and condemning him as a "reactionary", James nevertheless acknowledged that he "made the American Negro conscious of his African origin and created for the first time a feeling of international solidarity among Africans and people of African descent".[15]

Garvey made a seemingly conscious decision to pursue a course of self-isolation during his last years in England. His numerous contributions to *Black Man* (many issues were almost entirely written by him), including transcripts of speeches, editorials, poems, Socratic dialogues, news items and polemical attacks, contained his usual hyperbole and grand visions. Largely ignoring the racial issues in Britain that captured the attention of groups like the League of Coloured Peoples, Garvey was determined to remain centre stage on the world arena, devoting his energies to promoting the Five-Year Plan passed by the Seventh International Convention of the UNIA held in Jamaica just before Garvey resettled in England, reminding his readers of the need for strong black leadership, praising British civilization as a constraining force against Fascism, and, in a startling about-face from his earlier exaltation of Ethiopianism, vilifying Haile Selassie for surrounding himself with European advisors during the Italo-Abyssinian war, no doubt because Selassie snubbed Garvey when he arrived as an exile in London in 1936.

Although Walrond only wrote several articles and one short story for *Black Man*, he was the second most frequent contributor to the journal. His articles differ in tone and subject matter from Garvey's. They reveal the limits and the scope of his commitment to Garveyism.

Two of Walrond's articles, the first and the last, dealt specifically with England. "The Negro in London", which appeared in March 1936, contrasted the romantic image of the mother country held by blacks in the colonies with the reality experienced by black seamen living in segregated enclaves in Cardiff, Liverpool, Tyneside and London. Walrond undoubtedly learned of the situation of these seamen through the activities of the League of Coloured Peoples and its journal, *Keys*, and through articles by E.D. Morel, who regarded their presence as a threat to the social fabric of British society. In the early years after the First World War, Morel had in the British left-wing newspaper the *Daily Herald* condemned the use of black troops in the occupied Rhineland because of their alleged sexual proclivities, prompting an angry rebuttal from Claude McKay, who was in England at the time working for Sylvia Pankhurst's organization, the Workers' Socialist Federation.[16] Morel's diatribes against the black seamen bore much the same taint, accusing them of fostering "half-caste" progeny who could not survive Britain's inhospitable climate.[17]

Walrond's only comment on Morel's accusations was to note laconically that "[i]n communities where there has been a great deal of inter-mixing the feeling among the whites is one of subtle antagonism".[18] Otherwise, he sought to give a descriptive account of the economic barriers preventing them from entering the trades and industry. In London, Walrond noted, the situation was complicated by the presence of students, who were discouraged from settling permanently in England, and artists, particularly from the United States, who received a warmer welcome because, as Walrond put it, "the English have always been quick to recognize the genius of the Negro artist".[19] He concluded by noting the paradox that London, the centre of the British Empire and English liberty, should be so ignorant of racial matters and compared this sorry state with that of New York before the black migration from the South that resulted in the growth of Harlem as a black community.

The other article, "On England", written two years after, is a one-page scathing criticism of what Walrond described as England's most striking feature, "the love and worship of tradition".[20] This tradition was rooted in the class basis of English society, which makes a mockery of concepts like liberty and democracy. Walrond was especially incensed at the lack of representation and overt repression accorded the colonies. This short piece, in which Walrond offered examples of English hypocrisy at home and abroad, differed in tone from Garvey's attitude towards the Crown, which reflects his grudging admiration for the empire and his faith, however qualified, in British institutions.[21]

In some respects, Walrond seemed to be moving away from classical Garveyism, with its notions of black capitalism and racial politics, towards a more class-based, anti-capitalist world view.[22] However, due to the relative paucity of his output in the 1930s, evidence for such a development can only be gleaned from isolated passages in his articles. "The Negro Before the World", which appeared in March 1938, is a case in point. After summarizing the injustices committed against Africans and African Americans throughout history, he concluded:

> If the Negro is to be free he must rid himself of whatever illusions he may still have about the social and economic system that has grown up under capitalism and imperialism. A system that fattens off the laboring masses – black, yellow, and white – and that enriches the privileged few is one which he can never be reconciled to. Until and unless he takes up a firm stand against it, there can be no salvation for him: none of the things which he prizes in life, – a higher scale of living, the end of race and class hatred, the hegemony of the Negro over Africa – will ever be realized.[23]

This passage would perhaps be more appropriate for a George Padmore journal than a Garveyite publication. Walrond had started the article by suggesting that in the chaotic world of the 1930s, "[the Negro] may have to alter his whole outlook on the world he lives in".[24] Another indication of the kind of change Walrond had in mind can be found in "Fascism and the Negro" from March to April 1937. In this article, Walrond posed the same dilemma as Arthur Koestler had in 1931: in a world divided into two irreconcilable ideologies, Fascism and Communism, there was no middle ground. The choice must be for one or the other. Koestler, it will be remembered, chose Communism. Walrond observes that because of the growing consciousness of class and advancements in transportation, "[i]solation in the sense of race, nationality or geography has ceased to exist".[25] Without openly urging blacks to support Communism against Fascism, Walrond saw the threat of Nazism and the Italian conquest of Abyssinia as removing any hope for black neutrality. On the other hand, he also accused the Labour Party in England of failing to confront the colonial issue and to encourage solidarity between black workers in the colonies and white workers in Britain. Once again, Walrond seemed on the verge of declaring his allegiance to Communism, but, no doubt out of discretion, he stopped short of doing so.

It is only in the one article dealing solely with the Abyssinian conflict, "The End of Ras Nasibu", that Walrond appeared to be in line with Garveyite thinking. In reviewing the life of Ras Nasibu, one of Haile Selassie's advisors and the commander of Abyssinian forces in the Ogaden, Walrond emphasized his role as a modernizer who attempted to remodel Abyssinia's feudal institutions "along modern European lines".[26] In countless articles, Garvey had driven home the same theme of the economic development of Africa as a way of raising its level of civilization. The idea that colonized nations such as those in Africa had to conform to European standards of development in order to enter the family of civilized nations was a universal application of Bookerism that is not evident in Walrond's other writings. On the contrary, in *Tropic Death* and elsewhere he had shown himself to be sensitive to the folk cultures of colonized peoples. In his one article on literary matters, he displayed this sensitivity. "Can the Negro Measure Up?", from August 1937, focused on the life and work of the Jesuit priest Henri Gregoire, whose book *An Enquiry Concerning the Intellectual and Moral Faculties and Literature of Negroes* (1808) sought to repudiate the doctrine of racial inferiority by examining the lives of fifteen blacks distinguished in science, literature and the arts. Although Gregoire was clearly measuring the progress of blacks by European standards, Walrond emphasized the advances blacks had made in the struggle against capitalism, their support of nationalist movements, as well as their contribution in the cultural and artistic sphere.[27]

Taken as a whole, these articles reveal that Walrond maintained his distance from Garveyism even while contributing to the official organ of the UNIA. One can only speculate as to the motives for Walrond's renewing his association with Garvey instead of joining one of the rival black organizations in England in the 1930s that seemed to better conform to his views. Perhaps as a self-imposed exile on the main street of the British Empire, he sought refuge in the familiar. The question of why his projects to write a history of the Panama Canal and a series of fictional works on the Caribbean never materialized remains a mystery. A letter he wrote to the Guggenheim Foundation in 1940, the year of Garvey's death, however, gives a hint of his situation:

> Unfortunately, as a depression casualty I have had my ups and downs; my quest for security in a world in which nothing is stable led me astray. Yet even now, with everything more insecure than ever before, all my energies are being

directed towards one end, namely to produce something which would in some small measure justify the confidence which the Foundation so generously reposed in me twelve years ago![28]

Walrond received a small retainer from Garvey for his contributions to *Black Man*. His renewed association with Garvey in the 1930s could therefore be attributed to nothing more than a desire for financial security, however tenuous and irregular. It would certainly have been more ideologically consistent had Walrond decided to throw his support to the burgeoning radicalized pan-Africanist movements of C.L.R. James and George Padmore instead of to the declining Garveyite movement, which was pretty much a spent force even before Garvey's death in 1940. However, intriguingly, Walrond did contribute one short piece to the *Keys*, the journal of the League of Coloured Peoples, in 1935, a one-page review of Zora Neale Hurston's *Jonah's Gourd Vine* and Langston Hughes's *The Ways of White Folks*.[29] Obviously, such a short and inconsequential contribution hardly constitutes any form of allegiance to the League of Coloured Peoples. It is, however, worth noting that Walrond occasionally met with Padmore and James at Amy Ashwood Garvey's restaurant in London. His relationship with Padmore was close enough that he saw fit to pay his respects at his funeral in 1959.[30] On the other hand, James himself offered a reason that Walrond never saw fit to throw in his lot with the radical pan-Africanists, despite his close personal ties with them. Walrond had first met James in 1929 when he attended one of his lectures, "The Colonial Question in Manchester". When James attempted to engage Walrond in a discussion on Marx, Walrond interrupted him by saying, "Marx was not the one. Garvey is the man."[31]

Walrond outlived his former employer by more than a quarter century, and his meagre contributions to *Black Man* proved to be his final sustained output outside of the recently recovered *Roundway Review* pieces. Rarely a prolific writer, the smattering of small pieces in myriad publications after Garvey's death provides only scant evidence of the direction of his writing. Perhaps, had he had the funds and energy, he could have produced his work on the Panama Canal and a sequel to *Tropic Death*, writings that would have further distanced him from Garveyism. Walrond's association with Garvey in England in the 1930s was motivated to a certain extent both by financial necessity and a degree of nostalgia. However, Walrond's comments to James underscore that, even while he was associating with pan-Africanist movements in the United Kingdom, he maintained at least some sense of ideological kinship with the black nationalism of his former employer long after they had worked together in New York. Walrond's association with the League of Coloured Peoples, however tenuous, and his renewed association with Garvey in the 1930s, suggest that Walrond continued to wrestle with, if not reconcile, the ideologies of Marxism, black nationalism and pan-Africanism during his self-imposed exile in the centre of the British Empire.

NOTES

1. Marcus Garvey, *Black Man* 1, no. 6 (November 1934): 2.
2. For Garvey's years in Jamaica, see Judith Stein, *The World of Marcus Garvey: Race and Class in Modern Society* (Baton Rouge: Louisiana State University Press, 1986), 256–65.
3. Garvey quoted in E. David Cronon, *Black Moses: The Story of Marcus Garvey and the UNIA* (1955; repr., Madison: University of Wisconsin Press, 1969), 158.
4. Eric Walrond, "Developed and Undeveloped Negro Literature: Writers Desert Great Field of Folk-Life for Propaganda", *Dearborn Independent*, 13 May 1922.
5. Eric Walrond, "The New Negro Faces America", *Current History*, February 1923, 786–88 and "Imperator Africanus, Marcus Garvey: Menace or Promise?" *Independent*, no. 114 (January 1925): 8–11.
6. George Lamming, *The Pleasures of Exile* (London: Allison and Busby, 1984), 24–25.
7. Michelle Ann Stephens, *Black Empire: The Masculine Global Imaginary of Caribbean Intellectuals in the United States, 1914–1962* (Durham: Duke University Press, 2005), 79–82. Curiously, Stephens makes no mention of Walrond in her otherwise wide-ranging study. She does, however, discuss him in her article "Eric Walrond's *Tropic Death* and the Discontents of American Modernity", in *Prospero's Isles: The Presence of the Caribbean in the American Imaginary*. ed. Dianne Accaria-Zavala and Rudolfo Popelnik (London: Macmillan, 2004), 167–78.
8. Winston James, *Holding Aloft the Banner of Ethiopia: Caribbean Radicalism in Early Twentieth-Century America* (London: Verso, 1998), 70–71.
9. Robert Bone and Louis Parascandola, "An Ellis Island of the Soul: Eric Walrond and the Turbulent Passage from Garveyite to New Negro", *Afro-Americans in New York Life and History* (July 2010): 4–5.
10. Marcus Garvey, "The British West Indies in the Mirror of Civilization", in *Mar-

cus Garvey and the Vision of Africa, ed. John Henrik Clarke and Amy Jacques Garvey (New York: Vintage Books, 1974), 82.
11. Marcus Garvey, "A Journey of Self-Discovery", first published in *Current History*, September 1923, reprinted in Clarke and Garvey, *Marcus Garvey*, 73. See also Stein, *World of Marcus Garvey*, 28–32.
12. Eric Walrond, *Tropic Death* (New York: Boni and Liveright, 1926), 85.
13. V.S. Naipaul, *The Middle Passage* (London: André Deutsch, 1962), 29.
14. Quoted in Roger E. Kanet, "The Comintern and the 'Negro Question': Communist Policy in the United States and Africa, 1921–1941", *Survey* 19, no. 4 (Autumn 1973): 93. In her study of the impact of the Soviet Union on African American writers, Kate Baldwin notes that the Soviets had little understanding of the differences between the Garvey movement and Padmore's pan-Africanism, preferring to regard them both as ideological comrades-in-arms against Western imperialism. See Kate Baldwin, *Beyond the Color Line and the Iron Curtain: Reading Encounters Between Black and Red, 1922–1963* (Durham: Duke University Press, 2002), 243.
15. C.L.R. James, *A History of Negro Revolt* (New York: Haskell House, 1969), 69–71.
16. In "The Negro in the Armies of Europe", *Black Man* 2, no. 3 (September–October 1936): 8–9, Walrond notes the opposition of England, Germany and the Soviet Union to French use of black troops and concludes that "the French . . . accord the Negro the fullest scope for development in the army, as in civil and political life", although he recognizes that blacks have "been made to do the spade-work in the European conquest of Africa".
17. See chapter 6 of Paul B. Rich, *Race and Empire in British Politics* (Cambridge: Cambridge University Press, 1986).
18. Eric Walrond, "The Negro in London", *Black Man* 1, no. 12 (Late March 1936): 9.
19. Ibid., 10.
20. Eric Walrond, "On England", *Black Man* 3, no. 10 (July 1938): 18.
21. See for example Marcus Garvey, "Italy and Germany", *Black Man* 2, no. 2 (1937): 1–2.
22. In his unpublished paper "Anticolonial on the River Avon: Eric Walrond's Black British Writing", James Davis rightly points out that even while writing for a Garveyite publication, Walrond's militant views were more Marxist than black nationalist.
23. Eric Walrond, "The Negro Before the World", *Black Man* 3, no. 9 (March 1938): 5.
24. Ibid., 4.
25. Eric Walrond, "Fascism and the Negro", *Black Man* 2, no. 6 (March–April 1937): 3.
26. Eric Walrond, "The End of Ras Nasibu", *Black Man* 2, no. 5 (January 1937): 13–14.

27. Eric Walrond, "Can the Negro Measure Up?", *Black Man* 2, no. 7 (August 1937): 9–10.
28. Quoted in Kenneth Ramchand, "The Writer Who Ran Away: Eric Walrond and *Tropic Death*", *Savacou: Journal of the Caribbean Artists Movement* 2 (September 1970): 74.
29. Cited in Eric Walrond, *"Winds Can Wake Up the Dead": An Eric Walrond Reader*, ed. Louis J. Parascandola (Detroit: Wayne State University Press, 1998), 348. Parascandola notes that another article in *The Keys* from 1938 signed E.W. could be attributed to either Walrond or Eric Williams (344).
30. See introduction in Louis J. Parascandola and Carl A. Wade, eds., *In Search of Asylum: The Later Writings of Eric Walrond* (Gainesville: University Press of Florida, 2011), lviii–lix, n40.
31. Walrond quoted in Frank Stewart, "Eric Walrond, *Tropic Death* and the Predicament of the Colonial Writer", *Studies in the Humanities and Sciences* (Japan) 38, no. 2 (1998): 75.

SELECTED BIBLIOGRAPHY AND WORKS OF INTEREST ON ERIC WALROND

Agatucci, Cora. "Eric Walrond (1898–1966)". In *A Bio-Bibliographical Critical Sourcebook*, 429–39. Westport, CT: The Greenwood Press, 2000.

Barton, Rebecca Chalmers. *Black Voices in American Fiction, 1900–1930*. Oakdale, NY: Dowling College Press, 1976.

Bassett, John E., ed. *Harlem in Review: Critical Reactions to Black American Writers, 1917–1939*. Selinsgrove, PA: Susquehanna University Press, 1992. [Pages 65–67 list reviews of *Tropic Death*.]

Berry, Jay A. "Eric Walrond". In *Dictionary of Literary Biography*, vol. 60. *African American Writers from the Harlem Renaissance to 1940's*, edited by Trudier Harris and Thadius M. Davis, 296–300. Detroit: Gale, 1987.

Boelcskevy, Mary Anne. "Walrond, Eric". In *African-American National Biography*. http://www.oxfordaasc.com.

Bogle, Enid E. "Eric Walrond (1898–1966)". In *Fifty Caribbean Writers: A Bio-Bibliographical Sourcebook*, ed. Daryl Cumber Dance, 474–82. Westport, CT: Greenwood Press, 1986.

Bone, Robert A. *Down Home: A History of Afro-American Short Fiction from Its Beginning to the End of the Harlem Renaissance*. New York: Putnam, 1975. Reprinted as *Down Home: Origins of the African-American Short Story* (New York: Columbia University Press, 1988).

Bone, Robert A, and Louis J. Parascandola. "An Ellis Island of the Soul: Eric Walrond and the Turbulent Passage from Garveyite to New Negro". *Afro-Americans in New York Life and History* (July 2010): 34–53.

Brown, Sterling. *The Negro in American Fiction*. New York: Atheneum, 1969.

Brawley, Benjamin Griffith. *The Negro in Literature and Art in the United States*. New York: Duffield, 1930.

Calverton, F.V. "Grounds Swells in Fiction". *Survey Graphic* 67, no. 3 (1 November 1926): 159–61.

Carter, Linda. "Eric Walrond". In *Encyclopedia of the Harlem Renaissance*, edited by Cary Wintz and Paul Finkelman, 2:1230–32. 2 vols. New York: Routledge, 2004.

Chude-Sokei, Louis. *The Last "Darky": Bert Williams, Black-on-Black Minstrelsy, and the African Diaspora*. Durham: Duke University Press, 2006.
Du Bois, W.E.B. "Five Books". *Crisis* 33 (January 1927): 152–53.
Dunkley, Larnell Jr. "White Patronage". In *Encyclopedia of the Harlem Renaissance*, edited by Cary D. Wintz and Paul Finkelman, 1253–56. New York: Routledge, 2004.
Edwards, Brent Hayes. *The Practice of Diaspora: Literature, Translation, and the Rise of Black Internationalism*. Cambridge, MA: Harvard University Press, 2003.
"Eric Walrond, Back in City, Feels No Homecoming Thrill". *New York Amsterdam News*, 9 September 1931, 11.
Fabre, Michel. *From Harlem to Paris: Black American Writers in France, 1840–1980*. Urbana: University of Illinois Press, 1991.
Frederick, Rhonda. *"Colón Man a Come": Mythographies of Panamá Canal Migration*. Lantham, MD: Lexington Books, 2005.
——— . "Mythographies of Panamá Canal Migrations: Eric Walrond's Tropic Death". In *Marginal Migrations: The Circulation of Cultures within the Caribbean*, edited by Shalini Puri 43–76. Oxford: Macmillan, 2003.
Gloster, Hugh M. *Negro Voices in American Fiction*. New York: Russell and Russell, 1976.
Green, Elizabeth Lay. *The Negro in American Literature: An Outline for Individual and Group Study*. College Park, MD: McGrath Publishing, 1928.
Hathaway, Heather. *Caribbean Waves: Relocating Claude McKay and Paule Marshall*. Bloomington: Indiana University Press, 1999.
Herrick, Robert. *"Tropic Death*: Review". *New Republic*, 10 November 1926, 332.
Hill, Robert, comp. and ed. *Black Man: A Monthly Magazine of Negro Thought and Opinion*. Millwood, NJ: Kraus-Thomson, 1975.
Horne, Gerald. *Race Woman: The Lives of Shirley Graham Du Bois*. New York: New York University Press, 2000.
Hughes, Langston. "Marl-Dust and West Indian Sun". (Book review.) *New York Herald Tribune Books*, 5 December 1926, 9.
Hutchinson, George. *The Harlem Renaissance in Black and White*. Cambridge, MA: Belknap Press, 1995.
Ikonné, Chidi. *From Du Bois to Van Vechten: The Early New Negro Literature, 1903–1926*. Westport, CT: Greenwood Press, 1981.
James, Winston. *Holding Aloft the Banner of Ethiopia: Caribbean Radicalism in Early Twentieth-Century America*. London: Verso, 1998.
Lewis, David Levering. *When Harlem Was in Vogue*. New York: Vintage Books, 1982.
Martin, Tony, ed. *African Fundamentalism: A Literary and Cultural Anthology of Garvey's Harlem Renaissance*. Dover, MA: Majority Press, 1991.
——— . "The Defectors: Eric Walrond and Claude McKay". In *Literary Garveyism: Garvey, Black Arts and the Harlem Renaissance*, by Tony Martin, 124–38. Dover, MA: Majority Press, 1983.

Nance, Ethel Ray. Transcript of Oral History Interview with Ann Allen Shockley, 18 November 1970 and 23 December 1970. Fisk University Library.
Newton, Velma. *The Silver Men: West Indian Labour Migration to Panama, 1850–1914*. Kingston: Institute of Social and Economic Research, University of the West Indies, 1984.
Niblett, Michael. "The Arc of the 'Other America'": Landscape, Nature, and Region in Eric Walrond's *Tropic Death*". In *Perspectives on the "Other America": Comparative Approaches to Caribbean and Latin American Culture*, edited by Michael Niblett and Kerstin Oloff, 51–72. Amsterdam: Rodopi, 2009.
Parascandola, Louis J., ed. *"Look for Me All Around You": Caribbean Immigrants in the Harlem Renaissance*. Detroit: Wayne State University Press, 2005.
———. *"Winds Can Wake up the Dead": An Eric Walrond Reader*. Detroit: Wayne State University Press, 1998.
Parascandola, Louis J., and Carl A. Wade, eds. *In Search of Asylum: The Later Writings of Eric Walrond*. Gainesville: University Press of Florida, 2011.
Parascandola, Louis J., and Maria McGarrity. "'I'm a . . . Naughty Girl'": Prostitution and Outsider Women in James Joyce's 'The Boarding House' and Eric Walrond's 'The Palm Porch' ". *CLA Journal* 50 (2006): 141–61.
Pedersen, Carl. "The Caribbean Voices of Claude McKay and Eric Walrond". In *The Cambridge Companion to the Harlem Renaissance*, edited by George Hutchinson, 184–97. Cambridge: Cambridge University Press, 2007.
Perry, Margaret. *Silence to the Drums: A Survey of the Literature of the Harlem Renaissance*. Westport, CT: Greenwood Press, 1976.
Philipson, Robert. "The Harlem Renaissance as Postcolonial Phenomenon". *African American Review* 40, no. 1 (Spring 2006): 145–60.
Purchase, Genive Kellyonique. "Rediscovering Eric Walrond". MA thesis, Morgan State University, 2006.
Ramchand, Kenneth. "Andrew Salkey, 30th January 1928–28th April 1995". *Wasafari* (Autumn 1995): 82–84.
———. "The Writer Who Ran Away: Eric Walrond and Tropic Death". *Savacou: Journal of the Caribbean Artists Movement* 2 (September 1970): 67–75.
Reid, Ira De A. *The Negro Immigrant: His Background, Characteristics and Social Adjustment, 1899–1937*. New York: AMS Press, 1970.
Richardson, Bonham. *Panama Money in Barbados, 1900–1920*. Knoxville: University of Tennessee Press, 1985.
Rossum, Deborah J. " 'A Vision of Black Englishness': Black Intellectuals in London, 1910–1940". *Stanford Electronic Humanities Review* 5, no. 2 1997: 1–18. http://www.stanford.edu/group/SHR/5-2/rossum.html
Silbermann, Seth Clark. " 'Youse Awful Queer, Chappie': Reading Black Queer Vernacular in Black Literatures of the Americas, 1903–1967". PhD diss., University of Maryland, 2005.

Steele, Philip. *Down Pans Lane: The History of Roundway Hospital, Devizes 1851–1995*. Bradford on Avon, UK: Redwood Books, 2000.

Stephens, Michelle A. *Black Empire: The Masculine Global Imaginary of Caribbean Intellectuals in the United States, 1914–1962*. Durham: Duke University Press, 2005.

———. "Eric Walrond's *Tropic Death* and the Discontents of American Modernity". In *Prospero's Isles: The Presence of the Caribbean in the American Imaginary*, edited by Dianne Accaria-Zavala and Rudolfo Popelnik, 167–78. London: Macmillan, 2004.

Stewart, Frank E.L. "Eric Walrond, Tropic Death and the Predicament of the Colonial Expatriate Writer". *Studies in the Humanities and Sciences* (Japan) 38, no. 2 (1998): 29–88.

Story, Ralph D. "Patronage and the Harlem Renaissance: You Get What You Pay For". *CLA Journal* 32, no. 3 (1989): 284–95.

Stovall, Tyler. *Paris Noir: African Americans in the City of Light*. Boston: Houghton Mifflin, 1996.

Thurman, Wallace. "Negro Artists and the Negro". *New Republic*, 31 August 1927, 37–39.

Tolson, Melvin B. *The Harlem Group of Negro Writers*, edited by Edward J. Mullen. Westport, CT: Greenwood Press, 2001.

Underwood, Edna Worthley. "West Indian Literature: Some Negro Poets of Panama". *West Indian Review* (March 1936): 36–37, 57.

Wade, Carl A. "African-American Aesthetics and the Short Fiction of Eric Walrond: Tropic Death and the Harlem Renaissance". *CLA Journal* 42 (June 1999): 403–29.

———. Review of *"Winds Can Wake Up the Dead": An Eric Walrond Reader*, ed. Louis J. Parascandola. *Wasafiri* 30 (Autumn 1999): 69–70.

Wade, Carl A., and Louis J. Parascandola. "In Search of Asylum: Eric Walrond's Roundway Review Writings, 1952–1957". *Journal of Caribbean Studies* 19, nos. 1 and 2 (2004–5): 21–42.

Walrond, Eric. "Avec Eric Walrond". Interview with Jacques Lebar. *Lectures du Soir*, 14 January 1933.

Watkins-Owens, Irma. *Blood Relatives: Caribbean Immigrants and the Harlem Community, 1900–1930*. Bloomington: Indiana University Press, 1996.

Wintz, Cary. *Black Culture and the Harlem Renaissance*. Houston: Rice University Press, 1988.

INDEX

Abyssinia, 209–10
African Blood Brotherhood, 80, 86, 127n93
African diaspora: difference in unity, 103, 105–6; race-call of Africa, 155; racial "revolutionary romance", 60; racial solidarity and, 72–75; unrepresentable diversity of, 75
African Times and Orient Review, 205
Ali, Duse Mohamed, 205
American Caravan, 42, 169
American Hunger (Wright), 128
American Philosophical Association, 157, 158
An American Tragedy (Dreiser), 152
Anderson, Sherwood, 152
anticolonialism: alliance with Communism, 129; authority of English state, 179–80
apprentice fiction. *See* Walrond, Eric – apprentice fiction
Aramata, Hiroshi, 138
Argosy All-Story Weekly, 153
articulation: as difference within unity, 103, 105–6
atavism, 51–52, 164n33

Baldwin, James, 177–78
Banana Bottom (McKay), 82
Banjo (McKay), 81, 85, 87–88, 94
Barbados, 19, 20, 110; "Drought", 23, 26, 46, 130–31, 136–38, 143, 144; "Panama Gold", 23, 29–32, 112–17, 138–41, 144; "The Black Pin", 23, 25, 26, 28, 38, 46–47; "The Vampire Bat", 23, 25–26, 28
Barbusse, Henri, 129
Barrett, Lindsay, 29
Batouala (Maran), 61–62
Becoming Black (Wright), 103–7
Bennett, Gwendolyn, 168
Bennett, Louise, 29
black art: forms of, 62
Black Empire (Stephens), 9, 100, 107–8, 122
black identity. *See* identity
black immigrant modernism, 81, 85
black internationalism, 102–3, 124n22
Black Man, 5, 11, 33, 202, 203, 205, 207, 209, 211
black transnationalism, 8–9, 67–68, 106–7, 122, 206–7; African American racial solidarity and, 72–75; black empire narratives, 100–102, 122; gendered tropes of, 106; race-based unity, 107–8
blackface minstrelsy, 57–58
blackness: cross-cultural diversity of, 69; cultural invisibility and, 57–58, 59; gendered language of, 59; as signifier of diaspora, 73; of Spanish-speaking world, 64–66; as unity of diversity, 104

black-on-black cross culturality, 72–75; of colonial modernity, 89, 90; intraracial tension, 86, 87
Bone, Dorothea, 171
Bone, Robert, 8, 10, 35–53, 149–66, 191; biographical research on Walrond, 170–71, 184–85n12; *Down Home*, 170; *The Negro Novel in America*, 170
Boni and Liveright Publishers, 7, 169, 170; "The Big Ditch", 4, 6, 167
Bowen-Struyk, Heather, 138
Brathwaite, L. Edward Kamau, 29
Briggs, Cyril, 122, 123n3, 127n93, 130
British Guiana (Swan), 173
British Guiana: cultural features of, 172–73; "The White Snake", 23, 25, 26, 28, 50–51
Brooklyn (New York): black immigrant population, 188, 192–94, 198, 201n37; immigrant communities, 198
Brooklyn and Long Island Informer, 3, 188, 189
Brown, Sterling, 85

Cadogan, Edith Melita (wife of Eric Walrond), 1
Cadogan, Edith Melita (wife of Walrond), 168
Campbell, Grace, 130
Cane (Toomer), 21, 52, 78, 95
capitalism: confrontation with peasant economy, 139–40; reification of lifeworld, 142–43; separation of nature and society, 134–36; unevenness of capitalist modernity, 130–31
Carew, Jan, 172
Caribbean diaspora: constructions of cultural history, 183; cultural diversity of black modernity, 88–89; diasporic nostalgia, 74–75, 77–78; émigré writers, 19

Caribbean identity: foreignness of black migration narrative, 76–77; immigrant "way of seeing", 91–92; stereotype of, 4; in *Tropic Death*, 4, 23
Carnegie, Charles, 122; *Postnationalism Prefigured*, 100
Century Company publishers, 159
Césaire, Aimé, 105
Chang Hyok-chu: "Hell of the Starving", 138
Chapman, Esther, 163n13
Cheng, Ann Anlin, 177
Ch'oe So-hae: "The Death of Pak Tol", 138
Chude-Sokei, Louis, 9, 64–65, 72–99; invisibility of Caribbean immigrants, 57–58, 59
Clarté, 129
class difference: discrimination of, 6; in England, 6, 33; "Panama Gold", 29–32
colonialism: anglophone Caribbean realities, 107; authority of English state, 179–80; colour consciousness of, 9, 49–50; European standards of development, 210; intersections of racial types, 82; legacy of hatred and, 49; mythology of white civilization, 174, 186n24; narratives of nation and, 106–7; neo-colonialism of US, 175, 181, 187n38; New World cultural forms and, 69; race consciousness and, 61–62; racial politics of, 21; vs imperialism, 23–24
colour consciousness: of art, 62; in Britain, 207; in the Caribbean, 65, 112, 115; of colonialism, 9, 49–50; as crisis of identity, 38–40; as politics of the skin, 62–64, 66–67; racial passing and, 58; of the white gaze, 61–62
Communism: alliance with anticolo-

nialism, 129; Garveyism and, 206–7, 213n14; vs Fascism, 209
Conroy, Jack, 10
Crisis (NAACP), 21, 86, 168, 194
Crosswaith, Frank R., 130
Cuba: racial discrimination in, 65
Cullen, Countee, 5, 85, 168, 169; "Incident", 177
cultural invisibility: of Caribbean immigrants, 57–58
Cunard, Nancy, 5; correspondence with McKay, 82, 83, 85
Current History, 86, 153, 203

Davis, James, 11, 167–87, 188–201
Davis, Robert H., 153–54
Denning, Michael, 128–29, 142
depression, 33–34, 108, 109, 111, 176–77, 186–87n28
diasporic nostalgia, 74–75, 77–78
diasporic politics: black identity and, 60–62; of transnationalism, 72–75
difference in unity, 9; of African diaspora, 103, 105–6, 124n22; and black solidarity, 107–8
Domingo, W.A.: "Gift of the Black Tropics", 86, 194
Douglas, Aaron, 150, 168
Down Home (Bone), 8, 170
Dreiser, Theodore, 152
Du Bois, W.E.B., 5, 105, 168, 170, 203; African Blood Brotherhood, 80; *Crisis*, 21, 194; "literary prostitutes", 84; Pan-African Conference speech, 102; pan-Africanist movements, 74; *The Souls of Black Folk*, 61, 78; 'Talented Tenth', 130, 155
Dunkley, Larnell Jr, 10, 150, 151, 161

Eastman, Crystal, 84
Eastman, Max, 83, 84

Edmondson, Belinda, 59; Caribbean intellectual as gentlemen, 173–75, 185–86n19
Edwards, Brent: *The Practice of Diaspora*, 102–3, 105, 109
Elder, J.D., 29
empire: masculinist discourses and, 106–7
England: Caribbean migration to, 192, 200n17; class structure in, 6, 33; Garvey in, 202, 204–5; role of tradition in English society, 208; Walrond in, 5–7, 203–12
epidermalization, 67
Ethiopianism, 74, 207
exile (the): as universal figure, 203–4

Fanon, Frantz, 61, 105
Fascism: vs Communism, 209
father-son relationship: "A Cholo Romance", 44; "The Yellow One", 49; trauma of absent father, 37, 171–72, 185n14; "Tropic Death", 32, 33, 38, 120–21
Fauset, Jesse, 167
folk: dehumanization of, 10; primal world of, 28–29
folkways: and the supernatural, 25–26, 28
Forbes' Magazine, 153, 168
Ford, Henry, 203
"foreign Negro": assimilation process, 86–88; as flash agent, 90–91
Foucault, Michel, 60, 62
France, 5; Marseilles as escape from Harlem, 88; Prix Goncourt, 61; use of black troops, 208, 213n16
Frazier, E. Franklin, 85
Frederick, Rhonda, 9–10, 100–127, 131, 181
Friede, Donald, 169

Garvey, Amy Ashwood, 206, 211
Garvey, Marcus: back-to-Africa movement, 203; *Black Man*, 5, 11, 33, 202, 203, 205, 207, 209, 211; black transnationalism, 8–9, 67, 106; *Brooklyn and Long Island Informer*, 3, 188, 189; death of, 211; deportation from US, 202; in England, 202, 204–5; and McKay, 83; *Negro World*, 3, 21, 57, 83, 86, 153, 188, 189; *New Jamaican*, 202; newspapers, 3; opposition to Communism, 207; pan- Africanist movements, 74; racial politics of, 11, 21; reconciliation with Walrond, 5; "The British West Indies in the Mirror of Civilization", 205; Universal Negro Improvement Association (UNIA), 3; and Walrond, 11, 155, 168, 198; *Weekly Review*, 3, 189; white patronage, and "literary prostitutes", 83–84, 150
Garveyism, 67–68, 189; decline of, 206–7, 213n14; development of, 204–5; "Garvey Must Go" campaign, 80; "Imperator Africanus", 44, 49; rejection of by Walrond, 155, 168; "The Voodoo's Revenge", 44, 85
Gates, Henry Louis Jr, 63
gender: empire, and masculinist discourses, 106–7; interpretations of, 9, 10; as sociopolitical category, 104, 105
Gilroy, Paul, 67
Glissant, Edouard, 172; "foreign Negro" as flash agent, 90–91; *The Poetics of Relation*, 82
Gold, Michael: *Jews without Money*, 132
Gothic fiction, 35–53; "A Cholo Romance", 43–44; as antipastoral, 35–36; exoticized images of the Caribbean, 173–74, 186n22; "The Voodoo's Revenge", 43–44; "The White Snake", 50–51

Graham, Shirley, 5, 168
Gregoire, Henri: *An Enquiry Concerning the Intellectual and Moral Faculties and Literature of Negroes*, 210
Guggenheim Foundation: Fellowship award, 4, 5, 153, 169
Guillén, Nicolás, 155

Hall, Stuart, 103, 172
Harlem: black immigrant population, 194; Caribbean émigrés in, 170, 184n9; as city of dualities, 67; involvement with political movements, 130; as "sociological *el dorado*, 86–88; tropicalization of, 80–81
Harlem Renaissance, 1, 19, 21; black internationalism and, 102–3; black modernism, and racial solidarity, 9, 73–75; black transnationalism and, 101–2, 123n3; Caribbean writers, reception of, 75–76; interracial dynamics of, 151; micro-politics of, 83; "Negrotarians", 149; Walrond's place in historiography, 169–70, 184n9; white patronage, 10, 149–66; white patrons, personal agendas of, 149–50, 151
Harlem Shadows (McKay), 77, 80
Harmon, William E., 151
Harmon Award, 4, 169
Harris, Wilson, 172
Harrison, Hubert H., 130
Hearn, Lafcadio, 8, 36, 51, 157; "A Midsummer Trip to the Tropics", 48–49
Heinrichs, Jurgen, 151
"Hell of the Starving" (Chang Hyokchu), 138
Herrick, Robert, 45, 169
Hill, Robert, 2
Hitchcock, Frederick, 159
Holstein, Casper, 85, 153, 163n19

Home to Harlem (McKay), 21, 81, 85, 87–88, 94, 150
Hughes, Langston, 168; patron-artist relationship with Mason, 150; "The Weary Blues", 85; *The Ways of White Folks*, 211
Huiswood, Otto, 206
Hurst, Fannie, 151
Hurston, Zora Neale, 168, 206; *Jonah's Gourd Vine*, 211; Moe and, 158, 161, 165n43; "Negrotarians", 149; patron-artist relationship with Mason, 150, 155, 156, 164n33; "Spunk", 85; "The Pet Negro System", 156; *Their Eyes Were Watching God*, 158
Hutchinson, George, 151

identity: African American identity, assumption of, 58; alienation, and cultural displacement, 172; black diasporic identity formation, 103–7; Caribbean identity, 1, 172–73; determination of through difference, 103; diasporic politics and, 60–62; racial self-identification, 91–92; search for in Walrond's writings, 6, 37, 38; white/black duality, 174–75, 186n24; writing as exploration of, 36
immigrant communities: assimilation process, 6, 86–88; Caribbean immigrant culture in New York, 75–77; Caribbean "way of seeing", 91–92; displacement of, 4, 22; intra-racial tension, 86, 87; militant political spirit of, 191; as "other", 8; societal bullying of immigrants, 43; as vagabondage, 82, 89
imperialism: in New World plantation system, 131; of US in Panama, 19–20, 175, 181, 187n38; vs European colonialism, 23–24, 129

"Incident" (Cullen), 177
Independent, 203
industrialization: conflict between industrial and agricultural economies, 112; impact on folk communities, 29, 118, 126–27n82
intercultural interaction: African American New Negro and Caribbean New World Negro, 59; and colour consciousness, 9
International African Friends of Abyssinia, 206
The Invention of Africa (Mudimbe), 74

James, C.L.R., 10, 22, 132, 206, 207, 211; black transnationalism, 8–9, 106; *A History of Negro Revolt*, 207; "The Colonial Question in Manchester", 211
James, Winston, 109, 191, 204
Jameson, Frederic, 130–31; capitalist reification, 142–43
Jews without Money (Gold), 132
Johnson, Charles S., 21, 161; *Opportunity*, 84; *Opportunity* awards, 154
Johnson, James Weldon, 168
Jonah's Gourd Vine (Hurston), 211
Jones, R. Clifford, 80–81

Kenyatta, Jomo, 206
Keys, 208, 211
Koestler, Arthur, 209
Kyk-over-Al, 172

labour: commodification of, 2–3, 13n6, 20, 131, 137, 181
Lamming, George, 204; Caribbean immigrant "way of seeing", 91–92
landscapes: sepulchral descriptions, 66–67
language: local dialects and, 4, 23, 26–27

Larsen, Nella, 168
The Last "Darky" (Chude-Sokei), 9
League of Coloured Peoples, 6, 206–7, 212; *Keys*, 208, 211
Leighten, Patricia, 150
Lenin, Vladimir, 129
Lewin, Olive, 29
Lewis, David Levering, 5, 66, 73, 149, 161
Lewis, Sinclair, 152
Liberator, 83, 84
Locke, Alain: internationalist intentions of, 102; *The New Negro*, 3, 58, 85–86, 154, 194; patron-artist relationship with Mason, 150
Loti, Pierre, 8, 36, 51, 157
Lovelace, Earl, 29

Main Street (Lewis), 152
Mair, Lucille Mathurin (daughter of Eric Walrond), 1
Maran, René: *Batoula*, 61–62
Marx, Karl, 139; separation of nature and society, 134–35
Marxism, 5, 208–9, 213n22
Mason, Charlotte Osgood: patron-artist relationship of, 150–51, 155, 156, 164n33
Masters, Edgar Lee, 152
McKay, Claude, 42, 59, 73, 130, 168, 170, 201n37; "After the Winter", 80; *Banana Bottom*, 82; *Banjo*, 81, 85, 87–88, 94; black transnationalism, 8–9, 106; comparisons and contrasts to Walrond, 82–86, 88–90, 94; correspondence with Nancy Cunard, 82, 83, 85; death of, 22; in England, 208; "Flame Heart", 80; on Garvey, 83; Harlem Renaissance involvement, 19, 57; *Harlem Shadows*, 77, 80; "Home Thoughts", 80; *Home to Harlem*, 21, 81, 85, 87–88, 94, 150; "I Shall Return", 80; "If We Must Die", 77–78, 79–81; "Outcast", 80; "The Tropics in New York", 77–78; "To One Coming North", 77–78
melancholia, 63; of Bert Williams, 57; racial melancholia, 177–78
Mendes, Alfred, 132
Messenger, 21, 86, 130
The Middle Passage (Naipaul), 206
migration: alienation, and cultural displacement, 172, 205; Caribbean immigrant culture in New York, 75–77; Caribbean migration to England, 192, 200n17; Caribbean racialization and, 204; in childhood and youth of Walrond, 2, 37; as cultural reality of diaspora, 96–97; diasporic nostalgia, 74–75, 77–78; displacement of immigrant communities, 4, 22; Great Migration of American South, 76, 194; immigrant's ordeal of, 46–47; impact on self-identity, 120; need for home, 33; panoramic racial specularity, 92–95; patterns of immigration, 75; psychological effects of on colonized peoples, 109, 125n40; struggle for survival and, 48–49; transplantation and dislocation, 8, 38; US immigration narrative, 192–94; xenophobia and, 46–47
Miller, Kelly, 191
Mittelholzer, Edgar, 172
modernization: reifying impact of, 143
Moe, Henry Allen, 6; correspondence with Walrond, 10, 33–34, 109; Guggenheim Foundation and, 157–58, 164–65n41; Harlem Renaissance and, 161; relationship with Walrond, 151, 157–61; Zora Hurston and, 158, 165n43

Moody, Sir Harold Arundel, 6, 207
Moore, Richard B., 130
Morel, E.D., 208
mother-son relationship, 37; "Subjection", 39; "Tropic Death", 39, 118–20
Mudimbe, V.Y.: *The Invention of Africa*, 74

Naipaul, V.S., 22, 178–79; *The Middle Passage*, 206
Nance, Ethel Ray, 168
National Association for the Advancement of Colored People: *Crisis*, 21, 86, 168
National Urban League: *Opportunity*, 3, 19, 21, 84, 86, 155, 168, 169, 189, 194
nature: destruction of, 10; as dramatic agent, 26, 27–28, 46; production and reproduction of, 134; separation of nature and society, 134–36; transformation of in *Tropic Death*, 136–37; vs abstract space, 138–41
Nazism, 209
Negrismo, 74, 86
Negritude, 74, 86
Negro International: *Negro Worker*, 206
The Negro Novel in America (Bone), 170
Negro Worker, 206
Negro World, 3, 21, 57, 83, 86, 153, 168, 188, 189, 203
"Negrotarian" patrons, 149, 152
neo-colonialism: of United States, 19–20, 175, 181, 187n38
neorealism. *See* proletarian arts movement
Nettleford, Rex, 29
New Jamaican, 202
New Masses, 5, 130
The New Negro (Locke), 194; "Gift of the Black Tropics", 86; "The Palm Porch", 3, 85–86, 154; "The Paradox of Color", 58, 60–61, 62

New Negro movement, 19, 40; African American cultural expression, 21; black transnationalism, 67–68; development of black leadership, 203; trope of, 63
New Republic, 86, 153, 168
Niblett, Michael, 10, 128–46
Nichols, Julia and Charles, 188–89
Nigger Heaven (Van Vechten), 84, 168

obeah: as resistance to white culture, 36–37; rural vs urban life, 133; supernatural power of, 28; vs Christianity, 25
Ogbu, John: voluntary/involuntary minorities, 96
Opportunity (National Urban League), 3, 19, 21, 84, 86, 155, 168, 169, 189, 194
Opportunity awards, 85, 153, 154, 163n19
oppression: dialectical oppression, 92; discourses of racial freedom and, 60–62; proletarian arts movement and, 129; shared victimization of Old and New World blacks, 67–68
"otherness": of blacks, 104, 105; of immigrants, 8; the white Other, 63
Owen, Chandler, 21

Padmore, George, 6, 206, 207, 211
pan-Africanist movements, 6, 204–5, 211; American immigration policy and, 81; black internationalism and, 102–3; Communism and, 206–7, 213n14; diaspora of the "Black Atlantic", 74–75; as politics of relation, 91–92
Panama: knowledge of Afro-Caribbean history, 181–82
Panama Canal Zone, 19–20, 110; capitalist modernization, impact on nature, 136–37; commodification of labour, 2–3, 13n6, 20, 131, 137, 181;

Panama Canal Zone (cont'd) cultural diversity of black modernity, 88–89, 111, 125n50; emigration to, 29; gold/silver policy, 3, 132; neo-colonialism of US, 19–20, 175, 181, 187n38; "Subjection", 23, 39, 130–31, 136, 141, 144; "The Godless City", 68–69, 93–94; "The Palm Porch", 3, 23, 24, 85–86, 132–33, 136; "The Second Battle", 6, 11; "The Wharf Rats", 23, 24–25, 28, 125n50, 131, 133; trade unionism, 140

Panama Star and Herald, 20, 189

pan-Caribbean migrations: panoramic racial specularity, 92–95

Pankhurst, Sylvia, 208

pan-Latin American migrations: panoramic racial specularity, 92–95

Parascandola, Louis J., 1–16, 61, 65, 149–66, 171, 188–201; *In Search of Asylum*, 11; *Winds Can Wake Up the Dead*, 169

pastoral ideal: vs antipastoral, 35–36

patriarchal world view: of hetero-normative masculinity, 105; of white supremacy, 107

patron-artist relationship: personal agendas of white patrons, 149–50, 151

Pedersen, Carl, 11, 202–14

Pell, Henry, 7

The Penitent (Underwood), 151, 154–55

Perry, Samuel, 138

Phillips, Caryl, 57

Plymouth Brethren, 25, 36, 48, 189

The Poetics of Relation (Glissant), 82

Postnationalism Prefigured (Carnegie), 100

poverty: as cause for migration, 122; economic exploitation and, 25; ghetto life of, 26

The Practice of Diaspora (Edwards), 102–3, 105, 109

pretentiousness: as form of bigotry, 41–42; of urban bourgeois, 133, 191–92

primitivism: colonial stereotypes of, 150–51; in Gothic fiction, 43–44; obeah as resistance to white culture, 36–37

primitivist perspective: of white patronage, 10, 150–51, 155–56

proletarian arts movement, 10; bodily horror as theme, 137–38; *Clarté*, 129; Korean proletarian writers, 138; trade unionism, 128; workers' housing, 131–32, 133, 145n16

publishing: difficulties of black West Indian authors, 178–79

Pushkin, Aleksandr, 154–55

race: African American ideas of, 59; Caribbean immigrant "way of seeing", 91–92; and colour consciousness, 9; convergence of understandings on, 59–60; historical consciousness of, 60–63; patterns of immigration, 75; as politics of the skin, 62–64, 66–67; as sociopolitical category, 104

racial consciousness: of colonialism, 61–62; and community, 175, 186n25; "Cynthia Goes to the Prom", 189–91; "vanilla temptation" and, 41–42, 192; of Walrond, 123n2

racial discrimination: within African American community, 58; in Caribbean communities, 2, 21; in Cuba, 65; Jim Crow modes of in Canal Zone, 88–89; pretentiousness and, 41–42, 133, 191–92; in United States, 2, 21, 36, 40–44

racial grievance: vocabulary of, 177–78, 187n29

racial inferiority, 210

racial passing: as form of colour consciousness, 58

racial "revolutionary romance", 60
racial solidarity: African diaspora and, 72–75; as ethnological oneness, 84–85; global consciousness of, 204; in United States, 194
racism: as depersonalization, 41; intersections of racial types, 82; national origin, and ethnic differences, 194; white/European vision of black subjectivity, 101, 123n6
Ramchand, Kenneth, 8, 19–34, 143; on "Panama Gold", 112; on the short story, 1; *The West Indian Novel and Its Background*, 167–68
Randolph, A. Philip, 21
Reed, Amanda, 153
religion: church as agent of acculturation, 39; naive faith and, 27; obeah vs Christianity, 25, 28, 49; Seventh-Day Adventists, Caribbeanization of, 80–81
"Revolt from the Village" movement, 152
Rice Burroughs, Edgar, 153
Richardson, Bonham, 132
Robeson, Paul, 207
Rogers, Joel Augustus, 86; *From Superman to Man*, 77
Roundway Hospital, 5, 7, 109
Roundway Review, 7, 109, 160, 176; "From British Guiana to Roundway", 110–11; "Success Story", 6, 11, 188, 192–94; "The Second Battle", 6, 11, 159

Savacou, 168
Schomburg, Arturo/Arthur, 83, 201n37
Scott, David, 60
Scottsboro Boys, 6
In Search of Asylum (Parascandola and Wade), 11

Selassie, Haile, 207, 209–10
Senghor, Léopold Sédar, 105
sepulchral descriptions, 66–67
sexuality: as sociopolitical category, 104
Seymour, A.J.: features of Guianese culture, 172–73
slavery: black migration narrative of American South, 76; as legacy of colonialism, 6; relations of personal domination, 131; white/European vision of black subjectivity, 101, 123n6
Smart Set, 153, 168
Smith, Neil, 134
social organization: Canal Zone housing conditions, 131–32, 133, 145n16
social realism, 8; West Indian fiction of, 10
social relations: utopian potential of, 141–42, 143–44
The Souls of Black Folk (Du Bois), 61, 78
Spence, Eulalie, 201n37
Spoon River Anthology (Masters), 152
Springarn, Arthur, 151
Springarn, Joel, 151
"Spunk" (Hurston), 85
Stephens, Michelle A., 8–9, 57–71, 172, 175, 204; *Black Empire*, 100, 107–8, 122
Stewart, Dorothy (daughter of Eric Walrond), 171, 176
Stewart, Frank (grandson of Eric Walrond), 2; biographical research on Walrond, 171, 184–85n12
Stewart, Joan (granddaughter of Eric Walrond), 171
Story, Ralph D., 10, 149, 161
strike narrative, 142
Styron, William: on depression, 177
success: backsliding and, 38; pressures to succeed, 37
Success Magazine, 153, 180
Sunao, Tokunaga: *The Sunless Street*, 132

The Sunless Street (Sunao), 132
From Superman to Man (Rogers), 77
Survey Graphic (*Harlem: Mecca of the New Negro*), 85
Swan, Michael: *British Guiana*, 173

"Talented Tenth", 130, 155
"The Big Ditch" (Walrond), 4, 6, 51, 125n38, 159, 165–66n45, 167, 175
"The Death of Pak Tol" (Ch'oe Sohae), 138
"The Paradox of Color" (White), 58, 60–61, 62
"The Weary Blues" (Hughes), 85
Their Eyes Were Watching God (Hurston), 158
Toomer, Jean, 8, 80, 167, 168; *Cane*, 21, 52, 78, 95
trade unionism: impact on Caribbean labour, 140; proletarian arts movement and, 128
Tropic Death (Walrond). See also Walrond, Eric – works: acclaim for, 1–2; Caribbean folkways and the supernatural, 25–26; contemporary reviews of, 101, 123n2; dedication to Holstein, 85; economic exploitation, 25; folk cultures of colonized peoples, 210; foreignness of black migration narrative, 76–77; industrialization vs plantation economy, 45; influence on McKay, 81; intraracial hostility in, 89; language, and local dialects, 4, 23, 26–27; migration, and displacement, 22; mythic language of racial values, 95–96; nature as dramatic agent, 26, 27–28; obeah vs Christianity, 25; portrayal of working-class Caribbeans, 130; as a "return to beginnings", 51–52; sex, levelling power of, 24; sudden death, motif of, 45; transformation of nature, and capitalist modernization, 136–37
Trotsky, Leon, 130

Underwood, Edna Worthley, 198; as agent for Walrond, 153; as patron of Walrond, 151–57; patronage of Walrond, 10; *The Penitent*, 151, 154–55; as translator, 152, 163n13; *West Indian Review*, 155, 157, 163n13
United States: African diaspora, and racial solidarity, 72–75; Afro-Caribbean immigrants in, 192–98; black transnationalism, 67–68; Caribbean migration to, 3, 75–77, 188; colour consciousness in, 9; "foreign Negro" assimilation, 86–88; Great Migration of American South, 76, 194; interracial context of conflict, 61; invisibility of Caribbean immigrants, 57–58; neo-colonialism of, 19–20, 175, 181, 187n38; in Panama Canal Zone, 2–3, 88–89, 131; pastoralizing of American South, 78
Universal Negro Improvement Association (UNIA): in England, 202; *Negro World*, 3, 21, 57, 83, 86, 153, 168
Up From Slavery (Washington), 205

vagabondage, 82, 89
Van Vechten, Carl: *Nigger Heaven*, 84, 168
Vanity Fair, 168

Wade, Carl A., 1–16, 149–66, 171; *In Search of Asylum*, 11
Walrond, Eric: biographical research on, 170–71, 176, 184–85n12; biographies of, 169–70; Brooklyn (New York) years, 188–89, 198–99, 201n41;

character of, 5; childhood and youth, 2, 19–21, 37–40, 73, 108–9; death of, 7, 22; depression, 33–34, 108, 109, 111, 176–77, 210–11; in England, 203–12; as *évolué*, 36; fluidity of national identities, 108–9; as manager of calypso revue, 5; Marcus Garvey and, 3, 5, 11, 67–68, 203–4, 205, 211–12; marriage, 1, 168; Marxist world view, 134–35, 208–9, 212, 213n22; as outsider, 2, 19, 38, 122, 151, 198–99; physical description of, 168; racial discrimination experiences, 2, 3, 109; rejection of Garveyism, 155, 168, 198, 203, 205–6; Roundway Hospital, 5, 109; self-identification as Panamanian, 180

Walrond, Eric – apprentice fiction, 7, 11, 40–44; "A Cholo Romance", 43–44; "City Love", 6, 38, 42–43; "Miss Kenny's Marriage", 41–42; "The Silver King", 153; "The Stolen Necklace", 153; "The Voodoo's Revenge", 43–44, 85; "Vignettes of the Dusk", 41, 92

Walrond, Eric – journalistic career: *Argosy All-Story Weekly*, 153; *Black Man*, 5, 33, 203, 205, 207–8, 209, 211; *Brooklyn and Long Island Informer*, 3, 188, 189; *Crisis*, 21, 86, 168; *Current History*, 86, 153, 203; *Forbes' Magazine*, 153, 168; *Independent*, 203; *Messenger*, 21; *Negro World*, 3, 21, 57, 83, 86, 153, 168, 188, 189, 203; *New Masses*, 5; *New Republic*, 153, 168; *Opportunity*, 3, 19, 21, 84, 86, 155, 168, 169, 189, 194; *Panama Star and Herald*, 20, 189; proletarian arts movement, 130; *Smart Set*, 153, 168; *Success Magazine*, 153, 180; *Vanity Fair*, 168; *Weekly Review*, 3

Walrond, Eric – literary career: acclaim for, 1–2, 4, 168, 169, 183–84n3; *American Caravan*, 169; anti-tropical representations of Caribbean, 78–80; apprentice fiction, 7, 11, 40–44; atavism, 164n33; autobiographical aspects in work of, 32–34, 36–40, 117; on Bert Williams, 80; childhood influences, 19–20; comparisons and contrasts to McKay, 82–86, 88–90, 94; decline in productivity, 178–79; descriptions of landscapes, 110; in England, 5–7; "foreign Negroes", 80; genealogical connection between the Americas, 68; as Gothic writer, 173–74; Guggenheim Fellowship, 4, 32, 153, 169; Harmon Award, 4, 169; language, and local dialects, 4, 23, 26–27, 93, 156, 195; in New York, 11, 19, 110–11; *Opportunity* awards, 85; in Paris, 5; patronage of Underwood, 151–57; relationship with Moe, 151, 157–61; Rosenwald Fellowship, 161; *Roundway Review*. See *Roundway Review*; sepulchral descriptions, 66–67; social acceptance of, 84–85; "The Big Ditch", 4, 6, 51, 125n38, 159, 165–66n45, 167, 175; unfulfilled talent of, 171–73; Zona Gale scholarship, 4, 169

Walrond, Eric – works. See also *Tropic Death* (Walrond): "A Cholo Romance", 43–44; "A Fugitive from Dixie", 205; "A Senator's Memoirs", 62–63; "Can the Negro Measure Up?", 210; "City Love", 6, 38, 42–43; "Cynthia Goes to the Prom", 188, 189–91; "Drought", 23, 26, 46, 130–31, 136–38, 143, 144; "Fascism and the Negro", 134–35; "From British Guiana to Roundway", 110–11; "I Am an American", 64–66, 92; "Imperator Africanus", 44, 49, 203; "Miss Kenny's Marriage", 41–42, 188, 191–92; "Morn

Walrond, Eric – works (cont'd)
ing in Colon", 156; "On Being a Domestic", 153; "On Being Black", 63–64, 91–92, 153; "On England", 208; "Panama Gold", 23, 29–32, 112–17, 138–41, 144; "Subjection", 23–24, 39, 130–31, 136, 141, 144; "Success Story", 6, 11, 188, 192–94; "The Black City", 92; "The Black Pin", 23, 25, 26, 28, 38, 46–47; "The Color of the Caribbean", 92; "The End of Ras Nasibu", 209–10; "The Godless City", 68–69, 93–94; "The Negro Before the World", 209; "The Negro in London", 207–8; "The Negro Literati", 92; "The New Negro Faces America", 67–68, 92, 100, 199, 203; "The Palm Porch", 3, 23, 24, 85–86, 132–33, 136, 154; "The Second Battle", 6, 11, 159; "The Silver King", 153; "The Stolen Necklace", 153; "The Stone Rebounds", 66; "The Vampire Bat", 23, 25–26, 28; "The Voodoo's Revenge", 43–44, 85, 93, 154; "The Wharf Rats", 23, 24–25, 28, 131, 133; "The White Snake", 23, 25, 26, 28, 50–51; "The Yellow One", 23, 28, 49–50; "Tropic Death", 23, 26, 28, 32, 33, 38, 39, 44, 47–48, 117–21, 131, 141; "Vignettes of the Dusk", 41, 66–67, 92, 192

Walrond, Ruth (mother of Eric), 2, 20, 33, 159

Walrond, William (father of Eric), 2, 20
Washington, Booker T., 19, 38, 203; *Up From Slavery*, 205
Watkins-Owens, Irma, 3, 86, 88–89
The Ways of White Folks (Hughes), 211
Weekly Review, 3, 189
West African Students' Union, 206
The West Indian Novel and Its Background (Ramchand), 167–68
West Indian Review, 155, 157, 163n13
Westernization: impact on folk communities, 29
White, Walter, 169; "The Paradox of Color", 58, 60–61, 62
white patronage, 10, 149–66; colonial stereotypes of primitivism, 150–51; patron-artist relationship, 149–51; primitivist perspectives of, 155–56
Williams, Bert, 57, 58, 59, 63, 80
Williams, Ethel Ray, 161
Winds Can Wake Up the Dead (Parascandola), 169
Winesburg, Ohio (Anderson), 152
women: as central figures of diaspora, 94–95; community definitions of womanhood, 114; portrayals of, 29, 33, 102
Workers' Socialist Federation, 208
Wright, Michelle: *Becoming Black*, 103–7
Wright, Richard: *American Hunger*, 128
W.W. Norton Publishers, 170

Zona Gale scholarship, 4, 169

CONTRIBUTORS

LOUIS J. PARASCANDOLA is Professor of English, Long Island University, Brooklyn. His publications include *"Winds Can Wake Up the Dead": An Eric Walrond Reader*, *"Look For Me All Around You": Anglophone Caribbean Immigrants in the Harlem Renaissance* and, with Carl A. Wade, *In Search of Asylum: The Later Writings of Eric Walrond*.

CARL A. WADE is former Senior Lecturer at the University of the West Indies, Cave Hill, Barbados. He is co-editor (with Louis J. Parascandola) of *In Search of Asylum: The Later Writings of Eric Walrond*.

ROBERT BONE was Professor Emeritus, Teachers College, Columbia University, New York. Bone was one of the pioneering figures of African American literature and the author of many books and articles including *The Negro Novel in America* and *Down Home: Origins of the Afro-American Short Story*.

LOUIS CHUDE-SOKEI is Associate Professor of Literature, University of Washington, Seattle. He is the author of *The Last "Darky": Bert Williams, Black-on-Black Minstrelsy, and the African Diaspora* and the forthcoming *The Sound of Culture*.

JAMES DAVIS is Associate Professor of English, Brooklyn College, New York. He is the author of *Commerce in Color: Race, Consumer Culture, and American Literature, 1893–1973* and the forthcoming *Quite to Himself: Eric Walrond, the Harlem Renaissance and the Caribbean Diaspora*.

RHONDA D. FREDERICK is Associate Professor, Boston College, Boston, and Director of the school's African and African Diaspora Studies Program. She is the author of *"Colón Man a Come": Mythographies of Panamá Canal Migration*.

MICHAEL NIBLETT is Research Fellow at the Yesu Persaud Centre for Caribbean Studies, University of Warwick, England. He is the co-editor of *Perspectives on the "Other America": Comparative Approaches to Caribbean and Latin American Cultures* and the author of *The Caribbean Novel since 1945*.

CARL PEDERSEN is Adjunct Professor of American Studies, Center for the Study of the Americas, Copenhagen Business School, Denmark. He is the author, most recently, of *Obama's America*.

KENNETH RAMCHAND is Professor Emeritus, University of the West Indies at St Augustine, Trinidad, and Colgate University, Hamilton, New York. His publications include *West Indian Poetry, An Introduction to the Study of West Indian Literature,* and *The West Indian Novel and Its Background*.

MICHELLE A. STEPHENS is Associate Professor of English and Latino and Hispanic Caribbean Studies, Rutgers University, New Jersey. She is the author of *Black Empire: The Masculine Global Imaginary of Caribbean Intellectuals in the United States, 1914–1962*.

www.ingramcontent.com/pod-product-compliance
Lightning Source LLC
Chambersburg PA
CBHW032056230426
43662CB00035B/582